The Burdens of Sister Margaret

The Burdens of Sister Margaret

INSIDE A SEVENTEENTH-CENTURY CONVENT

Abridged Edition

Craig Harline

YALE UNIVERSITY PRESS  NEW HAVEN AND LONDON

Yale Nota Bene

Revised and abridged edition first published as a
Yale Nota Bene book in 2000 by Yale University Press,
© Craig E. Harline, 2000.
All rights reserved.
An earlier version of this work was published in 1994 by
Doubleday, © Craig E. Harline, 1994.

Designed by Sonia Scanlon
Set in Minion type by Keystone Typesetting, Inc.
Printed in the United States of America by R. R. Donnelley,
Harrisonburg, Virginia.

Library of Congress Cataloging-in-Publication Data
Harline, Craig E.
The burdens of Sister Margaret : inside a seventeenth-century convent /
Craig Harline. — Abridged ed., Rev. and abridged ed.
         p.   cm.
Includes bibliographical references (p.   ) and index.
ISBN 0-300-08120-0 (cloth : alk. paper) — ISBN 0-300-08121-9 (pbk.)
1. Smulders, Margaret, d. 1648. 2. Franciscan sisters—
Belgium—Louvain—Biography. 3. Monastic and religious life of
women—History—17th century.   I. Title.
BX4705.S6628 H372 2000
271'.97304933—dc21
00-020784

A catalog record for this book is available from the
British Library.

10 9 8 7 6 5 4 3 2 1

For information about this and other Yale University Press publications,
please contact:
U.S. office   sales.press@yale.edu
Europe office   sales@yaleup.co.uk

CONTENTS

BOOK TWO
How Margaret Sought Her Revenge and Became the Watchdog of Reform All at Once

BOOK THREE
How Margaret's Hard-Won Triumphs Partly Fizzled Out

Contents

TO THE CURIOUS READER

To outsiders the convent is a mystery. A Belgian television documentary of the 1950s articulated what many curious people have wondered since the fourth century A.D.: "What are they doing there behind those walls?"

The mystery could hardly be otherwise. The convent is by nature private. The women who enter there reject the world most of us love. Their dress ignores fashion. Their regime emphasizes restraint. Their walls declare separation. And their records, through which we must try to know them, were long dominated by official papers and corporate ideals, rather than individual sentiments and actual experience. When we do know details of inner life, it is usually because of the exceptional—a scandal or a saint—since these generated more documents and rumors around convents than did "ordinary" nuns.

These truths were confirmed to me repeatedly over several summers as I dug around, full of hope, in the archives of convents from the old Spanish Netherlands (roughly modern Belgium), trying to find records that would divulge in some detail how these women lived. Most of the time, I found only beautifully decorated volumes containing the house rules, or towering stacks of tedious legal documents, or fat registers that recounted the wondrous deeds of a potential saint. Rarely was there a personal, human letter.

Imagine my surprise, therefore, when one day I miraculously saw—not quite in vision—the blessedly revealing bundles of a convent called Bethlehem, which stood centuries ago in the old university town of Leuven. After five minutes of thumbing, I realized that here was what I had been searching for.

It wasn't simply that these bundles were hundreds of years old, for there were thousands of such papers in this archive. Neither was it simply that the bundles were thick, for dozens of convents could boast these, even from the Middle Ages. And it certainly wasn't fame that drew me in, for Bethlehem was among the simplest of the two dozen monastic institutions in and around Leuven. What rendered the documents in these bundles unusual was that they contained far more than official records: here was page after page written by the sisters themselves.

Instead of documents that grudgingly surrendered the occasional tidbit about the feelings of sisters, instead of sterile generalities by official visitors about the spiritual state of the convent, instead of the usual warm trail of prescriptions that led to the familiar cold trail of practice, here was breathtaking detail and passion. I marveled at the survival of these papers, their prolixity, the noise of a convent sworn to regular periods of silence, and the diverse points of view revealed. Also appealing was that most of the documents had to do with decidedly routine aspects of conventual life, more the "garden-variety" sort of nuns I had been looking for—though as in any community or family the sensational surfaced in Bethlehem as well.

The records of Bethlehem were thickest for the years between 1600 and 1650, an especially dynamic time in European religious history, right after the early Reformation. Besides Protestant versions of religious Reform, by Martin Luther, John Calvin, or even King Henry VIII of England, there was of course a Catholic Reformation, featuring Pope Paul III, Ignatius Loyola, the Most Catholic King Philip II of Spain, or the monumental Council of Trent (1545–63). But historians for long knew more about these giant landmarks on the religious scene than about the vast terrain of how Reformations actually worked. What did Reform, in all its varieties, mean to the ordinary clergy or laity of a particular time and place? It's a question that obviously involves many groups, confessions, individuals, and even centuries, but under scrutiny here are the women of convents, or "female religious."

These women always constituted a minority of Catholic Europe, but they were an important minority, numerically and psychologically. In places their total surpassed the male orders; by the mid–sixteenth century there were perhaps ten thousand women religious in all the Low Countries (roughly the modern Netherlands and Belgium), triple the number of males. And that ordinary laypeople and ecclesiastical and municipal authorities expressed such frequent opinion over how female religious ought to behave hints that convents exerted an influence out of proportion to their mere numbers. Thus when it became clear that the plain Franciscan nuns of Bethlehem had confronted the major religious issues of the day, in such recorded detail, I judged that their experience might help illustrate in vibrant color an important part of the Catholic panorama. More than what it told about this convent alone, here was a lively example (in some ways typical and others not) of that form of religious life which most in the Roman religion still regarded as the ideal for women, and which like many institutions during this age came under severe pressure to reform—in other words to maintain cloister more strictly, sing more attentively, pray more fervently, work more diligently, dress more modestly, love more generously, and obey more speedily.

This up-close picture of conventual life in the Age of Reformations is admittedly set within a small space, includes a very few people, and treats a mere handful of the many decades affected by the famous Council of Trent. Yet as with most close studies, there are connections to bigger themes and movements. Since these connections are usually embedded in the narrative rather than made explicit, I will state them briefly here.

To the Reader

First, the events in Bethlehem may in many particulars be unique to the seventeenth-century Spanish Netherlands, or even to this convent alone, but the basic challenges evident there dominated the experience of most Catholic religious, in whatever land, from the early Middle Ages onward. One can make a forceful argument that special friendships versus common love, dissent versus obedience, the rights of the individual versus the demands of the community, distinguishing between temporal needs and extravagance, and maintaining separation from the world while living within it, have *always* been the central tensions and challenges of monasticism.

Second, the experience of these nuns, and every other nun before and since, was influenced heavily by the very fact that they were women. As various historians have shown, the requirement of stricter cloister for women than men, along with the tradition of not ordaining women, caused nearly automatic differences in material life between male and female religious, led to different expectations for each gender, and contributed as well to differences in political and ecclesiastical influence. This is not to mention the difference that women—the nuns of this story not excepted—were long believed to be more inclined than men to witchcraft.

Third, rivalry in and around Bethlehem was not always a matter of the (female) convent versus the (male) hierarchy, but sometimes sister against sister, clergyman against clergyman, and even sisters and clergymen together against other sisters and clergymen—all complicated by alliances with laypeople as well.

Last and most generally I suggest—in the spirit of other recent studies but I hope in my own way—that instead of accepting such a sweeping term as "Catholic Reformation" as self-evident and then using it to define ideas and actions of the players, it is more helpful to let the players, in all their glorious frailty and cleverness and inconsistency, breathe life into the term. Despite the large role of the church bureaucracy in trying to implement Reform, the process was not simply one-way, decided by those at the top and obeyed by those at the bottom; rather it involved the wills and desires of millions of such humble characters as Sister Margaret Smulders and the other nuns of Bethlehem. Neither was Reform a clear blueprint, drawn up forever and universally by the Council of Trent, but rather a set of guidelines that allowed for regional and local variations; in fact a major part of Reform was to debate these guidelines, in word and deed. Moreover, not all debate in Bethlehem or other communities was about Reform at all; the eternal trials of female monasticism often had little to do with the most recent episode of general Church Reform. Of greatest interest and significance to me, therefore, has been to set the characters in motion, to see the shaping and reshaping of religious life by real individuals rather than incorporeal labels.

But enough of bald assertions and abstractions. I'd rather devote the rest of the book to the far more enjoyable task of illustration.

This new edition is about two-thirds the size of the original hardcover, published in 1994. Most of the condensing is in Book 2, which treated in great detail the unusually rich letters written by the nuns of Bethlehem between 1628 and 1633 about the nature of life in their convent. For the new edition, I decided to review the contents of those letters in less detail within the text but to post them in full on a Web site, so that students and other readers can examine them for themselves. The address of that Web site is http://sistermargaret.byu.edu

A Note on Usage

I have used *clausura* as is or rendered it as "cloister," rather than "enclosure" or "claustration." Some use "cloister" to refer loosely to all kinds of female religious institutions or to a convent, but I use "cloister" in a specific sense, akin to the Dutch word *slot:* that part of a convent closed to outsiders and restricted to nuns. This usually included the choir of the church, the dormitory, refectory, infirmary, workroom, and certain gardens.

Though each term is acceptable, I use "grille" rather than "grate" to describe the barred area in the parlor wall through which nuns and outside visitors conversed.

All biblical references are to the King James version—an imperfect choice on various counts, but to my ear still the most poetic English translation, not to mention well suited to the time when this story took place.

The official language today of the Netherlands and northern Belgium is Dutch *(Nederlands)*. Between each region there are variations in usage, similar to the variations in English between the modern United States and Britain, yet in the seventeenth century such variations were even stronger. Many outsiders used "Flemish" to refer to the language of the entire area, but it more precisely described the dialect of the County of Flanders, in the west, while *Duets* or *Diets* described the dialect of the Duchy of Brabant, in the center, where the convent of Bethlehem was located. For the sake of convenience, I use "Dutch" to refer to all dialects of the family. The reader should also be aware that residents of the southernmost provinces of the Spanish Netherlands spoke dialects of French.

Place names are given in the language of the locale in question. Thus the Dutch "Mechelen" is used rather than the French Malines, the Dutch "Leuven" in preference to the French and English Louvain, and the Dutch "Gent" and "Brugge" and "Ieper" rather than the French and English Ghent and Bruges and Ypres. The only exceptions are Brussels and Antwerp, English renditions so common that it would be silly to displace them.

Family names at this time were spelled at whim, so I have just as whimsically chosen a favorite version and stuck with it. Given names I usually leave in the Dutch or French or Latin original, unless they are not easily recognizable. Thus I have retained Anna, Adriana, Maria, Johan, and Catharina, but changed Margriet, Magriet, and Margareta to Margaret, and Petrus to Peter.

Dramatis Personae

JACOB BOONEN (BO-nun): Archbishop of Mechelen from 1621 until his death in 1655; "Ordinary" superior over Bethlehem during most of the years of Margaret's troubles.

JOOST BOUCKAERT (yoast BOO-cart): Pastor of the famous pilgrimage shrine at Scherpenheuvel from 1610; Dean of Diest from 1619; Bishop of Ieper from 1639 until his death in 1646; loyal confessor and patron of Margaret Smulders from 1624.

MARIA CONINXLOO (the *o*'s as in *low*): Veiled sister of Bethlehem from 1619 until her death around 1670; critic of Mother Superior (or Mater) Adriana Truis and supporter of Vicaress Catharina Rijkeboer.

MATHIAS HOVIUS: Archbishop of Mechelen from 1596 until his death in 1620; Ordinary superior over Bethlehem during Margaret's early troubles; responsible for removing Henri Joos as confessor.

HENRI JOOS (yoas): Confessor of Bethlehem from around 1604 to his expulsion in 1618; Pastor of Mol from 1624 until his death in 1638; brother of Maria Joos, family of Lesken Joos.

LESKEN (ELISABETH) JOOS: Lay sister of Bethlehem from 1609;

responsible for the infirmary; niece or cousin of Henri Joos; supporter of Adriana Truis.

MARIA JOOS: Veiled sister of Bethlehem from 1609 until her death around 1660; Bursaress from 1629; sister of Henri Joos; supporter of Adriana Truis.

BARBARA NOOSEN (NO-sun): Veiled sister of Bethlehem from around 1595 until her death in 1625; Mater from 1619.

CATHARINA RIJKEBOER (RYE-kuh-booer): Veiled sister of Bethlehem from 1617 until her death in 1635; Vicaress from 1626; a reluctant critic of Adriana Truis.

JOANNA SCHOENSETTERS (SCHOON-setters): Lay sister of Bethlehem from 1623; cook; the only lay sister in the convent who opposed Adriana Truis.

MARGARET SMULDERS: Veiled sister of Bethlehem from 1606 until her death in 1648; excluded from the community twice (1616–18, 1624–36); leading critic of Adriana Truis.

ADRIANA TRUIS (trouse): Veiled sister of Bethlehem from 1605 until her death in 1668; Bursaress from around 1613 to 1629; Mater, or Mother Superior, from 1625 to the end; friend of Henri Joos.

ANNA VIGNAROLA: Veiled sister of Bethlehem from 1624 until her death around 1673; Vicaress from 1635 to 1668; Bursaress after 1650; Mater from 1668; leading supporter of Adriana Truis and Henri Joos.

PETER VAN DER WIEL: The longtime Archdeacon of the cathedral chapter of Mechelen and Vicar-General of Archbishop Jacob Boonen; a regular official visitor to Bethlehem until his death in 1643.

Prologue

REMEMBERING

A guest room in the convent of Bethlehem, May 1618, the month of Mary. When with the noon meal of soup and an egg there came through the grille news that visitation was imminent, the nun's first thought was of the usual maddening delays, but right behind was the rousing knowledge that the Archbishop's men always did come eventually, so rather than wring her hands she would use every spare moment from now until they arrived to write about the foibles of her sisters, for oh the stories she could tell. She would not tell all because there wasn't enough ink and paper in the convent, and because she didn't want to ruin absolutely the reputation of her house, but she would divulge enough to show that the others had no business casting stones at her.

Not that she was without sin. In fact she doubted whether hers could ever be forgiven. But if salvation was not for this one, then neither was it, she reasoned, for those sanctimonious hypocritical spendthrifts who had banished her to this guest room. Did any well-intentioned, grace-seeking, middle-aged nun such as herself deserve the humiliation of being expelled from the cloister in which she had promised to live all her days? And to be thrown into a guest room right next door was worse than going leagues away, for the closeness sharpened the cuts of all the small humiliations that accompanied exile and reminded her daily of their loathing. Even the house confessor refused to comfort her—not that she would let him, mind you, but his public rejection piled on her disgrace, and the failure of a specially arranged Jesuit confessor to arrive when promised added to her reproach. She wondered why, since she had shown no signs of past troubles for three years now and since others had also fallen into error at times, they should continue to despise her so and deny her another chance to live among them? Surely they would understand and forgive her failings if they would only recognize their own, which were legion.

She couldn't see much, but she was still allowed in choir, she had a dependable source of news from inside the convent, and from her room in exile she could observe what seemed an endless stream of outsiders calling upon all-too-willing nuns. Plenty of what she saw and heard went quite against the Archbishop's recent reforms, and for that matter against centuries-old monastic standards. These transgressions would have to be told, and this time in more enduring fashion and detail than she—or most any nun—had ever attempted before. For the past two decades, in every interview with every ecclesiastical visitor who came to Bethlehem, she had made the customary promise on her oath and conscience to disclose what she knew to be right or wrong in the place. But now she would go beyond the usual brief oral testimony and add to it a written chronicle listing chapter and verse of the convent's ills. Something this extreme had to be done or their state would continue as before, in lukewarm mediocrity and worse. And there was of course her own unhappy situation in the guest room to consider, a situation which might improve if the Archbishop were convinced that her sins were hardly greater than those of the others. She was no spiritual author, like Teresa of Avila writing her famous autobiography, or even like the regionally revered Maria Petyt of Gent, but she would prove herself an incomparable spiritual reporter.

After making arrangements with her only friend, Sister Catharina, for a fresh supply of paper, and as she fingered her secret relic and gazed at her new picture of St. Joseph, she began with little delay. There was no need or want for any grand scheme, nor any notes, nor any careful outline of points to be made, for what she intended to say had burned long within. Searing memories and a bottomless reserve of unhappy anecdotes would carry her along for more than a month, until in the end there would emerge thirty-two large, emotional, tightly spaced, winding pages—order, polish, and finery be damned. She cared not at all about catchy introductions, smooth transitions, simple sentences, or tight conclusions, but only that the Archbishop should know the house's abundant problems, especially those caused by the woman recently put in charge, Mater (or Mother) Adriana.

What would he think of Adriana's lavishing unaffordable gifts on male and female friends, playing favorites, and alienating her second-in-command, the Vicaress? Words spilled out: Mater spoke "so curtly and with such spite" to Vicaress that Margaret was amazed. Mater also shamelessly cavorted at the grille, that barred area in the parlor reserved for speaking to outsiders, with a former confessor. "How her heart quickens when she may speak of him or hears talk of him. Such often begins innocently enough, but it often ends with a bad smell." If these weren't enough, then what of Adriana's disgraceful weakness for workmen, with whom she spoke "behind and before, above and beneath, early and late," often on frivolous subjects that had nothing to do with the work being done?

Or what of Mater's pampered young protégée, Sister Anna? Mater and Sister Anna often walked with each other "like fools in love; they take each other by the arm, fling their arms around each other's neck, walk hand in hand as if they're about to dance in the churchyard, and think that no one sees them." If Mater would love the rest even one-hundredth as much as she loved Anna, "it would be enough." How could the Archbishop stand for Anna's preoccupation with the elaborate, expensive decoration of a stuffy choir so full of candles that wax residue covered the floor? Or her dangerous infatuation with a young chaplain who came to perform Mass? Or her excessive devotion to the same confessor so esteemed by Mater? Or for that matter her devotion to any outsider? Whoever visited, Anna was "right there with them, religious, worldly, all sorts of people from whatever nation or quarter they come. Even if they speak with or see her only once, all want to be friends with her and be with her. We sometimes say among us that if a dog came off the street she'd be friends with it in a second."

Would any visitor be impressed with the convent's choir, where the services by the nuns were "done with such great haste, slovenliness, and speeding past others," that it was more like a farce than the Divine Office, and where she who "slobbers most and fastest has the biggest prize and praise"? Or with insolent Sister Maria, who "barks like a dog" at the Vicaress? Or with the last member of Mater's circle, a lower-status lay sister no less, who went in and out of the convent at will, ordered around the veiled nuns, and repeated distracting news and scandalous stories from the convent's past? Even as Margaret wrote, and also on days when she did not, she heard some of the sisters clanging about in the guest room below her, preparing to receive another special outside friend, cheating devotions and the common work.

Only Sister Margaret Smulders knew fully what distant and recent memories, what intense feelings, motivated her to write one of the most formidable accounts of monastic life composed by any nun of this era. Only she knew exactly where her hopes for a proper convent ended and her desire for revenge began. But the phenomenal length of her letter alone suggests that there was more to this story than the casual narration of defects in monastic decorum, for nuns usually reported even the most grievous faults in a thrifty, dense page or two. Other clues, from Margaret's past, reveal still more clearly how she had landed in this unenviable position outside the convent, and why she began her watch as a lonely sparrow upon the housetop.

Book One

How Just About Everyone Came to Loathe Sister Margaret

1
Beginning

The young nun from 1604 to 1616. The murkiest part of Margaret's early years is how she came to the religious life in the first place.

As with most sisters who entered Bethlehem, nothing is known of her childhood and adolescence except her place of origin, Stalle, near Brussels. Nothing is known of her family except the names of her parents, Andries Smulders and Maria Andries. Nothing is known of her social standing except the paltry income she brought with her to the convent, six florins per year. And though her age at entry in 1604 is known, nothing can be deduced from it, for by this time twenty-one was rather typical for a young woman setting out to become a nun.

Only one pitiful scrap remains to suggest that she, like many in these heady decades after the Council of Trent, had been genuinely drawn to the convent, rather than forced into it by daughter-rich parents who preferred a cheaper convent dowry to a marriage dowry, or by some nasty uncle-guardian who stood to receive her inheritance when she left the world behind. At her interview for profession in April 1606, Margaret told the Archbishop's representative that she had long had inclination to enter this particular convent, that no one was compelling her to stay, and that she desired to remain there all her days so as "better to serve God."

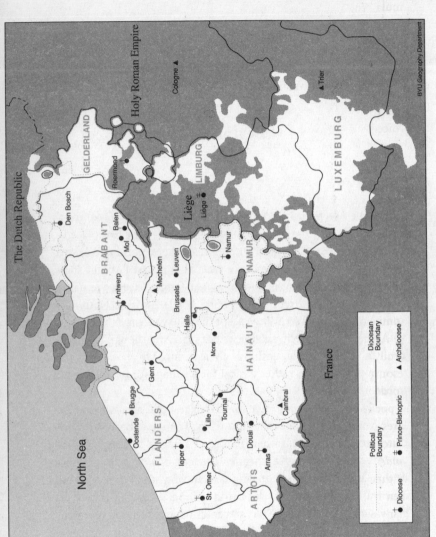

The Spanish Netherlands

North Sea

The Dutch Republic

Holy Roman Empire

GELDERLAND

Roermond

Den Bosch

BRABANT

Balen
Mol

Antwerp

Mechelen

Brussels · Leuven

Halle

Gent

Brugge

Oostende

FLANDERS

Ieper

Lille

Tournai

Douai

Arras

St. Omer

ARTOIS

Mons

HAINAUT

Cambrai

LIMBURG

Liège

Namur

NAMUR

LUXEMBURG

Cologne ▲

▲ Trier

France

BYU Geography Department

Political
Boundary

Diocese

Diocesan
Boundary

☩ Prince-Bishopric

▲ Archdiocese

Others in Bethlehem spoke similarly, even going beyond the formula required, to assure the interviewer that they entered freely: there was no family pressure, no economic cause, no romantic reaction to an unhappy love affair. Perhaps it was all cliché. Who could say? One could say only with great imprecision that, despite the ideal of voluntary entry promoted by the decrees of Trent, a whole spectrum of emotions was in play as a woman began the religious life. Important for Margaret was that when given the chance, she voiced the sentiment that the decision to become a nun was hers.

Also murky is how Margaret ended up in this particular house of some twenty Franciscan nuns. Even in an unassuming convent, even in these utopian times, competition for places made connections useful, especially if the ratio of applicants to entrants was anything like the three to one in Pescia, Italy. That most nuns in Bethlehem were not natives of Leuven but came at some distance from Brugge, Gent, or Brussels also suggests that patronage mattered. One can only wonder how Margaret came to know of Bethlehem, how keen the competition for entry was, and how her family gained the acquaintance of a patron who possessed the right to nominate a young woman of his or her choosing to this place.

Another influence on Margaret's decision would have been her family's financial and social position, which usually matched the resources and prestige of the convent one had in mind. In other words, Margaret surely set her sights on Bethlehem because it was as poor as she. During recent years it had, with many other structures in the southern Netherlands, suffered from war with the Dutch. Once upon a time, the seventeen provinces of all the *Nederlanden* (which simply meant Low Countries) were loosely united by their common ruler, the emperor Charles V (1500–1558) and then his son Philip II of Spain (1527–98). But during the 1560s many provinces rebelled against Philip, partly in the name of new Protestant religions and partly in the name of traditional Netherlandish liberties. By 1585, provinces in the south at last proclaimed their loyalty to Spain and were thus called the Spanish Netherlands, while provinces of the north declared independence and became the new Dutch Republic. Of consequence to Bethlehem was that north and south continued fighting until 1648, bringing not only political change but physical destruction—even to such obscure convents as this one.

Yet war alone had not made Bethlehem humble: it had been so from the start, in 1402, when a certain Laurent de Vroede left a run-down house and garden in Leuven for "poor sisters of the third order of St. Francis." The house was located in a fairly remote space, outside the old walls of the city but inside the new—a neighbor's house was part barn. For decades the sisters were without a real church; a converted room somewhere in the structure served as a makeshift choir where they could sing, pray, and hear Mass. But at least there was space to grow from this typically modest beginning. Rising demand for entry and new resources from pious bequests resulted in a small new church by the sixteenth century. Following a common pattern of evolution, the sisters steadily added surrounding houses—which were bequeathed to them or built with donated funds. Still, the physical quality of the convent, the status of this branch of the Franciscan order, and the social background of most sisters long remained as plain as Flemish cream cheese. Unattractive to the great, Bethlehem appealed mainly to middling or barely middling sorts of families who sought a place for their unmarried daughters, or, at its most ideal, to young women who felt called to the way of St. Francis of Assisi.

Christian women had been drawn to the idea of separation from the world since the origins of monasticism in fourth-century Egypt. The first monastic "rule," or set of prescriptions, designed specifically for women was composed in the early part of the fifth century. Over the next millennium countless orders were born, each with a distinct emphasis, and many with male and female branches of the family. Though some orders abandoned their female side, by Margaret's time the presence of women in the religious world had not only dramatically increased but come to be taken for granted, even by detractors. Indeed, the variety of monastic families from which a woman might choose was by now so bewildering that establishing the provenance of a specific group was no mean achievement.*

Bethlehem's past was as convoluted as any. It belonged to the so-called third order of the Franciscan family, founded in the early thirteenth century. Originally the third order consisted solely of laypeople who because of worldly responsibilities were unable to literally leave the world and join Francis's first (male) or second (female) orders, but who sought a more devout life in the midst of temporal cares. Members expressed devotion by the wearing of penitential clothing, adherence to a regime of prayer, periodic abstinence from food, regular confession, and the practice of humility and heroic almsgiving, all from one's own home.

But most who sought piety in this time still found its deepest expression in the traditional world-forsaking monastic style of the first and second orders: the taking of solemn vows of poverty, chastity, and obedience; living in community under a normative rule; observation of silence; communal singing of the Divine Office (prayers for seven times of the day); and among women the practice of strict cloister. Gradually these traditional forms of monastic practice were imitated by third-order Franciscans as well, until in 1377 a "regular" or monastic branch of the third order was given its own rule, to distinguish it from the lay versions of the third order. Some of the new third-order female houses continued with one of the identifying marks of Franciscans: care of the sick or the education of girls. But some female houses accepted cloister and became fully contemplative—distinguishable from their cousins of the second order only by lower social status, not the nature of their rule.

*I use the term "monastic" broadly, to include all those religious separated literally or figuratively from the world. Franciscan and Dominican friars were not monks, and neither were Augustinian canons and canonesses, but all were part of the professional religious world.

Both active and contemplative types of third-order female religious appeared in the Low Countries by the end of the fourteenth century. Most came to be called Grey Sisters, because of their grey habits. Most were still devoted to education or care of the sick. But the convent in Leuven, after 185 years of sick care, became in 1587 one of the few contemplative houses of Grey Sisters in all the land. This more withdrawn style surely influenced Margaret's decision as much as the house's modest standing.

On her way to Bethlehem, she did not travel empty-handed. Poor convents could not demand too much of new members, but one had to bring along something. In Margaret's case this included four wimples of high-quality grey cloth, yards of material for work bodices, petticoats, and blouses, three-dozen "nose-cloths," eight pillowcases, ten aprons, a mattress, blankets, bowls, chair, cushion, kettle, candelabra, broom, small table, breviaries, stockings and shoes, and still other items recently bought or to be purchased soon (such as the six black veils she would need after her profession as a nun). Most important of all, however, she brought a desire to remain in Bethlehem the remainder of her days.

Perhaps she had visited Leuven before, or perhaps she knew nothing of the 750-year-old city at all and caught her first glimpse of the five-towered skyline on that trip to enter Bethlehem. If she didn't know then, she would have learned later about its proud past: its great artists Bouts and Metsys, its acclaimed university, its having played host to countless counts, distinguished dukes, and other great nobles, even breakfasting the boy Charles Habsburg, the future Charles V, when he attended their carnival in 1509. She learned darker parts of the city's identity, too: recent unsuccessful resistance against foreign troops, the flooding of the town by its giver of life, the River Dyle, or the raging of the plague. Together these reduced Leuven's population of 19,000 in 1525 to 14,000 by 1565, and then the barely urban figure of 10,000 by 1600. But Leuvenaars persisted. Their chief industries of agriculture, viticulture, and brewing prospered, and their secondary industries of tanning, stove making, and marble working survived. And nearly 1,000 religious still populated the two dozen male and female convents of the city. As Margaret passed through the gates, which were fortified by triangular bulwarks to discourage invaders, then rode through the streets, she would have noticed the gabled, small-windowed, three- and four-story houses on both sides, becoming gradually denser until they reached the city center with its marketplaces and magnificent Gothic town hall. Then left and through another gate, on the interior wall, until she reached the street that led to Bethlehem, where she arrived a few blocks later.

The convent's chief claim to fame was a modest one: it possessed some relics of St. Renildis, a martyr from the region who, according to the nuns, was especially effective as a protector against all accidents to arms and legs. Unlike some renowned monasteries around Europe, Bethlehem produced no saints, housed no illustrious relics such as a saint's tooth, a thorn of Christ's crown, or a lock of hair from one of the 11,000 virgins. It could never match a big place such as medieval Cistercian Hertogendaal with its seventy-seven sisters or the contemporary Cistercian Beaupré with its seventy-two. It didn't have sisters who went out full of zeal to establish branch houses and lead new monastic currents. It included none of the great of society. It boasted no buildings of architectural significance or even unity. Its choir was undistinguished. Its handiwork was known locally at best. It had no great spiritual writers, not even a modest library, nor a competent illuminator of devotional works. Unlike San Marco's in Florence it could never have afforded to hire such a celebrated painter as Fra Angelico to beautify its walls and cells. Its nuns produced no accounts of any marvelous spiritual visions and experiences, nor could they converse in Latin, as could certain women at legendary medieval nunneries. It was meaner than almost every other house of religious in Leuven, too close to the street for true quiet, and too close to the river that carried behind the convent's rear walls foul-mouthed sailors and flooding waters. It was undoubtedly similar to most nunneries of the age in

LOVANIVM.

J. van der Baren, *A View of Leuven*, 1604. St. Gertrude's is the second large church from the left. Bethlehem, located just to the right of Gertrude's, is not visible in this panorama, because it was situated behind the elevated fortress in the middle foreground.

Stedelijk museum Vander Kelen-Mertens, Leuven

The Convent of the Annunciation Sisters, Leuven. This convent, though
undoubtedly more distinguished and architecturally unified than
Bethlehem, is probably a reasonable point of comparison in
size and appearance.

Stedelijk museum Vander Kelen-Mertens, Leuven

having but a local function and reputation, and in its middling
relics and mediocre choir. Still, though a small glimmer in the
monastic constellation, Bethlehem could take pride in belonging to
an elite in Catholic society as a whole, for the Grey Sisters of
Bethlehem practiced the form of religious life still regarded as
supreme for Catholic women: solemnly vowed, chaste, poor, and
obedient, whose members spent most of their time praying and
singing to God, with periods of manual labor and study in between, forever shut behind walls and locked doors.

Whatever brought Margaret to this monastic family and these
unassuming surroundings, once there she began the two-stage probation required by her order. This called for one year as a postulant,

which meant the continued wearing of worldly clothes while living near the nuns to learn the cadences of religious life, especially choir. After this, the nuns voted to receive Margaret as a novice, which meant another year of trial, culminated by bestowal of the novice's habit, made of "common cloth" and excluding the scapular and cord worn by professed nuns. During this year as a novice she would have continued to live separately from the veiled nuns while she received still more vigilant instruction on how to become one of them. During this year she would have learned to read and write. And during this year she most certainly learned the order's rule and the house's statutes: to deaden worldly desires within her. To be submissive and attentive in chapter (the weekly meeting for business and the correction of faults). To avoid private conversations with professed nuns. To learn the seven hours of the Divine Office. To be reverent in choir, avoiding the temptation to smash little worms with her thumb and then smear them on the choir stalls, keeping instead her eyes fixed ahead or on her book rather than looking about with flying glances like a wild deer in the woods or a coarse peasant, pronouncing all words fully and devoutly rather than rushing through or raising her voice too high, and bowing with the whole body to the knee rather than merely nodding the head. To be kind to cosisters, alien to all contention, silent in the dormitory, sober at meals. To master her evil passions. To treat the convent's property with care. To be modest in movement, so that when one member of the body was used the others were rested, that when using any member she did so in moderation, so that in laughing her teeth should not show and in speaking she should not move her hands, grind her lips, shake her head, lift her eyebrows, stick out her arms, or use her shoulders, and that in drinking she should use both hands, without sighing, blowing out, smacking the lips (all signs of gluttony), looking around, or talking.

To encourage her to remain, Margaret learned stories of those who had not. Several books related cautionary anecdotes: two novices pleaded with their parents to return to the world, but then died from plague after doing so. Another novice left his monastery, went dancing, then died when a tile fell from a roof and hit him on the head. Yet another wandering novice was a well-trained singer who left his monastery thrice, but on the last journey he was punished by God with an ailment in the throat that left him not only unable to sing but dead. With examples like these floating around, one wonders just how free novices felt to quit, even in an age that insisted on true vocation. No wonder that the historian Geneviève Reynes would later call Trent's requirement of voluntary entry into convents "timid, incomplete, and poorly enforced," particularly in regard to girls in their midteens who possessed more "reverential fear" for their parents than did young women of even slightly greater age. As many as one-third of the nuns who professed in France during the seventeenth and eighteenth centuries may have done so, according to Professor Reynes, against their own will and because they feared conflict with their parents. Such a figure may be impossible to verify, but what was a young woman to say who had been told that it was in her family's best interest for her to enter the convent, who even if she exited the convent legally faced censure socially, and whose family would have to scrape together a new and more costly dowry for her now-difficult-to-arrange marriage? At the other end of the spectrum of motivations were courageous examples of those who defied parents and siblings in order to profess, such as Clare of Assisi fleeing her seven brothers, or five-year-old Anne-Bathilde de Harlay of Paris who, after visiting an aunt in a local convent in 1616, was so drawn to the place that she refused to leave and professed at age eleven, causing anguish to her mother and father.

For whatever reasons, Margaret endured her novitiate and in 1606 decided to forsake the world and profess. This required not only an interview with the superior of the convent, and with the Archbishop of Mechelen or his representative, but the approval of the nuns. Mater therefore presented Margaret's name in chapter three times, after which Margaret came forward three times before the sisters, fell prostrate, and humbly asked to be received. Soon after her twenty-third birthday, a majority voted to accept her. Did she have to wait weeks or even months for the ceremony to take place, as occasionally occurred when bishops and deans were dis tracted? No one bothered to say, but the ceremony took place before the year was out, the same year that a great tempest visited Leuven and much of the Spanish Netherlands: the storm's heavy winds, which knocked out even church bells, were still talked about decades later. Margaret and those around her may well have looked back upon the violent weather that surrounded her profession as ominous.

At some point before the ceremony, Margaret formally granted her meager worldly goods to the house, and had her hair cut short. In most convents nuns were in practice required to offer monetary "gifts" upon professing, in part for the convent's general fund and in part to support themselves. But in these decades after Trent women like Margaret, who could hardly afford such gifts, benefited from decrees encouraging convents to abolish all de facto entry fees and railing against the notion that one had to be of certain financial standing in order to make a proper vow of poverty. That such decrees had been issued before and would be again reflects how difficult it was for conventual ideals to bear the weight of temporal reality, but for the moment they were strong enough in consciences to help Margaret Smulders.

During the profession ceremony, Margaret appeared at the door that divided the choir from the church while the Dean anointed the scapular, cord, and veil, the final symbols of her new life. Before putting them on Margaret, he required her to make her profession in his hands: "I Sister Margaret swear to God Almighty, the Holy Virgin Maria, St. Francis, and all of God's saints, obedience to the Archbishop of Mechelen and the Mater of this convent according to the third order of our Holy Father Francis which was confirmed by Pope Leo X, and eternal chastity, renunciation of my possessions, and eternal cloister until death." Then came the draping of the scapular, the placing of the black veil over the grey wimple on her head, the pronouncement of the crowning glory of marriage with Christ, *"Veni sponsi Christi, accipe coronam quam tibi dominus praeparavit in aeternum,"* and the promise to her of eternal life if she fulfilled these vows. Mater and sisters led her to her place in the choir, whence came forth prayers and hymns of the Holy Spirit, the Virgin, and the stigmata of Francis, concluding with the exhortation of Francis: "May God bless and watch over you, show his works and mercy in you, submit your will to his, and may he give you peace."

There was one last step: the profession feast, which in Margaret's case must have been less fine than most, even by the standards of this house, but it was good enough for her and God. Thus at age twenty-three, much older than the typical nun from earlier medieval times, Margaret became a bride of Christ, legally dead to the world. In the summer of 1606 she took her place in the nuns' dormitory, choir, chapter room, and refectory as a full-fledged member of the house.

For the next decade there was no hint that Margaret was anything but ordinary. Indeed, in light of her later difficulties she may have looked back on these early days with fondness. But at some point things began to go terribly wrong, more wrong than Margaret had ever imagined they might when she first set out on the pathway to perfection.

2
Demons

The parlor of Bethlehem, September 26, 1616. The Archbishop's Vicar-General had but one question for the nuns during his brief official visit today: should Sister Margaret Smulders be allowed to return to the convent? No documents remained to tell when Margaret had first left Bethlehem—perhaps weeks, months, or even years before. But whenever it occurred, this was a grave matter for a nun who just ten years before had vowed never to go out.

Only nine of the fifteen or so sisters in the convent were called forward to share their sentiments on the matter. A few, knowing the rarity of such visitations, seized the moment and volunteered opinions on other topics that troubled them as well, such as the excessively "sober regime" in the convent. But always, from the other side of the grille, the Vicar-General came back to his chief question: should Margaret return?

There was no debate, because almost all were against. The sisters would accept Margaret if the Archbishop insisted, but given the choice they would emphatically rather not. Some suggested the convent would do better to support Margaret at an outside location—a costly solution, but worth it. Two stated that they would rather live solely "on bread and water" than see Margaret return.

One sister felt it in the best interest of Margaret's "strength" to stay out. Others referred to spiritual symptoms, noting that the community was, thanks to the diligent efforts of their good confessor, more peaceful in Margaret's absence, and that "past vexations" had, praise God, disappeared with her.

What could Margaret have done to so upset the peace and arouse such hostility? One nun hinted that the root of alienation was Margaret's quickness to find fault in others. An elder sister leveled a more tangible complaint: Margaret had so alarmed outside friends and benefactors with her behavior that if she returned then these friends would never dare visit again, or bring their badly needed alms with them. And even if friends did visit, they would only be stirred up to gossip with other outsiders about Margaret and her troubles, thus inflaming the convent's wounded reputation. Besides, Margaret's return would vex their confessor, who had done so much to restore peace; he might even quit the place should she come back.

But most serious of all against Margaret were accusations of a wholly sinister nature. Sister Anna Marcelis alleged that prior to Margaret's departure "images were scattered about" in the cells and that nearly every evening there had appeared before the convent a strange dog, its head in the ground "so that it was hardly visible." With Margaret gone, continued Anna, these events had ceased. The meaning of such claims could not have been lost on the Vicar-General or on other nuns—cats, foxes, black sheep, bulls, spiders, vultures, bears, black pigs, and especially ferocious dogs were often associated with the devil and evil magic. Anna even recalled that Margaret had once volunteered to teach her the "magical arts." Sister Magdalena Remmens had a similar tale: when she and another lay sister* were sent on pilgrimage for the salvation of Margaret, they were terrorized on one lonely road by strange, silent

---

*"Lay sister" was the name given to those religious who took no vow of cloister and thus were free to perform the convent's necessary outside

"dancing apparitions." And at night in the dormitory, Magdalena and others would hear "great noise" and see that the rays of the moon—also associated with sorcery—caused the cell of almost every sister to glow with unusual brightness. Magdalena concluded, as had Anna, by noting that these events had stopped in Margaret's absence.

Obviously, there was serious resentment against Margaret. She threatened the convent's temporal well-being by offending outsiders. She broke one of the cardinal rules of monastic life by causing discord and upsetting the peace within. But she struck at something more fundamental still, at the very essence of religion and humanity, when she was linked to the feminine malady par excellence of the sixteenth and seventeenth centuries: witchcraft.

The nuns of Bethlehem, like most people of this time, saw evidence of the usually invisible otherworld all around them. If God noticed every sparrow that fell and numbered every hair on one's head, and the devil was just as vigilant in his opposition to God, then nothing happened by chance. A comet, an earthquake, a miracle, an illness, sexual impotence, a pig that became lame, a cow that stopped giving milk, the birth of an ill-formed child—these were all interpreted as omens of God's displeasure or as manifestations of His opposite, Satan.

God had His angels and the devil his demons, but both worked through human agents as well. God's grace could be found around Catholic Europe at numerous shrines, where the relics and divine powers of deceased holy people were made manifest, or in future saints who still lived among believers, healing and blessing. The devil was active too, in dreary or neglected places, and within humans in the form of witches or demoniacs. The distinction between

---

affairs and errands. They took vows, but of a lesser kind than the veiled nuns, and were generally of lesser status, before and after entering. There were usually six lay sisters in Bethlehem.

the two kinds of evil agents, a distinction developed only during the fourteenth and fifteenth centuries and not always cared about by nonexperts, was that the demoniac was involuntarily possessed, and thus less culpable, while the witch entered willfully into a pact with the devil—becoming his servant in exchange for power over the elements. During the early modern period, it seemed to many that evil agents of either sort were more active than holy agents. Not that Satan was more powerful than God and His allies, but rather that God allowed Satan to act in the world as a result of human proclivity to sin, or in order to illustrate His ultimately greater control by crushing evil spirits in very public rituals.

In this drama of supernatural evil, women stood at the center, front, back, and sides of the stage. As if the whole of womankind had not already been burdened enough over the centuries with a long list of "ills caused," the systematic definition of witchery would eventually leave them another: according to the male experts (such as the Dominican Inquisitors Heinrich Kramer and Jacob Sprenger, authors of the influential *Malleus Maleficarum*, or "Witches' Hammer," first published in 1485), women were more likely than men to become witches. This, explained these celibate men, was largely because the female sex was more lustful and thus more easily enticed by the carnality of the devil, always one of his major lures. Women were not thoroughly evil, obviously, for enough among them had led lives of extraordinary holiness. But women were more extreme than men, tending to be very good or very bad.

This unbreakable connection between women and witchcraft was quite new. Though belief in evil spirits was present in Christianity from the start, until the late Middle Ages men and women were, as far as can be determined, about equally accused of malevolent magic. But by 1550 the notion that women were more prone to witchcraft had triumphed in most of Europe. Indeed the notion was embellished—a female witch now not only engaged in the usual exchange of her soul for supernatural power, but she became as well the devil's sexual servant. By night the witch flew to secret locations where the "Devil's Sabbat" was celebrated, a giant orgy of blasphemy, child eating, and copulation between the devil and his eager servants. Such a fantastic scene was the product not of the popular imagination but of official hunters and definers of witches: theologians, lawyers, inquisitors, and other intellectuals. Yet the idea of the Sabbat caught on in wider circles as more and more people were brought to trial, as they heard more and more details from their learned accusers, and as ordinary people made more and more charges against perceived witches. In the end, roughly 80 percent of the tens of thousands of people charged with witch-craft during the sixteenth and seventeenth centuries were women; most people charged escaped execution, but among those put to death women again far outnumbered men (nine of ten in the Low Countries).

Another contemporary explanation of Margaret's condition was possession. Experts were silent on whether women were also more susceptible than men to this affliction, but they did agree that certain types of women—including nuns—undoubtedly were. In-deed the most notorious examples of possession in the age involved convents, as Margaret's coreligious knew only too well. Between 1600 and 1650 entire nunneries in France and the Spanish Nether-lands would experience wild, publicized bouts of possession, lead-ing some to speak of an "epidemic of diabolical possession" in the female convents of the Low Countries.

When the sisters of Bethlehem implied that Margaret was con-nected to the netherworld, whether as eager witch or unwilling de-moniac, they were therefore not pulling ideas out of thin air: such ideas were all around them. In fact, these particular sisters had more reason to fear than most, for they could draw upon scandals espe-cially close to home. Soon after profession or even before, each nun of Bethlehem must have picked up the darkest bit of convent lore.

In 1601, one of their very own had been executed for witchcraft. The first fires for witches in the Low Countries were lit toward the end of the fifteenth century, and they burned brightest from the 1580s into the first few decades of the 1600s—precisely when Bethlehem's witch emerged. But it was no consolation to these anxious women that "their witch" was but one of many. To them this was an ugly, extremely sensitive subject, perhaps explaining why no sister referred explicitly to it during the 1616 visitation. But various other records preserved anyway the dismal story of the Grey Sister of Bethlehem named Marie Everaerts.

Marie's troubles began in 1599, when, at the order of the Archbishop of Mechelen, she was imprisoned within Bethlehem for unspecified but "weighty crimes." During her two years of imprisonment, her troubles grew worse, for it was then that she supposedly went over to the devil for good and committed her long string of sinister misdeeds. At her trial in 1601, Marie confessed to entering into the characteristic pact with the devil (obedience to him in return for supernatural powers over the elements, so that she might afflict those around her), swearing off the Christian faith, letting the devil carry her away to a dance, eating human flesh in the meeting of the witches, taking on a "familiar" (usually a cat or other animal that served as intermediary between the witch and the devil), worshiping the devil with bowed knee as her God, flying away at night to engage in carnal relations with him, even in holy places, and giving "different consecrated hosts to the enemy."

Such fantastic confessions were quite typical by this time among convicted witches—especially those who, like Marie, confessed under torture. Most pertinent to the nuns of Bethlehem was Marie's further admission that with her new powers she had carried out assorted fiendish attacks upon them (as well as other nuns and clergymen), and her claim that she had first learned about witchcraft from one of her cosisters, named Marie Switten. Once, said Marie Everaerts, she was borne away by the devil to a tree outside the walls of Mechelen (her native city) and saw there Marie Switten and another nun, or at least the devil in their images, dancing and offering up unholy sacrifices. Marie Everaerts also insisted that she had long known and observed that Marie Switten was a witch, partly because of various marks on her body.

Because of this confession, because she showed no signs of remorse for her alleged crimes, and because the Archbishop's court could not carry out capital punishment, the local municipal court took over the case and condemned Marie Everaerts to be strangled and burned (the usual punishment in such hopeless cases). The executioner performed the deed on February 27, 1601. Marie Switten, for reasons unknown, was punished less severely—merely required by the Archbishop's court, in June 1602, to leave the convent of Bethlehem and take up residence in an unspecified "respectable place" in the city of Cologne, where she was to try to observe her religious lifestyle as much as possible.

That the nuns of Bethlehem connected the two Maries to Margaret Smulders was inevitable. In a later letter to the Archbishop, the Mother Superior of Bethlehem led the way: "The story is still told that we had a witch here; it's been twenty-three years, but I hope to God that Sister Margaret isn't such a one." Another sister decades later could still write chillingly of the ancient horror, advancing the opinion that guilty nuns probably became infected in Cologne during the 1580s, after the community had been forced into exile there by marauding troops: by the time the nuns returned to Leuven, in 1587, the damage had been done. Because of it, the community suffered for the next fifteen years—and now perhaps even beyond.

Surely this troublesome past explained why during his interviews of 1616 the Vicar-General found in Bethlehem so many worries about witchery. Few sisters would have cared at this point to look more closely and determine whether Margaret was a "true" and willing witch, like Marie Everaerts, or simply involuntarily possessed. If secular and church judges often confused possession with witchcraft and tended to see the latter, then why should nonprofessionals have bothered with such fine distinctions?

The Archbishop heeded the fears of the nuns of Bethlehem; Margaret did not reenter the convent at this time. But there was more to the story of the demons and to her departure, and it was locked in the heart of Margaret herself. When she chose to reveal it over the next two years, it would, as she hoped, serve to vindicate her and bring about her return to the convent after all. But it would also serve to galvanize the sentiments of other sisters against her, even more than in the past.

3
Confessors

June to December, 1618. Margaret never thought of herself as a witch, an active servant of the devil. At the time she first left Bethlehem, she wasn't even sure she was possessed, a lesser condition to which she would later admit. But regardless of the nature of her devilish ailment in those early years, Margaret always insisted that it was not the cause of her departure. Rather, she left Bethlehem for an even more scandalous reason: the sexual advances of the house confessor, the man who had supposedly done so much to restore peace in her absence.

There were at least two truths-universal about female convents: every convent needed a confessor, and every confessor was male. Though religious women might serve as spiritual advisors, such a role was sanctioned by personal holiness, not hierarchically bestowed authority. Moreover, such a relationship was never sacramental, since nuns, though part of the professional church, were not allowed to hear confession, perform Mass, or preach. For all these functions—and for general advice and assistance—convents called in a priest, whose appointment as a convent's confessor was in theory controlled by the local Bishop. Usually the nuns paid the confessor a salary, or even provided lodgings, to assure themselves of regular service.

How well the system worked depended very much on the people involved. Some confessors were clearly satisfactory and served for years in convents, but there were also those who neglected Mass, failed to preach, were outright scandalous, or alienated some of the nuns. With Henri Joos, their own chosen confessor, the Grey Sisters of Leuven long felt luckier than most. He was not lightminded, like the confessors of Santa Chiara in Pescia, Italy. He was not offensively familiar, like the confessor of a convent in Nevele, near Gent. He was not, like many confessors, accused of blabbing secrets, or of "constricting consciences." He did not so anger nuns in his care that they screamed in his face. He was never one to rush someone during confession, as a nun in Brussels complained to her confessor: "You're a murderer, you button up my conscience, and you busy yourself in confession like you're using a broom." No such charges were leveled against Henri Joos during fourteen years of service in Bethlehem.

Originally from Balen in the eastern Spanish Netherlands, the confessor had come to Leuven in the 1590s as a student at the university, where he earned a bachelor's degree in theology. After completing his studies, he won in 1604 a most respectable position as Vice Pastor of St. Gertrude's parish, just a block away from the convent of Bethlehem.* Soon after his arrival, Henri Joos learned the miserable state of the nearby convent, became acquainted with some of its nuns, and generously offered to help.

Given the poverty of their house at the time, and given the very recent affair of the witch Marie Everaerts, it's no wonder the sisters, including the newly entered Margaret Smulders, so appreciated the condescension of Henri Joos, who assisted them "with compassion

---

*St. Gertrude's was not only a parish church but attached to an Augustinian monastery; the Abbot was at the same time Pastor of the parish, but given his many responsibilities he always delegated his parish work to a Vice Pastor, for a couple hundred florins a year, plus beer and wood. Hence, in practice Henri Joos was the Pastor of the parish.

and alms." He saw that they had no permanent confessor and little money to pay for one. Out of Christian charity, said some sisters, he practically volunteered to take on that position in addition to his duties in the parish of St. Gertrude's. It was quite possible that he served the nuns "pro Deo," with no annual fee, not unheard of in poorer convents. And it was quite certain that he diligently represented the convent when its leaders sold an orchard or transferred an annuity, that he gave alms, and that he said Mass and heard confession faithfully. His reputation beyond Bethlehem was also good. Visitations to the parish of St. Gertrude's by the Archbishop's men were full of praise, beginning with the very first when the Dean wrote "the Pastor is commended" and "well liked by his parishioners," that there were "no scandals," and that "all commune."

But Henri Joos would not appear anytime soon on the calendar of saints. Even without Margaret's accusations, this might have been discerned from his account books: though required by the Council of Trent, these books were too tidy and detailed to reflect an intense longing for higher spheres. He proudly recorded catching a fraudulent iron-caster, he lovingly noted the precious ornaments on St. Gertrude's altars, and he neatly reckoned to the last stiver his expenditures for jewels, green and red cloth, leather, and golden angels. Certainly attention to temporal matters was necessary: someone had to look after damage caused by the winds of 1606, care for ruined graves in the cemetery, repair the organ, track Easter contributions, buy a couple of tasteful new chairs for the vicarage, and see that the church roof was repaired. Such tasks did not necessarily preclude profound spirituality, but Henri Joos relished the earthly too much for this.

Still, to most sisters of Bethlehem he was more than merely dutiful, more than an able temporal administrator, but a certain candidate for heaven. Henri Joos surely enjoyed his position as confessor as well, for when in Bethlehem he was almost king, free of the requisite bowing and scraping owed his superiors in St. Gertrude's. So highly regarded was he in the convent, and so sure of himself, that when he presented his sister and cousin for entry into Bethlehem, in 1609, the nuns did not hesitate to accept them. Only Margaret and a certain Sister Lesken felt less enamored of the man, and their sentiments went untold for years. When they finally emerged, the confessor who had served Bethlehem for so long, and who enjoyed such lasting favor, would be unceremoniously removed.

Sister Lesken Nijns, who had professed in Bethlehem in 1605, just a year before Margaret, leveled the first serious but imprecisely noted charges against Henri Joos in June 1618. These she sent through her messenger, a Pater Dhollander of Leuven, to Bethlehem's superior, Mathias Hovius, Archbishop of Mechelen. In line with many other instances of sexual scandal in this time (outside of formal trials), her charges were recorded only obliquely and key documents were destroyed. But that the charges immediately captured the attention of the inhumanly busy, aging Archbishop, and that they were soon connected to more specific sexual charges leveled by Margaret Smulders, suggested the case's gravity and nature.

By July 4 the Archbishop had heard enough to instruct Mater Judoca quietly to ban Henri Joos from Bethlehem. The Archbishop also sent a secretary to Leuven to deliver personally to Henri Joos a notice of his removal as the convent's confessor. This did not mean that Archbishop Hovius necessarily believed Lesken Nijns; in fact when the Archbishop permitted her in August to come to his residence and tell her story in person, he wrote in his journal that he thought her less than truthful. Moreover, after removing Henri Joos the Archbishop made him a most attractive proposal: how would he like to come immediately to Mechelen and assume a position as lector, or reader, in the Archbishop's beloved seminary? The ex-confessor was interested indeed, and he traveled to Mechelen to tell the Archbishop so.

What was one to make of this proposal? When a priest required discipline, the zealous Mathias Hovius never shied from imposing it. But since the facts in Sister Lesken's case were still vague to him,

Mathias Hovius, Archbishop of Mechelen, 1596–1620

Koninklijk Instituut voor het Kunstpatrimonium, Brussels, © IRPA-KIK Brussel

his primary concern was to stop the wagging of tongues. Thus he kicked Henri Joos upstairs, to get him out of Bethlehem without giving offense to the faithful, or propaganda meal to Protestants in Holland. The sisters were simply to imagine that their gifted confessor was upwardly mobile.

But the plan was more complicated than the Archbishop had hoped. Henri Joos's parishioners in St. Gertrude's and his nuns in Bethlehem both sent delegations to Mechelen to plead against his transfer from Leuven. And when Henri Joos dawdled in Leuven instead of taking up his position at the seminary, bells began to ring in minds and the fiction to fall apart: if the confessor was still in town, then why could he not, reasoned the sisters, come to hear their confessions, or at least visit? And what was so important that Lesken Nijns, sworn to eternal cloister, had to leave the convent in the middle of all this to talk to Archbishop Hovius in Mechelen?

By late August the fiction was in shambles, for the women of Bethlehem sent to the Archbishop a stack of depositions praising the character of Henri Joos. That the depositions were about character, and no longer the question of a transfer from Leuven, confirmed that the nuns now realized the true charges against the confessor, and their source. So angry were they at Lesken Nijns, and so eager the Archbishop to keep Lesken from telling her tales further, that he arranged for her transfer to a convent far away in Den Bosch, near Holland.

Though Lesken was discredited and departed, the Archbishop still refused to allow Henri Joos to return to Bethlehem as confessor, or even as casual visitor. The man was simply becoming an annoyance. Among other things, the Archbishop thought the ex-confessor a bit too untroubled by events. He also thought him presumptuous for continuing to call at Bethlehem, even when ordered not to. And he thought Mater Judoca wrong for receiving him, or sending lay sisters to wait upon him in his lodgings in Leuven. Hence it wasn't long before the Archbishop regretted having ever dangled the plum at the seminary. By the end of October 1618, the Archbishop had soured completely on Henri Joos.

There was one more likely reason why the Archbishop turned against the former confessor by this time, and her name was Margaret Smulders. During all this tumult around Sister Lesken, Margaret was of course out of Bethlehem. But it was very likely that she spent this time in Mechelen, probably among the Black Sisters, who had old ties with the nuns of Bethlehem.* For in the middle of the crisis provoked by Lesken Nijns, Archbishop Hovius suddenly called Margaret to his residence, on July 14, 1618, and she came immediately. That the overloaded Archbishop summoned at this particular moment an obscure, long-exiled, disgraced nun was surely no coincidence: he knew Margaret's whereabouts, and he suspected that she had intelligence about a particularly sensitive and cloudy issue currently before him.

The Archbishop's notes from his first meeting with Margaret on July 14 were fairly vague. Subsequent interviews with Margaret were likewise vaguely recorded. But of the last and most important interview, in mid-October, the Archbishop wrote that Margaret "affirmed by oath that the things which she had told me personally and written to me about were true." There was no more specific reference, as usual, but the vague antecedents, the fact that these conversations occurred at the same time as those regarding Lesken Nijns, and that Henri Joos fell out of favor this very month, all suggest strongly that they had to do with the former confessor.

*In fact the name "Bethlehem" belonged originally to the Grey Sisters of Mechelen, whose convent was ruined by Protestant troops during the 1580s. Because the nearly depleted Grey Sisters of Leuven had plenty of room, the Archbishop decided in 1587 to merge the two houses rather than build a new structure in Mechelen. The sisters from Mechelen brought not only their name to Leuven but their contemplative lifestyle, leadership, and documents. Some of those documents made plain the longtime connections between the Grey and Black Sisters of Mechelen when both convents were located in that city.

It was likely that Margaret gave the Archbishop on this occasion the same explanation she would give later in 1624 to another confessor. "Everyone is of the opinion," wrote this confessor, that Margaret left the convent in 1616 so she might be freed from the demons that possessed her. But the real reason she left, he continued, was to flee Henri Joos, who had "with carnal affection" so "often" importuned her. Here was the most specific evidence left of the entire case, and which gives meaning to so many cryptic references made elsewhere by the Archbishop. Margaret went on to tell this confessor that the importuning and the possessions were connected. Enough words remained on the confessor's torn letter that one of two things might be surmised about Margaret's claim: her possessions had occurred *after* the advances of Henri Joos, or even *because* of them.

These claims mattered both because of the gravity of sexual importuning, and because they show that the supernatural events surrounding Margaret were understood by her to have been demonic possession rather than witchcraft—a distinction that negated her complicity. In fact it put the blame not only on the devil but on Henri Joos. For someone of Margaret's station would have been familiar with the assumption that evil spirits often entered victims at the direction of a human agent rather than of the devil himself. A possessed woman named Spadens testified in 1618 that "a certain man had me by the neck, and blew into my mouth, and kissed my lips in three places leaving blue spots, and spoke certain words which I didn't understand." Ever since then, she had been ill and experienced mysterious accidents and sensations, so that she was stiff as a board and had to be clothed by others (a temporary catatonic state was common among the possessed).

Margaret would have been familiar as well with the notion that those who removed demons could also invoke them, like undercover agents who, after living in a world of vice, embrace it. There were plenty of turncoat exorcists around. A Dean's meeting in Antwerp in 1615 lamented that some clergy involved in exorcism had become infested with demons themselves. The next year a Capuchin confessed to the Archbishop's court in Mechelen that he had not only performed unauthorized exorcisms but gone over to the enemy and afflicted others with evil spirits. Some traitorous exorcists even used their powers to seduce unsuspecting women. Witnesses a century earlier in Spain testified against an exorcist who boasted that he could not only inflict and cast out demons but use these powers to seduce female subjects. Was Henri Joos capable of such? He certainly had opportunity, for even his supporters admitted that he had performed private exorcisms over Margaret and Lesken: though such exorcisms were supposed to occur before witnesses, to avoid temptation and the appearance of wrongdoing, it was easy for the unscrupulous to ignore that guideline and even to take advantage of their subject. In one sensational case a decade before, nuns of a convent in Brussels revealed that the exorcism methods of their confessor had included his undressing himself, undressing them, touching their exposed "private parts," and placing his tongue in their mouths. Now Margaret was suggesting that Henri Joos had taken advantage of her—in regard to both the inflicting of demons and the making of carnal advances.

Historians of monasticism have for long been too ready, perhaps, to find sexual fears and scandals behind every trouble in convents. But in Margaret's case a sexual overture was indeed in question, and in other cases was certainly not unheard of. One historian has pointed out that "the idea of devils 'possessing' the sexually unchaste is particularly common in monastic writing," a connection and legacy that likely affected Margaret as well. The episodes of conventual possessions in the Low Countries, noted earlier, involved a strong dose of sexuality. So did the notorious events in Aix-en-Provence, France, between 1609 and 1611, and later in Loudun, where several nuns accused a confessor of performing sorcery upon them in order to seduce them. "The demons gave me very evil desires and feelings of quite licentious affection for the persons who might have helped my soul," testified a lead witness in such a case. Even St. Anthony, that champion fighter of demons, was tempted always by two things when the devil attacked: loss of chastity and acquisition of wealth. Clearly, possession was about not merely being taken over and frightened but sexual temptation as well.

Hence, Margaret was quite up to date if she believed that an exorcist could also invoke demons. She was in good company in believing that where evil spirits were concerned, sinful acts or desires of the flesh were right behind. And she would not have been alone if her memory of what happened with Henri Joos was vague and troubling, or if she somehow connected her possessions to his importuning. Most important in all this, however, was that Archbishop Hovius seemed to believe her. In fact the Archbishop's actions after October 1618 show that he was more inclined to believe Margaret than he was Lesken Nijns. For though at first he wanted Margaret to leave Bethlehem, as Lesken had, he did this out of sympathy for Margaret rather than anger. Moreover, the Archbishop changed his mind in the end: because he believed her story enough, thought her innocent enough, or perhaps merely found her poor enough, he decided to return Margaret after all to her own convent of Bethlehem. Writing to Mater Judoca on October 20, the Archbishop reminded her of his ban on Henri Joos and ordered her and the entire convent to prepare to receive Sister Margaret "peacefully."

Naturally this put Mater Judoca in a dither. It was bad enough to have lost their beloved confessor, or that Lesken Nijns had slandered him, but the thought of Margaret returning was too great for nuns to bear. They knew her ability to cause discord and her suspicious past with demons. And surely they suspected by now that Margaret, like Lesken Nijns, had told stories against Henri Joos. Judoca wrote immediately to the Archbishop to request a personal audience, at his residence. So serious was the matter that he granted the request, and on November 2, 1618, "revealed the whole affair" to Judoca—which thus included the things he had been told in recent weeks by Margaret Smulders.

Only the nuns of Bethlehem knew what Mater Judoca reported to them upon her return to Leuven. But given her warm opinions of Henri Joos in the past, she probably told the story in a light most favorable to him, and unfavorable to Margaret. Whatever she said, the sisters were soon forming their own versions of events anyway. The most common was expressed as late as 1672 by one of the ex-confessor's dogged supporters, Sister Anna Vignarola. According to Anna, the good confessor served Bethlehem generously for years. Then, "two daughters" entered who appeared capable enough to profess but who in truth were "evil." Soon after their profession the house was wracked night and day by noise and desolation. Only Henri Joos, privy to the confessions of the two women, knew the true source of these disturbances, and he was not allowed to break the seal of the confessional. Out of the goodness of his heart, he read exorcisms over the afflicted nuns, "in secret," to protect their honor. But through their "evil instruments and jealousy" these two daughters spread rumors about the man and brought him to "ruin." Eventually he was "scandalously removed from the community" by Archbishop Hovius, who was "poorly informed" because the charges were brought "too late." The goodness of Henri Joos was therefore repaid with evil, wrote Sister Anna.

Unfortunately no one will ever know for sure who was right about Henri Joos—a conclusion all too familiar in such intimate cases. But given Anna's depth of feeling and unflagging passion about her version of events, as well as the equally impressive insistence on a contrary version by Margaret and Lesken Nijns, it was easy to see that here was the single most important question in Bethlehem for decades. What mattered here and in most such scandals was not the scandal per se, but how it affected life within the community. In the convent of Bethlehem this scandal defined almost everything for years to come—for those who liked Henri

Joos, and those who did not. Clear to the majority was that their popular confessor was gone and the dreaded Margaret about to return. Clear to Margaret was that she had been misunderstood and Henri Joos wrongly exonerated. Neither side would ever forget.

With the rumors that Margaret must have known were flying in Bethlehem against her, it's no wonder she was reluctant to go back. On November 23, 1618, the Archbishop called Margaret to him and "exhorted her to return promptly." Three weeks later he again ordered Mater Judoca to receive Margaret, who would be reintroduced in the convent by a certain Pater Gummarus. No one bothered to record exactly when Margaret finally returned, but return she did, probably in December 1618, having been away at least two years. Her reception was surely less than pleasant.

Mater Judoca died within months of Margaret's return, around February 1619, presumably still a believer in Henri Joos, and after asking the Archbishop that all papers of the case "be burned." The Archbishop and his Vicar-General, determined to swing the balance of power away from Henri Joos's supporters, came to Bethlehem in May to oversee the election of Judoca's successor. When the secret ballots were cast, the Archbishop was dismayed to see that Henri's sister, Maria Joos, had won a majority of votes. Without revealing the outcome to the nuns, he decided to ask whether they would not simply accept the candidate of his choice as their Mater. The nuns, many of whom must have been suspicious, consented. Archbishop Hovius then chose a woman whom he knew would at least refrain from attacking Margaret, and who was neutral toward Henri Joos: Sister Barbara Noosen.

Perhaps due to the episode with Henri Joos and the headache of the election, Archbishop Hovius soon grew weary of Bethlehem. By late 1619 he took the unusual step of offering to relinquish jurisdiction over it, to the local male Franciscans, but his turf-guarding cathedral chapter, which possessed a say in the matter, disallowed it—and the Archbishop was too tired to fight them. In May 1620 he died, aged seventy-eight, episcopal control over Bethlehem indifferently intact.

Before expiring, however, Archbishop Hovius told Henri Joos that the position at the seminary was no longer available. The Archbishop also sent negative messages to Henri Joos's superior in St. Gertrude's, to try to force the ex-confessor out of his position as Pastor in the parish as well. By the summer of 1623, Henri Joos had seen enough of Leuven. Thanks to family connections, he was put forward for the pastorship of Mol, about a day's walk northeast of Leuven in the diocese of Den Bosch, and near his family and place of birth. The parish did not have the prestige of St. Gertrude's, but there were attractive compensations: it was large and respectable, the salary was good, his bishop lived far away, he was the most important clergyman in town, he would have a Vice Pastor beneath him, and there was the chance at a fresh start among people to whom he was not a complete stranger but from whom he had been gone long enough to add to his mystery and stature. After much wrangling about distribution of tithes, he was at last appointed. The document of nomination, composed far from Leuven, offered much praise for his twenty years of service in St. Gertrude's and made a sentimental note that he was returning to Mol because he wished to be near the area of his birth. It said nothing about his service in Bethlehem.

As a parting blow, Henri Joos's superior in St. Gertrude's asked him to compile a full account of his temporal dealings from beginning to end (this despite the fact that Pastor Joos had submitted annual accounts regularly). Thus he put together at the end of a six-by-eight-inch leather-bound notebook a well-ordered list of his own expenses and credits, showing clearly that he had spent more than he had received. And what language for a tedious account book, with familiar Latin epigrams on the final page: "That which you do, do prudently and think of the end; the end crowns the work." His last words, however, provide a more fitting conclusion to the question of whether he had behaved unseemly with certain sisters of Bethlehem: in this, and presumably all things, he desired "no other compensation for my labor than the reward I expect from God almighty."

Besides Margaret Smulders and Lesken Nijns, who else was in a position to determine his just recompense?

4

Despair

Bethlehem, January 17, 1624. The matter of the demons and the episode with Henri Joos went far toward explaining Margaret's unhappiness in Bethlehem. But there was more to come, for the years after her return in 1618 did not go well at all. The same old demons came back to afflict her. The same old sisters, and a few new, continued to resent her. So burdened did Margaret feel that on this night she tried to kill herself.

The crisis began a day earlier, when Margaret told the new Archbishop of Mechelen, through the Dean of Leuven, that she was terrorized by "great noises" at night: objects were thrown down and dashed to pieces and coverings on her bed ripped off. Though petrified, Margaret did not dare mention the disturbances to anyone else, nor ask for another religious to sleep in her room, for she did not wish to confirm their suspicions about her links to demons. She simply wished to be moved to another room. In the meantime, her spiritual state was abysmal, for the convent's new confessor, a local Franciscan, had heard tales about her from other sisters and refused to comfort her.

Not content with merely relaying a message through the Dean, Margaret wrote the Archbishop directly as well—the first of her many marginless, rambling missives that would land on his table. It was hopeless to try to describe in such short space, she explained, the afflictions that came over her at night, "for a very long time is necessary to do so, so complex is the matter." In fact she had dared speak to no one on the subject these past eighteen months, and apparently did not trust the Dean of Leuven enough to tell him all the details. What she hoped for now was an audience with the Archbishop, since, being newly appointed, he did not yet know her full story, since explanation came easier in person, and since one never knew what eyes might read her letters on their way to Mechelen. Could the Archbishop not speak with her at length, Margaret pleaded, or appoint someone to the task? "I am prepared to talk to your reverence or your vicar at any time you may name," even about the "origins" of her troubles. If the Archbishop decided to delegate the task, Margaret even had someone in mind: a Capuchin friar called Johan Evangelista, a man with whom she had once spoken "as openly as if she was in the presence of the Lord." But now she heard that he had moved to Antwerp, too far away to deal with her regularly. "Had the matter been pursued by him, I dare say I'd already be freed from all burdens, for it's a very discreet man, much experienced in these things."

Until she could speak with Father Evangelista or the Archbishop, Margaret would remain "marvelously afflicted." The community had "evil suspicions" about her, from not only the old days but now a more recent event as well: around Christmas last, she explained, some items had gone missing from the cell of a troubled postulant. A few sisters blamed the theft "on me," while others "say that I give the devil power to do it." But Margaret claimed she had never done such things or "even had the desire" to do them, "I take God as my witness." Margaret admitted that she did not get on well with the postulant in question, and had even voted against her first entry into the convent. But if the events of recent weeks were the work of fiendish spirits or of humans, God only knew. The "accusations consume my flesh and blood, and I suffer so day and night from the devil and his sinister instruments, that it is often almost impossible for me to endure it all, and I fear that I might succumb, although I am by nature stubborn, which comes by the grace of God." She implored the Archbishop to intervene, before her resolve collapsed, "or it is to be feared that it will go badly with me, through the constant temptation." She desired with all her heart to "live as a religious ought." Don't delay, she beseeched, "for I'm now in a perilous state, having made no confession since New Year's" and having no desire to confess until the affair should be settled. "It will be damnation to the community on the one hand and me on the other, through hate and envy."

On the night of January 17 and 18, perhaps the very night she wrote her plea to the Archbishop, Margaret, despairing of an answer, took a knife to her stomach and tried to end her life. Mater Barbara Noosen and Margaret's only friend, Sister Catharina, told the Archbishop of the event, and added that Margaret was "miraculously healed" on St. Paul's day, January 25. Whether other sisters knew of the attempted suicide is unclear, but even without this they had still other reasons to resent Margaret, and to seek the intervention of the Archbishop. For on the very St. Paul's day that Margaret was healed, still more items went missing from the room of the postulant named Barbara Beli.

January 27, 1624. Barbara Noosen was lamenting her elevation as Mater five years before. By appointing her, Archbishop Hovius had hoped to avoid the factionalism that dominated elections, but instead Barbara's very want of popular election had caused disaffection from her. And under the circumstances of the appointment she could not help but be seen as an opponent of Henri Joos—a position out of line with the majority of sisters in the house.

Though her installation had been memorable, with the Archbishop handing her the keys of the convent and placing a crown on her head in the midst of singing and bell ringing, Barbara's only consolation since was that her reign had been good for her soul: she had learned empathy for other Maters.

Today was her latest trial. Nineteen of the twenty veiled and lay sisters (everyone but Margaret) now approached Mater Barbara for permission to send to the Archbishop a petition about their recent troubles. All knew that such a step was risky. For though each sister had the right to correspond privately with the Archbishop (all other letters, in and out, had to pass through Mater's hands), he did not like pressure from all at once, which resembled a public protest. That the nuns were prepared to send it anyway was a measure of their desperation; according to one sister, they "thirst for nothing else" but to have Margaret out.

Sister Adriana Truis, the most determined opponent of both Sister Margaret and by now Mater Barbara, had composed the twenty-five lines of the petition in her square letters, leaving the usual large left margin. In the name of all she pleaded "once more" that the Archbishop put an end to "this matter." Now "it seems daily to grow worse instead of better," for only two days before, while the community was saying morning prayers, the coverings on the bed of the postulant Barbara Beli were torn off and her clothes thrown out the window, just as in weeks past. The sisters were not upset merely about soiled clothes, but rather that something or someone sinister was believed to be behind it all. For like other religious, the women of Bethlehem supposed that the devil made the desecration of religious clothing a favorite pastime. They therefore sought the Archbishop's "fatherly care," and made the usual promise of prayers for his soul if he helped them.

After reading the piece, Mater Barbara was asked not only to approve but to put her name to it, placing her in a most difficult position. To sign would be to incur the displeasure of the Archbishop. But to refuse would win her the wrath of her flock, with whom she had to live and eat and pray and work and breathe, and without whose tacit support the hardships of monastic life would be rendered harder still. So she contrived a plan to placate both.

Despair

45

First, she went ahead and signed the petition, positioning her "Sister Barbara Noosen, Mater Unworthy," somewhere in the middle of the available space. Those standing by pointed out that as Mater, her name should appear at the head of the list. Perturbed, she crossed out, then signed again. She watched as the names of the remaining sisters were added beneath hers, according to date of profession, oldest first. Half couldn't write at all, a few wrote barely legibly, but no matter—Adriana Truis and Maria Joos were glad to help. A couple put an "X" beneath their name, others simply had Adriana and Maria sign for them. It was a formidable document, and neatly put together.

The petition entrusted to her for sending, and the sisters now gone, Mater Barbara executed the second part of her plan: she would include with the petition a private letter explaining to the Archbishop why she had signed. Barbara had little use for the likes of Adriana Truis, whom she found mean, stingy, and overly fond of outsiders: as Mater she wished to distance herself from the petition. In her typically perfunctory fashion, hopping from one thought to the next, ignoring punctuation, and spelling most irregularly even for this day of irregular spelling, Barbara therefore explained that she had signed the petition only to "make them content." It was true the community had reason to be upset, for the occurrences of late were troubling indeed. But a petition went too far, especially because the nuns themselves were largely to blame for the state of things: their actions, after all, had brought "the afflicted one to desperation." Their talk of the stolen items in the postulant's room, that Margaret was behind it all or "at least gives the enemy power to do it," only caused Margaret to despair. It was all Barbara could do to prevent a despondent Margaret from making once more "the same attempt" on her life. The sisters could "fill up each others' heads" and then walk away, lamented Barbara, while she had to "hear and suffer all this noise and keep silent, or there would be no peace." Salvation, "on both sides," was in great peril.

At the same time Mater Barbara was writing, Sister Catharina

Rijkeboer also retired to scribble a brief note to the Archbishop. One of the younger nuns, Catharina was among the few to support Mater Barbara on most issues in the house, and the only one to treat Margaret in a manner that approached friendship. She, too, wished to preserve good relations with the Archbishop and thus felt it necessary as well to explain why she had signed the petition: to keep the peace. Using every inch of her short sheet and writing with more sophistication than Barbara, Catharina recounted how from "both sides" she was deluged with requests for help. From one side, she said, came the pleas of Sister Margaret, who "promises me earnestly that she'll do her best" to once again lead a regular monastic life. But from the other the community begged Catharina to "help us in our time of need." There would probably be no peace from them, she guessed, until Margaret was out for good, for "it's gone on so long, and is now worse than ever." If this tempest was on account of Margaret, then, concluded Catharina, "perhaps we need throw her into the sea with the prophet Jonah," but only God knew. As far as Catharina was concerned, she would remain neutral and seek the will of God. She added almost as an afterthought the news of Margaret's attempt on her own life. She folded the letter, then secretly gave it to the same messenger bearing Mater Barbara's.

Mechelen, the Archiepiscopal Palace, late January 1624. Though elevated to the Archbishopric of Mechelen only in 1621, Jacob Boonen was already renowned as the "almsman of the poor." During his four decades as Bishop there and elsewhere he would offer not only his considerable prestige to a multitude of causes but his plentiful florins too. The means to do so came only partly from his episcopal benefices, for his archdiocese, in rank the first of the seventeen bishoprics in the land, was not the first endowed. Most of Archbishop Boonen's money came instead from his mother, Gertrude, an heir of the merchant Van Heetvelde's of Leuven. Most of his empathy probably came from his mother as well, as she was renowned for her piety. When Jacob was but six, and his two sisters

Jacob Boonen, Archbishop of Mechelen, 1621–1655

Koninklijk Instituut voor het Kunstpatrimonium, Brussels, © IRPA-KIK Brussel

not much older, Gertrude heard the news that her husband had been poisoned and executed by the Dutch. Sought out some time later by the penitent assassins, now kneeling at her feet, Gertrude readily forgave them.

If he owed virtue and wealth to his mother, Jacob Boonen could thank his paternal family for a head start on fame. Father Cornelius and grandfather Jacob had both sat on the prestigious Council of State in the Spanish Netherlands, a career for which young Jacob also seemed destined. At age twenty-two, after graduating with distinction in law from the University of Leuven, he began working in the eastern Netherlands as a lawyer specializing in Dutch affairs. But upon moving back to his home town of Mechelen, he set out on the high-church road to influence—not for convenience or power, for he had access to either without a clerical collar, but because of vocation: during an emotional moment of prayer before a local miracle-working image of Our Lady, he vowed to enter the clergy. Rapidly appointed to a host of ecclesiastical offices, he was finally ordained a priest in 1611 at age thirty-eight, then in 1616 became Bishop of Gent. Finally, after the death of his old patron, Mathias Hovius, he moved from Gent in 1621 to become the fourth Archbishop of Mechelen, where he remained to his death.

For the next three decades, Jacob Boonen would be *primus* not only in the seven dioceses that composed the church province of Mechelen but in the entire Spanish Netherlands, prompting one devotional author to compare him to Moses, leader of all the land. Thanks to his new position, Archbishop Boonen would also sit in the Estates (or provincial assembly) of Brabant and display the old family talent for politics, a talent that would make him a member of Archduchess Isabella's Council of State and eventually a major envoy.

But this involvement in the political world did not make Jacob Boonen a throwback to medieval or contemporary prince-bishops who cared more for war and intrigue than their flocks. Regularly he visited lesser monasteries and parishes, and he wrote attentive

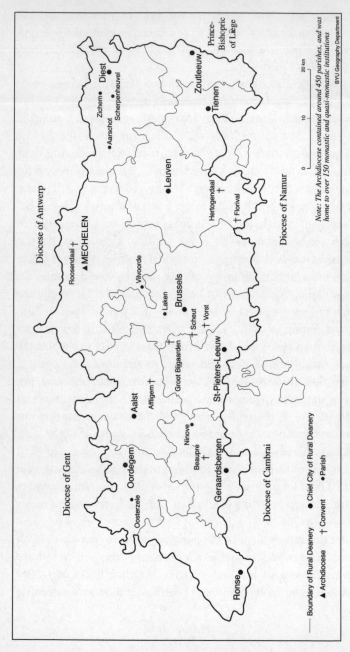

The Archdiocese of Mechelen, with selected deaneries, parishes, and convents

Diocese of Antwerp

Prince-Bishopric of Liège

Diocese of Namur

Diocese of Gent

Diocese of Cambrai

Diest
• Zichem
• Aarschot
Scherpenheuvel
Aarschot

Zoutleeuw

Tienen

▲ MECHELEN
Roosendaal †

Leuven

Hertogendaal †

† Florival

Vilvoorde

Laken •
Brussels
† Scheut
† Vorst

Groot Bijgaarden †

St-Pieters-Leeuw

Affligem †

Aalst

Ninove
Beaupré †

Geraardsbergen

Oordegem
Oosterzele

Ronse

Note: The Archdiocese contained around 450 parishes, and was home to over 150 monastic and quasi-monastic institutions

0   10   20 km

BYU Geography Department

— Boundary of Rural Deanery   ● Chief City of Rural Deanery   ● Parish
▲ Archdiocese   † Convent

reports about them. Personally he investigated candidates for ecclesiastical posts as well as complaints about the clergy's underpreaching, overdrinking, incontinence, and petty rivalries. Worriedly he read the report of a chaplain in Brussels that a multitude of people were quite unaware that Christ was the Redeemer. Disappointedly he heard problems of the archdiocesan seminary, of deficiencies in the members of his own household, of haggling convents and confessors, of "temptresses" in Brussels, or the indolence of the Bishop of Arras, to the south, who never left his rooms or preached. Perhaps at this early date Jacob Boonen was not yet the archetypal Bishop, a Carlo Borromeo of Milan or a Matteo Giberti of Verona, but he was very conscious of that ideal and strove after it eagerly.

In spite of his zeal, at the episcopal palace of Mechelen even the most compelling affairs of a nun in Leuven could be drowned out in a roar of requests for his abundant expertise and charity. Margaret's problem, though serious, was no doubt secondary to more pressing concerns: the threat of invasion from the Dutch, establishing a home in Brussels for penitent women, and trying to get a new common catechism for the whole church province into print and usage. Sister Margaret of the Grey Sisters was one of many squeaky hinges—annoying, clamoring for repair, but hard actually to get around to fixing. Most of the time his aides handled such cases, but when he deemed a case important enough, he got involved himself. And in Bethlehem the moment for intervention had arrived.

Examining all the documents, the Archbishop was confronted with disturbing facts and gaps. Who could have ransacked Barbara Beli's room on the day of January 25? There were a number of this-worldly explanations: Margaret attempted suicide on the 17th, but according to Mater Barbara she was healed on the 25th. Was she healed enough to have risen from her bed while the others were in choir? And why would Margaret have done it? To make it look as if the source of evil in the convent was the postulant rather than herself? Could Barbara Beli have pillaged her own room, knowing that others would suspect Margaret, and thus get revenge for Margaret's having voted against her entry? Yet Barbara Beli was supposed to have been in choir with the others when the ransacking occurred.

Then came otherworldly explanations. He would not ignore the sisters' claims on this point, but he had sat on too many tribunals to believe every cry of sorcery. He would undoubtedly have echoed the opinion of one of his Vicar-Generals, who stated that accusations of possession or witchcraft should not be made lightly. This was especially true, said the Vicar-General—citing a common opinion among the experts of the day—"when it comes to women, for they often give evidence of great powers of imagination." But neither did the Archbishop disbelieve in evil spirits; he had taken care in the most recent edition of the diocesan pastoral handbook to personally amend one of the formulas against demonic infestation and to add five new formulas against possession. And he was certainly aware of the famous scandals involving evil spirits in France and the Low Countries. Perhaps they were at work in Bethlehem too.

A clearer understanding of Margaret's case would emerge only months later. For the moment, lacking the details he would have liked and knowing Margaret's reluctance to speak with anyone else, the Archbishop took the safe path of calling in the expert, the man whom Margaret claimed could cure her, if only given the chance.

5

The Specialist

Leuven, the friary of the Capuchins, February 23, 1624. Margaret was wrong about the abode of her ideal confessor, Johan Evangelista. In truth, he lived only blocks away from her in Leuven, in the new— and according to some brothers overdecorated—Capuchin friary.

The Capuchins (so-called because of their pointed hoods) were born in Italy in 1528, to revive strict observation of the Franciscan rule and good preaching. The order spread gradually to northern Europe, so that by the late sixteenth century a Bishop of Antwerp could declare that the Capuchins edified "everyone." The friary in Leuven took shape in the 1590s, thanks, said chroniclers, to the usual litany of miracles. When one woman, for instance, refused to sell her home, which stood on grounds envisioned for the new friary, God, who did not "forget his friends," turned her "into a corpse." Soon after, the deceased's daughter declared, like Pharaoh, that she was ready, after all, to let the house go. The house was purchased, the friary built, and then enlarged by 1619.

From within one of the thirty-five cells, the friar gazed into the garden below and pondered his past and recent experiences with Sister Margaret of Bethlehem. He was willing to report his sentiments on her situation, as Archbishop Boonen had requested, but

Hagiographical portrait of Johan Evangelista

Capuchin Monastery of Antwerp

doubted that he could do much good. This, however, was modesty, for he was no ordinary Capuchin. Gerardus Verscharen van den Bosch, who had professed in 1614 at age twenty-five under the religious name of Johan Evangelista, was by 1623 already Guardian, or superior, of the friary in Leuven. Here in 1624 his name was being tossed about for the vacant, destitute bishopric of Roermond, where only someone such as a poverty-loving Capuchin could cope. He would also make his mark through three tracts on the inner life: while he lived, these circulated only privately among monks and nuns, but when published they caused scholars to name him one of the three great Capuchin writers of the Low Countries. Finally, he was renowned for his austere personal habits, which demonstrated his rejection of this world and his pursuit of the next: daily meditation, two hours of sleep a night, and assiduous prayer and study—all reflected in the heaven-looking, mercy-seeking, hagiographic portrait of him painted soon after his death from the plague in 1635. In life as well as death, therefore, Johan Evangelista was revered as an authority on matters spiritual, especially in regard to the professional religious. This reputation, along with his promising meetings in the past with Margaret, brought him to the attention of Jacob Boonen.

How many times had the friar walked through his own front gate with its inscriptions of St. Augustine and scenes of the Passion, then over the bridge and on for a few blocks to the convent of the Grey Sisters? After two years of correspondence and visits, he could say with authority to the Archbishop that Margaret's afflictions were "most perilous and grave," to herself and to the community she had single-handedly brought into tumult. At his very first visit, he wrote, Margaret instantly revealed the depths of her heart to him, something she was loath to do with the house confessor or anyone else. From this it was obvious to him that, as Margaret had said already, her troubles were "most intricate" indeed.

These intricate problems must have included Margaret's account of strange noises, lonely nights, and her fears of demons, for one of Father Evangelista's first endeavors, he told the Archbishop, was to try to exorcise the poor woman. During one critical period that extended over several weeks, he visited her daily to perform the ritual. Though he did not think Margaret a witch, obviously he believed that demons were around her.

In arriving at this conclusion, surely he drew upon previous experience and the views of other experts of his time. Saints, witches, the possessed, even travelers, tended to behave as others of their kind, imitating types laid down by predecessors. Likewise those who treated the afflicted. As Joseph Klaits has noted, "Those assigned to counsel the possessed were usually religious personages who interpreted the sufferer's behavior in accord with their previous knowledge of demonic possession. They began their sympathetic therapy by reinforcing the suggestible victim's fear that he or she was suffering from a supernaturally induced disorder." Even the astute Johan Evangelista was susceptible to such suggestion. This did not mean that either he or Margaret fabricated the possession, or that it was any less real in their minds, but rather, as D. P. Walker has written, that their knowledge of other cases would "to a considerable extent condition their behavior." In 1629, for instance, a Netherlandish confessor would tell a woman that the devil had her around the neck, causing her to fall into a great faint so that she "lay there without speaking for five or six hours." In fact it would be surprising if Margaret's possession was not first suggested to her by either Henri Joos or a cosister in Bethlehem.

Father Evangelista and Margaret could draw from a plenitude of cases the chief characteristics of possession: (1) sudden ability to speak and understand exotic languages (usually Greek, Latin, or Hebrew); (2) clairvoyance; (3) unnatural body strength; (4) horror and revulsion at sacred things; (5) attempts at murder or suicide; and (6) long "swoons" or faints. Symptoms three and four were arguably the most common, and demonstrated usually by bodily and facial contortions and acrobatics, such as a French woman in 1599 whose face turned black, whose tongue protruded the length of four or five fingers, whose eyes rolled back and mouth gaped, while she leaped, arced, and twisted in different directions; it emerged that she was faking these possessions, but she obviously knew what investigators were looking for. As for Margaret's symptoms, one could point to the disturbances in the convent or her attempt at suicide. Father Evangelista himself could recall that more than once while waiting in the parlor for Margaret, Mater Barbara had come to inform him that Margaret was lying in a great swoon and could not meet him. And a later confessor would note Margaret's strange visage and her revulsion at his presence.

Yet even in such cases as Margaret's, when many of the usual signs were present, Johan Evangelista knew that detection was a tricky matter. The best minds of the day disagreed over how to distinguish among evil spirits, good spirits, and natural ailments. Even the first spiritual advisors of the eventual saint Teresa called her ecstasies "demonic delusions," while some sufferers were all too ready to think themselves full of demons when in fact they were afflicted, said experts, with merely "natural" maladies of the flesh. These people would have done better, continued experts, to consult a physician for their epilepsy, hysteria, and melancholy. Yet, to complicate things, it was common knowledge in medical circles that melancholy might *lead* to possession. Catharina Rijkeboer would later mention to Archbishop Boonen that Margaret experienced such a connection. So did a later nun named Catherine Janssens, who confessed that from a young age she had been "very desperate and despairing of the mercy of God, to such a degree that from then on she was possessed by the evil enemy." The best medical opinion of the time even concluded that especially nuns over forty, who had long been celibate and were consequently of drier "humor" than younger women, were prone to melancholy and thus most susceptible to possession.* In fact, celibacy at any age made possession more likely than otherwise. Father Evangelista knew also that a person brought to melancholy not merely by age or unsettled humors but by loneliness was a strong candidate for

---

*It had been believed since ancient times that the balance or imbalance of the body's four humors, or fluids (blood, phlegm, bile, and black bile), determined one's physical and emotional state; to be dominated by the "dry" humors was to risk melancholy.

possession. So was someone with serious financial trouble, which also applied to Margaret: she owed around forty florins, nearly a year's support, to "someone" outside the convent.

There was one more cause of possession, perhaps the most commonly believed of all: sin. It was elementary to Johan Evangelista that demons invaded with the permission of God, either to punish disobedience in the victim or to set the stage for public exorcisms, in which God's power was shown to be greater than the devil's. Since in Margaret's case all publicity was avoided, and since most cases focused on the sinfulness of the victim, it was easy to assume that hers was a case of punishment. After all, Sister Anna Vignarola called Margaret an "evil daughter," suggesting she did something to deserve possession.

The thought had surely passed through Margaret's mind, and Johan Evangelista's. Perhaps Margaret was burdened by an uncertain and self-abusive memory of her encounters with Henri Joos. Perhaps she blamed herself for having given audience to the devil at all, through succumbing to melancholy. When she wrote elsewhere of possession as "temptations," she surely meant in part the temptation to yield to discouraging moods. And there was temptation in that she might willingly surrender to the devil and be enticed into a more voluntary and sinister relationship with him, replete with the mysterious orgies and upside-down Sabbath of full-fledged witchcraft.

Father Evangelista was wholly aware of the standard signs and causes, the sinister ploys and counterploys, as he formed his conclusions about Margaret. And he was unaware of later psychological interpretations, such as the notion that possession was common in monastic environments because it signified desperate resistance to discipline and repression: "to be the victim of possession was a means of expressing forbidden impulses and attracting the attention of otherwise indifferent or repressive superiors." In such a state, the possessed could shout out statements and engage in behaviors that, under normal circumstances, would have resulted in punishment or alienation but that, when blamed on the devil, were virtually ignored. Yet Johan Evangelista could interpret Margaret's condition only with the tools of his time. Thus did he decide, he told the Archbishop, that she needed first the supernatural help of the church, in the form of exorcism.

He had therefore more than once donned surplice and vestments, readied his crucifix, holy water, incense, candles, and books of scripture and ritual. Ways to exorcise were many, even in this time of increasing uniformity. He would have avoided the more spectacular, such as seating Margaret in a chair, binding her fast to it, and making her drink a strange potion, "nauseating and intoxicating." Instead he recalled in his best clear voice the transcendent powers of Christ that had been shared with his apostles, including the power to withstand serpents and to cast out unclean spirits. He prayed that like power would be brought to bear against these forces that vexed this friend of the Lord. Blessed be the Father, Son, and Holy Spirit, he repeated often, crossing himself regularly as he went, and believing as most others that the very sound of the words and appearance of this sign could drive the foes out.

To encourage a miracle within Margaret, he turned literally to miracles from the Gospels, first pressing the Gospels to his brow, mouth, and chest, then to the brow of Margaret, as if the printed words themselves had power. While positioned before her, he read from Matthew the story of the boy whom only the master could cure, then from Mark Jesus' promise that his disciples would have the power to cast out demons, then from Luke the account of the man cured in the synagogue, and from John the assurance that the Evil Prince of this world would be overcome. Again the book to Margaret's head, the sign of the cross on her brow, pronouncement against this unclean spirit, enemy of all humanity, bringer of death, ravisher of life, enemy of justice, root of all evil, seducer of men, mother of envy, cause of discord, and father of poverty—all through the power of He who cursed Lucifer to crawl on his belly, revived Lazarus, was sacrificed in Isaac, sold in Joseph, slaughtered in the lamb, and crucified in humankind, who showed his power in Job, cursed Pharaoh, shut the mouths in the lions' den, conquered with David, and damned Judas Iscariot.

Holding up the crucifix, the friar commanded the demons to behold the wood of the most holy cross, urged Margaret to look as well, and implored her to try to say with him, "We adore you, Christ, and we bless you, because by your holy cross you have redeemed the world." He chanted the Kyrie Eleison, Our Father, and other orations, repeating formulas and prayers again and again. He called upon the God of the Angels, of the Archangels, of the Prophets, of the Martyrs, of the Saints (especially devil-fighting Anthony), of the Virgins, of the Sabbath, the God of Adonai, God omnipotent, the God who turned Sodom and Gomorrah to ash, the God baptized in Jordan. He recalled the power given to Paul and Peter and other saints, and the blood-soaked martyrs and the power of the holy sacrament against the persecutor of the innocents. And he blessed with the water on which sailed the ark of Noah, which sprang from Jacob's well, which was parted by Moses, which flowed in Jordan, which turned to wine in Cana, and on which Christ had walked.

Around these sessions, or as time went on, they must have talked in less dramatic fashion about the inner life in which he was so experienced and she—despite twenty years as a nun—quite naive. He may well have reviewed with Margaret the pattern laid down in his easy-to-follow, simplified devotional writings: *The Kingdom of God in the Soul,* on meditation and prayer, and *Eternal Life,* on preparing for and receiving the Eucharist. Like so many devotional works of the Flemish-Rhineland tradition, the first urged the reader to look for God within the soul, a task accomplished through prayer, meditation, and the exercise of virtue. This was as frightening as a first journey at sea, for it required one to leave the safety of familiar ground and ride strange, unsteady waters. Once embarked, the author advised, learn to unfurl your sails and catch the wind of God, to read the state of your soul like the skipper reads the sea floor, compass, and stars. Do not despair at times when you feel alone, when sorrow finds a place within you and tells you that you are empty and useless and without any special light from God.

In counseling Margaret, Father Evangelista may well have concluded that she was among those many religious who were content with merely being a religious in name—not necessarily evil, but too interested in worldly necessities and ways, "like sniffing dogs, sniffing curiously into what goes on here and there." Too few were willing to go farther, to sell all they had to buy the pearl of great price within themselves, so few that if he had not "seen it himself he never would have believed it." Daily there were books published, he continued, "which tell us that the end and perfection of this life lies in a union with God," but most religious had "no more appreciation for such than a horse or cow for gourmet food."

Whatever marked the discussions between Margaret and the friar, his efforts proved of little consequence, he admitted to Archbishop Boonen, "because of various vexations" from her sisters, "the demon," and the new house confessor, from whom Margaret was alienated as deeply as the last. Whatever good the friar's exorcism and counseling sessions did, they were reversed almost immediately when Margaret returned to her place in the community and confronted once more the enmity against her there. Losing hope, Father Evangelista told the Archbishop that he felt it best to cease his "simple and imbecile" methods, insufficient for such an "arduous business." This may have been the friar's way of putting the burden for Margaret's cure back on the Archbishop. Indeed, since he had heard that Archbishop Boonen was contemplating other methods to help Margaret, the friar had simply urged her to submit herself totally to the Archbishop's "paternal tutelage." Fortunately she was well disposed to this exhortation, and the friar expressed his confidence that His Illustrious Reverence would triumph and "free the dear little woman from the jaws of the most wicked wolf." Before relinquishing responsibility, however, Johan Evangelista expressed some final sentiments.

First, among the "vexations" and "impediments" to her recovery, one of the greatest was the constant slander against her within the convent. For this reason, he doubted she would ever be fully cured if she remained in Bethlehem—a sentiment, he was glad to note, that the Archbishop had come to share. As for where she should go, Margaret was willing to leave that to the discretion of the Archbishop; her only desire was for the guidance of a man to whom she could open her soul, for the "age-old tricks and machinations of the devil" would continue. Margaret's problems "require the total man," concluded Father Evangelista, someone who could give more than he. Her heavy needs, his massive responsibilities, and a recent warning from his order to avoid spending excessive time with female religious simply did not mesh.

Second, the Archbishop will recall, wrote the friar, that Margaret had sought permission to travel to Mechelen and tell the Archbishop in person her version of her past. Since that permission had been denied, she now asked Pater Evangelista to convey it for her. Most basic, he wrote, was the origin of her troubles: here the friar recounted Margaret's unpleasant encounters with Henri Joos, whom she blamed for her long dismal state. Also important, however, continued Pater Evangelista, was a more recent piece of "business" that engulfed her: the debt of forty florins. During her first exile from the convent, before 1616, Margaret had been forced to borrow money to support herself. When she returned to Bethlehem in 1618, her unnamed creditor pestered her for repayment. Because she had no money, her only means of paying off that debt was to contract another, with a second creditor, in 1622 or 1623. This second creditor she identified simply as "that wizard *(magus)* who frequently came to her." In making the loan, the *magus* took advantage of Margaret's wretched financial state and extracted from her a despicable condition: that if she failed to repay her loan by the coming Easter, of 1624, then she would have to consent to that "filthy act" that "already and for so long" he had required of her *(in turpem actum ad quem illam iam diu requisivit)*. Margaret pleaded with Father Evangelista and Archbishop Boonen to help her be free "from the rule of that man," and pay the debt.

Was Henri Joos "that wizard" who had demanded a "filthy act" from Margaret? She would not have hesitated to call someone who dealt suspiciously in the supernatural, priest or not, a "wizard." The absence in Father Evangelista's letter of a clear antecedent, as well as the lack of any other names in his letter besides that of Henri Joos, is also suggestive. Moreover, Henri Joos was still in Leuven in 1623 and continued to visit the convent illicitly, as he would also do after moving to Mol the following year. Finally, apart from Margaret's remark about Henri Joos's "frequent importuning" of her, there is no record of anyone else having pestered her about a "filthy act" for any period of time.

Along with the indirect suggestions in the friar's letter to Archbishop Boonen was a final consideration: from what other man could Margaret have gotten such a loan in 1622 or 1623? Especially since she knew few people in Leuven and, unlike many other nuns in Bethlehem, was rarely visited by family or friends. The Mont de Piété, or local pawnshop, was a possible source from which to borrow money, but what did she have to pawn? Later when she needed money she would turn to Archbishop Boonen—but not yet. Whether she liked Henri Joos or not, she was desperate for a loan, and she had more opportunity to ask him than anyone else who came calling, despite her uneasiness around him. Whether the *magus* was Henri Joos or someone else, there certainly occurred a pathetic but classic scene in which the humiliated Margaret, as the wretched debtor, sought out the opportunistic creditor who exacted a suitably desperate promise.

After mentioning Margaret's debt and the *magus*, Johan Evangelista closed his letter with the hope that the Archbishop now had a good idea of the matter. Upon receiving the missive, Archbishop Boonen made note of several parts and of the fact that Father

Evangelista could no longer care for Margaret. Not long afterward, the Archbishop announced his decision.

Bethlehem, March 14, 1624. The Archbishop's response could not come quickly enough for the nuns of Bethlehem, who were consumed by fear, not compassion, as they witnessed Margaret's "sorrow and desolation." And the daily visits to Margaret of such a man as Johan Evangelista, who was not the house's regular confessor, could only heighten their anxieties.

Sympathizing with this "miserable patient," Catharina Rijke-boer wrote secretly in late February to Archbishop Boonen that one root of Margaret's sorrow was, put in the gentlest possible way, the failure of the Archbishop to send any instruction. Margaret, with tears streaming down her face, had recently lamented to Catharina that she had been so open with Father Evangelista and allowed him to write the Archbishop about the "depths of her heart." Surely the friar's letter was lost, she feared, for the Archbishop had "carefully answered" all her previous correspondence in timely fashion. Now she feared that some stranger between Leuven and Mechelen knew her plight as well, from which Margaret "tasted extraordinarily great" shame, as well as reproach "from the enemy and his evil instrument."

Such fears were not unfounded. Even the great worried about losing letters and the risks involved in committing messages to paper. This had contributed to Margaret's remaining unconfessed since New Year's, which "burdened her conscience" and scandalized the convent, as "not one hour of life is certain" for any human being. All they wanted, Catharina continued, was word from the Archbishop. If he did nothing, then Margaret's recent "good will and intentions" would be wasted.

Finally the Archbishop acted, assuring them that he had received Father Evangelista's letter after all. First he sent a sum of money from his own pocket to relieve Margaret's onerous debt to the *magus:* no longer would she have to fear that man's threats and evil conditions. Along with that money, the Archbishop sent news of an unusual and arousing plan: Margaret, accompanied by her only friend Sister Catharina, was to leave the monastery once again—this time to seek her cure at the miraculous new shrine of Our Lady of the Sharp Hill, or Scherpenheuvel, some twenty miles away.

6

Pilgrim

Scherpenheuvel, late March to November 1624. Though it could be done, as Margaret herself had already proved, the departure of a veiled nun from any convent was no routine affair. When another sister of Bethlehem asked Archbishop Boonen in December 1624 for permission to visit the shrine of Laken, near Brussels, where she hoped to find a cure for headaches that caused her to "tear her eyes out," he refused, stating that a dispensation to leave cloister should be granted only "with great scrupulousness"—a decision praised by both the Dean of Leuven and Catharina Rijkeboer, who hoped it would discourage similar requests from other nuns.

That the Archbishop decided to send Margaret outside the convent, on pilgrimage, was a measure of his desperation. By now he had little to lose. He also had a great deal of confidence in the Pastor who directed this particular site. And of course he did not deny altogether the potency of the shrine itself, which offered another means besides exorcism in the dispossession of odious spirits.

All such shrines in Catholic Europe had as their chief function healing. In the Low Countries, Scherpenheuvel, to the northeast of Leuven, was now the rage. If Margaret had never read the new, popular collection of miracles reported there, she certainly knew of them. The lame, the blind, the troubled in spirit, all found their cures at Scherpenheuvel, while in less beneficent displays of power those who ridiculed the shrine were suddenly maimed. Sister Catharina Tserraerts of the White Ladies of Leuven had a left leg shorter than her right, but she saw the difference disappear after visiting the Scherpenheuvel. Anna Laureys, a Leuven Annunciation Sister, had suffered eighteen years from a terrible ringing in her ears, caused one day when she overexerted herself in choir; though she was not allowed to leave her convent, she was soon healed in a replica of the chapel of Scherpenheuvel, built for her in the convent's garden.

Not only bodily ailments could be cured at shrines, but spiritual ones as well, such as Margaret's. At the shrine of Our Lady of Hanswijk in Mechelen, a possessed girl of twelve was healed by a quick-thinking young boy who recognized the demon, saw that it was near the girl's navel, made the sign of the cross at that spot, and gradually led the beast up the body so that it finally came out her mouth in the form of a hairy worm. Or Margaret could have read in Thieleman's *Lives of the Franciscan Saints* how possessed persons who visited Francis's favorite church of Portiuncula were instantly freed of their demons.

No wonder that when she heard from Mater Barbara the news of the Archbishop's plan, Margaret was overjoyed, in the best spirits she had been for years. The thought of leaving Bethlehem under current circumstances was alone liberating, but heightening the anticipation were the reputed powers at Scherpenheuvel. In a new letter she thanked the Archbishop profusely for his "genuine fatherly care" and begged forgiveness for the trouble she had caused—yet she pleaded "please don't forget me," as he had recently in taking so long to respond to her, "for I cannot help myself." There was also the problem of money. Though grateful for the funds the Archbishop had sent to discharge her debt to the *magus*, "so that he would have no more cause to harm me," how was she to pay for her journey? Her annuity of six florins wasn't enough, though she would gladly use it anyway, even if she had to "live in poverty all my life in order to have a good soul." Many thanks, she repeated to the Archbishop, for all he had done for unworthy her. Though she could never hope to repay him, she asked one last kindness anyway: would the Archbishop please send a document, in Dutch, written and signed in his own hand, stating that she had his permission to leave the convent, and thus by implication to return? Then the others would have no grounds to prevent her from coming back. Margaret's fears on this point would prove only too true.

Joy among the rest of the sisters at the prospect of Margaret's departure was likely overflowing, except in Mater Barbara. It was not that she disputed the Bishop's wisdom in deciding to send Margaret, nor that she doubted the efficacy of the shrine, nor even that she thought Margaret's condition hopeless. Rather, she feared the scandal that might befall the convent "once again" should Margaret visit this very public place. How Mater wished that the "exorcisms could occur secretly in house, for when they're about to begin Margaret is often not herself, and the enemy puts her into a trance or cripples her." In popular Scherpenheuvel, such a scene could hardly be kept secret: "all the world will see and hear, and it will be a travesty for our convent." In other words, convents with possessed nuns were not likely to have many friends, or benefactors.

As for Margaret's expenses, they were too great for such a convent "in decline," and besides, how was Margaret to get there? Father Evangelista had advised against letting her ride in the public wagon, for fear of scandal, but who would provide a private coach? The only suggestion Mater could make to Archbishop Boonen now came too late—keep Margaret at home and put her for the time being in the convent's guest house, where she could live apart from the other nuns and where Father Evangelista would have easier access to her. But if His Reverence insisted that Margaret must go, then so be it.

Despite Mater Barbara's opposition, Margaret and Catharina soon set off for the shrine. Along with anticipation of such trips always went a sense of fear: not only of bandits but of evil spirits and demons, who had a liking for such out-of-the-way places as the road from Leuven to Scherpenheuvel. Only a few years later a woman accused of witchcraft would claim that her initial contact with the devil occurred on this very road. The devil's Sabbath was even said to occur in similarly remote locations: a large field, woods, a mountain, amid ruins, dunes, or at crossroads. But Margaret and Catharina passed through the woods unscathed and arrived at their destination. They lived briefly in Diest, near Scherpenheuvel, with a certain "widow," but eventually Margaret found lodging among the Hospital Sisters of that town, a less private but probably cheaper place. She would remain there for most of the year, with Sister Catharina by her side until late August 1624.

Rising abruptly out of the hilly region east of Brussels, the Scherpenheuvel at first appeared as another of those isolated places so eagerly frequented by the devil and his minions. Though holy sites also were found in such places—for God did many miracles on mountains—one chronicler of the Scherpenheuvel considered it a "wonder that the Mother of God would choose this raw and wild little mountain, in the area of a very poor and common city." It was another in a series of divine surprises, demonstrating once again that the godly was greater than the sinister, for here was triumph in the devil's backyard.

But it was more than location that made Scherpenheuvel stand out: it was the sacredness of the place that mattered. In medieval times, at the top of this uninhabited hill, there appeared on an ancient oak a miracle-working image of the Virgin. Like others around Catholic Europe, this image exuded grace and performed miraculous deeds on and from that spot. Whenever the image was removed by well-meaning or luck-hoarding peasants, it always returned on its own, making evident to all that intercession with the divine was to occur here, and confirming to all that grace was attached to place.

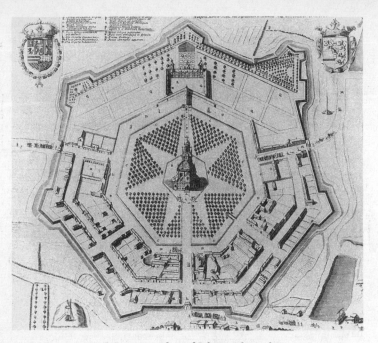

C. Lauwers, plan of Scherpenheuvel

From Sanderus, *Chorographia Sacra Brabantiae,* an eighteenth-century work
reprinted many times

For centuries the Scherpenheuvel was but one of many local
shrines to Mary around Europe, visited for quite ordinary problems. But after 1587 more and more Spanish soldiers in the area
visited, in 1602 the first formal pilgrimage was made, and a year
later Archbishop Hovius began to patronize the site, authenticate
its miracles, and organize its setting. True fame waxed only with the
enthusiastic, full-coffered support of the pious Archdukes Albert
and Isabella, co-rulers of the Spanish Netherlands since 1598, who
attributed progress in their war against the Dutch to the powers
of the new shrine. The conclusive sign of the Virgin's approval with
the Scherpenheuvel came in September 1604, when the Dutch gar-

rison in the strategic coastal town of Oostende capitulated to Albert's troops. To the archdukes the connection was obvious: the Virgin was expressing thanks for their devotions to her at the Scherpenheuvel. The shrine therefore became an object of their deepest piety, surpassing other favorite Marian shrines of the area, such as at Cambron, Chièvres, Scheut, or even Laken and Halle, to become *the* shrine of the Spanish Netherlands.

In order to emphasize this, the shrine was to be enlarged, crowned by a dignified new church atop the lonely hill, while around it would be constructed from the ground up an entire city, conceived of by the archdukes themselves. Villagers began to arrive soon after. The first stone of the new church was laid in July 1609, and the first Pastor came in 1610, along with numerous Underpastors to preach and hear confessions among the multitudes that now arrived. Accounts of miracles poured in, confirming the rightness of the archdukes' decision. By the time of Margaret's journey in 1624, the Scherpenheuvel was therefore the obvious place to send her.

When she approached the still-unfinished hill, she would first have seen the nearly completed round, domed Baroque church, fifty meters high, then the incomplete surrounding wall, begun in 1620, in the form of a septagon, representing the sacred, magical number seven but especially a seven-pointed star, symbol of the Virgin. Margaret might have seen workmen on the partly earthen wall, or children making holes in it to the irritation of authorities. Entering through the main gate opposite the front of the shrine, or one of the several side gates accessible by steps up the hill, she would have readily grasped that the interior of the city continued the star motif of the walls, with the still-earthen streets and houses laid out in seven clear sections. Beyond the rows of houses came a seven-sided wall surrounding an enclosed seven-pointed, star-shaped, sapling-filled garden, all of which in turn surrounded the star-covered church.

Just outside the garden wall stood peddlers of sacred and not-so-sacred objects, and crowds of pilgrims, soldiers, or the merely curious. Margaret probably passed by with eyes down to avoid distraction, or to keep from drawing attention to herself, as hoped by Mater Barbara. Perhaps she fixed her eyes on the church, oblivious to other pilgrims, who came from nearby or as far away as Italy, some borne on stretchers. This was a busy time of year but less so than summer. The temptation to be distracted did not cease once at the threshold of the church, for some pilgrims tried to sleep there, others milled around the large door, workers continued construction, and beggars looked for money or pillaged the offer boxes during services, often putting wax across the openings to catch coins before they fell through.

Margaret recognized the four evangelists above the entry to the church and then went inside, noticing first the chalk-white, star-filled ceiling. The interior was unfinished, but there was still plenty to see, and given the circular form she could see almost everything at once: the brand-new white marble high altar with the initials of Albert and Isabella prominently inscribed, the freshly painted Ascension of the Virgin above it, the red flagstone, the surrounding confessionals, the seven alcoves in the wall housing images of Old Testament prophets, the rows of silver candelabra and hanging lamps, the finely crafted baptismal font, and especially the pile of ex-votos—little wax models of body parts sent to the church in thanks by the cured, or brought there in anticipation of cures. At some point her eye would have rested on the object she and everyone else had come to see: in a silver alcove above the altar was the oaken Virgin, thirty centimeters by eleven, infant Jesus on her left arm, scepter in her right hand, clothed in proper liturgical colors in one of the many sumptuous gowns provided by Archduchess Isabella and other grateful donors.

Margaret would have visited the shrine frequently while in Diest. To what extent this aided her cure is unknown. More certain is that here or in Diest she and Catharina would have met Pastor Joost Bouckaert, the man who directed the shrine and gave it his stamp. He was the third of the prominent religious figures of the land, after Jacob Boonen and Johan Evangelista, to come into her life in 1624, and the one who would exert the most lasting influence upon her. In fact this trusted friend of the Archbishop may have been the real reason for the decision to make Margaret a pilgrim.

Joost Bouckaert was not only Scherpenheuvel's first Pastor but also Dean of Diest, and eventually Bishop of Ieper. This was the man renowned for his benevolence, but who in spite of fittingly poor health proved tenacious in begging and pleading and fighting for funds to complete his shrine. This was the man who was determined to make the shrine a "church for the entire fatherland." But most of all this was the man who from 1624 on became the chief patron, counselor, and protector of Sister Margaret Smulders.

With the religious life he was familiar, since as Dean of Diest he was required to make regular visitations of female convents in and around that city. He never recorded his first impressions of Margaret, but over the years he clearly was sympathetic to her. Neither he nor she ever recorded the details of her eight-month stay, or whether her treatments were as public as Mater Barbara had feared. But from April to November 1624 she certainly spent much of her time under his influence. One witness later commented on Pastor Bouckaert's expertise as a theologian, but an early historian of the church in the Spanish Netherlands noted that above all his ecclesiastical positions and academic degrees, Joost Bouckaert was a shepherd of souls.

The inner life, so important to religious, would have occupied the centerpoint of her healing and their discussions. He could have continued the teachings of Johan Evangelista, including his lessons on how to prepare for the Eucharist, his three ways to know that her soul was on the path to God, and his four ways to achieve the Kingdom of God within. But Pastor Bouckaert could also have gone far beyond this, now that there was time, inclination, and more works of devotion in print, and in translation, than ever before. The popular little book by the Spanish Franciscan Alcantara, so influential upon Teresa of Avila, suggested to the religious

Joost Bouckaert, Pastor of Scherpenheuvel

two weeks' worth of nuggets for meditation: personal sins one day, misery and brevity of life on a second, the hour of death on a third (which he promised would cause one to run to confession), the Last Judgment on a fourth, and of course the Passion, including the thought that Our Lord's crown of thorns was so enormous that the only way for his enemies to steal his robe was to rip the crown from his head, turning his body into one big, bloody wound. There were plenty of systematic, even mnemonic techniques for meditation, including Balbano's *Seven Meditations*, the Jesuit Androtius's relentlessly methodical *Devout Memorial of the Passion* with its twelve mysteries, each with five meditations and each meditation with five submeditations, and the famous Vervoort's popular *Wilderness of the Lord*, which provided forty days of meditations and prayers with a woodcut of a holy scene for each. There was the synthesis by Madrid, the *Golden Book to Learn the Art of Serving God Sincerely*, which the author claimed would outpace all other books because it showed how to put the others to work, warned that it "wasn't as heavy as it looked," and cautioned that reading it once wouldn't suffice in learning the two ways to serve God, the three steps to holy and perfect love, and the five steps to come to God.

Pastor Bouckaert could have given Margaret books of comfort, such as Spoelberch's reassurance that God's love was so great He had a special angel watch over each person, even great sinners, even anti-Christs. It's this angel who helps you fight against the devil in all temptations, Spoelberch assured. Think that God is prepared to forgive in an instant even great sins. Think that God doesn't punish twice for the same fault. Think that God doesn't overwhelm anyone above her power to be tempted—all of which would have soothed Margaret.

There were various *Lives of the Saints*, or accounts of miracles in evocative, faraway places in Italy, or the more recent and close drama of the martyrs in Gorcum, near Holland. There were more basic works specifically for religious, including Ferraria's treatise on the three monastic vows. Was she truly poor? Was her breviary too well decorated? Could she leave her cell open for thieves rather than lock it to protect objects which would only turn to dust? Was she obedient, a sufficiently dumb mule in accepting burdens, or did she resist them? When she heard her superior's voice, did she obey "as if it were God's"? Was she chaste, and did she love enough the three remedies against lust? And these works were only the beginning of Balsamo's recommended list of twenty-seven books every religious ought to read.

Even simpler writings would have worked, such as the pithy, self-deprecating *Contemplations of an Idiot:* Live purely, Consider your smallness, Be alone gladly, Keep peace with others, Think on the day, That passes no one by. She could have benefited from reading the *Spiritual ABC* of St. Bonaventure, or from elementary but profitable exercises at the end of her Book of Hours: pondering the Ten Commandments, the three divine virtues of faith, hope, and charity, the four cardinal virtues, the seven gifts of the Holy Spirit, the twelve fruits of the Holy Ghost, the eight steps to salvation, the seven deadly sins, and the four extremes of death, judgment, hell, and heaven. If Margaret felt primarily blame and guilt for her troubles, as she hinted elsewhere, then the seven penitential psalms would have been fitting: *Have mercy upon me, O Lord, for I am weak: O Lord, heal me. . . . My soul is . . . sore vexed. . . . I am weary with my groaning, all the night make I my bed to swim; I water my couch with my tears. . . . For mine iniquities are gone over mine head, as an heavy burden they are too heavy for me. . . . Mine enemies are lively, and they are strong: and they that hate me wrongfully are multiplied. . . . Mine enemies reproach me all day, and they that are mad against me are sworn against me.*

Precisely which writings and impressions were involved cannot be said, for the ways to do so were as numerous as the stars at Scherpenheuvel, but most assuredly did Margaret work at being healed. At some point she made her confession to Pastor Bouckaert and then took communion, something she had not done for months. She even seemed to begin to feel at home in the hospital of Diest, so much that Mater Barbara and Sister Catharina began during the summer of 1624 to talk of Margaret's staying on for good, while wearing her Franciscan habit under the new one and observing her original vows and obligations as much as possible.

Despite all these hopeful signs, and despite rumors that may have reached the nuns at Bethlehem about Margaret's convalescence, what was remembered best in the convent were Margaret's troubles. Indeed, while she was gone, the nuns of Bethlehem continued to rage furiously against her.

7

Fulminations

Bethlehem, June to November 1624. Mater Barbara could not enjoy long the peace that came when Margaret left for Scherpenheuvel in the spring. For within weeks of Margaret's departure, the postulant Barbara Beli decided to tell a most unsettling story to the house confessor, who called in the Dean of Leuven, who called in the Archbishop's Vicar-General to come and hear for himself.

When the nuns sent in January their petition about strange events in the cell of Barbara Beli, they strongly implied to Archbishop Boonen that Margaret and her supernatural allies were to blame. But no one could offer firm proof. With Margaret away in Scherpenheuvel, however, Barbara Beli felt safe enough to come forward and tell what she knew. The Vicar-General called at Bethlehem on June 5 to hear it.

The twenty-year old postulant began. She had first entered Bethlehem a year before, in June 1623. But it wasn't long before her life in the convent became most unpleasant, beginning around the previous Christmas when her hair shirt and "discipline" (an instrument of self-mortification) went missing from an unlocked chest in her cell, and when she thrice discovered a "rod," or switch, on top of her bed or between her blankets. Most disturbing of all was that her clothes and linens, usually folded neatly in a chest, had been scattered about the cell three different times. These events had remained a disturbing mystery until the past January 25, when Barbara returned to her cell after the midday meal to find not only that her things were scattered once again but that the culprit was still there: standing next to the just-emptied chest was none other than Sister Margaret Smulders, arisen from her sick-bed that very day.

Though everyone in the convent knew about the disturbances in Barbara Beli's cell, most suspected that something otherworldly lay behind them: no one knew that there was such a simple, human explanation. The reason no one knew was also simple: upon being trapped, Margaret immediately went on the attack and forbade Barbara from telling anyone what she had seen or "she would not escape alive." Margaret even exacted an oath of silence from her. There was more to the terror, continued Barbara. Occasionally during Mass, just after the elevation of the host when faces were on the ground in reverence, Margaret would kick her in the head. Mater eventually noticed these abuses and asked Barbara about them. Despite her oath of silence, Barbara finally revealed the story, no doubt after assurances from Mater that the oath she had made to Margaret was under such conditions no oath at all. Still, warned Mater, Barbara would indeed be wise to keep silent about these events, lest her chances of advancing to the next stage of conventual life, the novitiate, be jeopardized: for these events, suggested Mater, would arouse the other nuns not to sympathy but only fear. In their minds, anyone connected to Margaret was bound to bring trouble.

Barbara heeded this warning, and told the story only to her confessor. With her permission, however, the confessor passed it up the line to Mechelen, which was how she came to be standing before the Vicar-General today. Upon completing her tale, she volunteered to repeat it to anyone else in the Archbishop's hierarchy who cared to listen. The Vicar-General appreciated this, but warned her once more that in the meantime she would do well to keep all of this a big and terrible secret from the nuns.

Barbara Beli continued to keep quiet, enough so that in July 1624, scarcely a month after her interview, a majority of nuns in Bethlehem voted to admit her as a novice. Then, for reasons unknown, Barbara changed her mind: before the summer was out she decided that the other nuns should know of her experiences with Margaret after all, and so she told them, in every detail. Perhaps young Barbara, buoyed by her recent advancement and the absence of Margaret, supposed that her tales would now strengthen her ties with the many Margaret-despising nuns of Bethlehem. Perhaps Barbara was eager to lend ammunition to their efforts to keep Margaret out of the convent for good, since by late summer there were rumors that Margaret was on the mend in Scherpenheuvel and thus might return to Bethlehem. Or perhaps Barbara wished to dispel once and for all any possible suspicions that she and Margaret were somehow partners in sorcery. Whatever her motives, all that is certain is that the new novice Barbara Beli talked, and that the outcome was just as Mater had predicted: the nuns were not only confirmed in their disdain for Margaret but added Barbara to their list of undesirables.

Barbara was not expelled from the convent immediately, because there were no obvious grounds at the moment to do so. But when her probationary year as a novice was up the following summer, the chances that the others would allow her to profess and become one of them were about as slight as the most ascetic Franciscan nun.

If this disobedient novice wasn't trouble enough for Mater Barbara Noosen, more came knocking literally at the convent's door.

On June 25, 1624, there arrived a message from the local Franciscan Guardian in Leuven. This announced that at a recent regional meeting of the order, the friars had voted to stop serving as confessors in all female convents not directly under their jurisdiction. The decision would go into effect in three months. Naturally this would affect Bethlehem, where local Franciscans had, at the

Archbishop's request, been hearing confessions ever since the expulsion of Henri Joos in 1618. Now, however, the only condition under which the Franciscans would continue serving Bethlehem was if Archbishop Boonen relinquished to them his authority over the convent.

Just as there was a long tradition of confessors serving in nunneries, so was there a long tradition of confessors threatening to quit. During the boom years of the late Middle Ages, most confessors in female houses came from the male side of the monastic family. But enthusiasm among these men soon wavered. The Norbertine order not only broke up its unique double houses (men on one side, women the other) but ended the female branch altogether. The Dominicans ceased ministering to religious women soon after Dominic's death, though they eventually resumed. Some Carthusians concluded that the five female monasteries under their care were the five wounds of the order. Even the infinitely charitable Francis rarely visited, by the end of his life, Clare and her Poor Ladies of San Damiano. And male Franciscans generally came to regard the female second order, as well as the entire third order, as sources of embarrassment and trouble—an old sentiment only compounded by recent events in Bethlehem.

Such reluctance toward female houses was not universal. Some confessors were always eager to be associated with holy women. And Capuchins and Jesuits quite actively ministered to female religious. But for many males, female houses were often nuisances, or at worst full of tempting objects. By the seventeenth century women were still considered not only more likely than men to become witches or demoniacs but to be more lustful and seductive: think, said experts, upon Adam and Eve, Samson and Delilah, David and Bathsheba, Solomon's pagan wives, and ad nauseam. Care for nunneries also detracted from more public and spectacular activities, such as preaching and missions. Yet most tangible of all in the desire to discard nunneries was the confessors' increasing lack of control.

By the sixteenth century ultimate control over many female convents rested with local bishops. But when such convents could not afford to pay a confessor of their own choosing, a bishop would often ask members of the male side of the order to serve as volunteer confessors to their religious sisters—similar to the old medieval arrangement, but now under the bishop's thumb. Those monks and friars who consented to this arrangement often grew frustrated when nuns ran to bishops to appeal a confessor's unpopular advice or actions or discipline, thus negating the confessor's authority.

Bethlehem was a perfect example of this pattern. Henri Joos was needed there in 1604 because somewhere along the line the local Franciscan friars had become fed up with the situation. When Henri Joos left in 1618, the friars, at the Archbishop's request, reluctantly took up the role of confessors again because the house was so desperately in need. But all parties were soon unhappy. The Archbishop complained that the first friar was "wholly" unlearned. Some sisters complained that the unenthusiastic friars were not fulfilling their duties and hence agitated for permission to confess to the friars' chief rivals, the Jesuits. And the friars themselves of course complained that they had no real control: their words were by definition advice, not law, and their authority too limited to solve such problems as Sister Margaret. Surely this played a role in the order's region-wide decision on female convents: jurisdiction or nothing.

It was no coincidence that the Franciscans flung down this gauntlet at the same time Barbara Beli was telling one and all her stories of Margaret. Indeed, the local friars were already voicing to the sisters of Bethlehem the same irresistible promise they would repeat many times over the months and years: nudge the Archbishop to grant jurisdiction to us, and your problems, including Margaret, will be solved. Mater Barbara must have found the timing of the friars unsporting, but she recognized the seriousness of the situation and sent along a request to Archbishop Boonen that he decide as soon as possible whether he wished to retain jurisdic-

A Grey Sister and a Franciscan Friar, from an eighteenth-century costume book. The details of monastic dress varied not only between orders but even within. They also varied according to occasion—work, choir, and so on.

© Royal Library Albert I, Brussels (Prentenkabinet)

tion over Bethlehem or hand it over to the friars. She expressed no preference one way or the other, simply that the matter be solved, for the convent had been without a permanent confessor for six years now.

Most other sisters were far more partial than Mater Barbara toward the Franciscans. When in late August of 1624 the Archbishop sent the Dean of Leuven, Peter Lucius, to hear their opinions on the matter, sixteen of twenty favored granting total jurisdiction to the friars, and giving up the Archbishop. The Archbishop was simply too busy and far away, said many, to solve their problems. A few worried about the friars' reputation as great "constricters of consciences," since they prohibited sisters from confessing to anyone but a Franciscan. But in the end the desire for a

Fulminations

permanent confessor who might solve lingering problems out-weighed any concerns about style, and most sisters pleaded for the house to be placed under the friars.

The Archbishop instructed Dean Lucius to ask a second question as well in his August interviews with the nuns: should Sister Margaret be allowed to return from her long pilgrimage in Scherpenheuvel? Both Archbishop and convent knew by now the alarming—or, depending on one's fountain of mercy, hopeful—news: Margaret was healed and ready to come back to Bethlehem. In fact so improved was she that her companion, Sister Catharina, would be able to return to Bethlehem from Scherpenheuvel any day now. But as in 1616, almost no one wanted Margaret herself to return. Only Mater Barbara was positively willing to try, and old Aleidis Doelmans said she would do as the Archbishop pleased. But all others would, despite the convent's poverty, rather support Margaret at an outside location, rather suffer more poverty and want, rather "eat dry bread," rather fast one day more per week, rather give up part of their daily portion, rather do almost anything, than have her back. The tension within the convent, the strange events and fears, had all been "stilled" since her departure. "For the love of God," they prayed, "keep this person from us."

Dean Lucius dutifully sent along to Archbishop Boonen these opinions of the sisters, plus several comments of his own. Many nuns, he explained, still suspected Margaret of sinister things. The current Franciscan confessor promised to quit immediately if she returned. And if most sisters favored transferring jurisdiction, it was not because of any merit in the Franciscan method of governance, or even because the Archbishop was negligent, but because Mater Barbara had handled Margaret's case so ineptly. Thus the Dean ended his account.

Before making his decision about Margaret, the Archbishop sought as well the opinion of Margaret's new protector, Pastor Joost Bouckaert, in Scherpenheuvel—including his opinion on the recent revelations of Barbara Beli.

In the Pastor's view, Barbara Beli's charges against Margaret seemed unfounded. The accusations regarding Margaret's connection to sorcery were spurious, for the acts of which she was accused required more active powers than she had shown—implying, as Johan Evangelista had implied, that Margaret was not a witch but at worst possessed. Hence, insisted the Pastor, all of Beli's charges against Margaret should either be proven or dropped. Besides, through his extensive conversations with Margaret and Catharina, the Pastor had learned that Bethlehem's problems were far greater than Margaret alone. Though he had never visited the convent, the Pastor was, based on what he had heard, even bold enough to suggest several specific reforms for the place. Reduce the size of the grille in the guest room. Bolt the door to the confessional with locks (no doubt a result of Margaret's stories about Henri Joos). Order more alert watch over the main door of the convent. And halt the outbreaks of worldly dancing.

Whether the Archbishop acted immediately on the Pastor's reforms for Bethlehem is unknown, but they revealed two patterns that would continue over the years. First, in answering charges brought against her by other sisters, Margaret and her protector were quick to countercharge by pointing out the sisters' equally offensive weaknesses. And second, Pastor Bouckaert's vision of conditions in Bethlehem would forever be influenced by his special relationship with Margaret and his belief in her version of events. Unlike Johan Evangelista months before, Joost Bouckaert was not merely and neutrally sending information about Margaret to the Archbishop: rather, he was as convinced of her story as she was.

Assailed by such strong opinions from every side, it was no wonder the Archbishop continued to show himself indecisive about Bethlehem and Margaret. By October 1624, after the deadline imposed by the Franciscans, he still had not decided on the matter of jurisdiction, but simply persuaded the friars to continue their services temporarily. Nor had the Archbishop yet decided whether to keep Margaret out of Bethlehem for good. With no one else taking any conclusive action at this point, and believing herself cured, Sister Margaret therefore determined to take matters into her own hands, and return to Bethlehem by stealth.

8
No Balm in Bethlehem

*She weepeth sore in the night and her tears are on her cheeks: among
all her lovers she hath none to comfort her: all her friends are become
her enemies.*

—*Lamentations 1:2*

On the road to Leuven, November 4, 1624. The old road from Diest,
like every other road of the day awaiting satisfaction of the ancient
promise that crooked ways would be made straight and rough
places smooth, was a sometimes dusty, usually muddy, and always
narrow path that wound through half a dozen villages and encoun-
tered half a dozen other such paths until twenty miles later it finally
ran up, pocked and scarred, to the northeast walls of Leuven.

Anyone who saw the coach that rumbled through the gates of
Diest and then toward Leuven would have wondered what a veiled,
cloistered nun was doing on the road at all. This was a question of
which Margaret was painfully aware as she left the city behind. But

of greater import and depth as she bumped along was the need to clear her heart of whatever rancor remained from past offenses in Bethlehem. It was on this road, as she meandered past bleak, stubbled fields and hills less dramatic than the cliffs in a Bruegel landscape, that Margaret again told herself she was cured, for a few days before she had felt such "sweetness" within that her heart seemed ready to melt. It was on this road, in the midst of the usual November chill and mist, that she hoped her sisters would see the change, her new determination to live the rest of her days in peace with them and in submission to her superiors. But this hope alternated with fear of rejection, for they might not forget the past, or they might react badly upon learning that she, like a daring artist acting on her own in the hope that her patrons would be pleasantly surprised, had quit Diest without permission.

By agreement she was supposed to have remained in that town until at least Archbishop Boonen and Pastor Bouckaert—and preferably the sisters of Bethlehem as well—consented to her return to the convent. But because she was cured, because waiting for others to act might take forever (to the salvation of no one), and because her intent was "pure and sincere," Margaret felt justified in making arrangements on her own. If her sisters could only see for themselves her willingness to live "with a genuine humility" the rest of her days, "as the least in our convent," and "doing nothing, refraining from nothing, except as they pleased," they might be convinced.

The coach bounced ever closer to Leuven, past the Holy Trinity hill, past Jesuit-owned woods, past a split in the road where the driver took the path most likely to be least muddy, and then gradually downhill until Leuven drew into view. The western glimmers of light left in the day created a stark silhouette of the city's towers. Closer still and Margaret could hear the bells of those towers sounding the hour, at which she automatically made the sign of the cross and fortified herself with either Veni Creator Spiritus to the renewal of her spirit or Ave Maria in memory of the hour when God became flesh, just as when she heard the names Jesus, Maria, or Francis, or mention of the holy sacrament or sacred blood she always made a slight bow. The coach arrived just before the closing of the thick-stoned, oaken-doored Diest gate, finest on the city's walls, for it was built by fastidious Josse Metsys, brother of the famous painter Quentin. A few streets more, a few turns, and Bethlehem was before her.

Margaret descended from the carriage and tugged on the bell that hung outside the main entry to the convent. The Portress, sixty-five-year-old Aleidis Doelmans, probably first looked through the small opening in the heavy door. But whether she peeked or swung the door wide open, Sister Aleidis must have turned pale at the sight. Though not a bitter enemy of Margaret, she understood the enormity of this event, and sent immediately for Mater Barbara. Soon the entire convent learned the news, but it was Mater and her close helpers who came to handle the crisis.

Though Mater Barbara had expressed to the Archbishop a willingness to allow Margaret to return, it was on the assumption that such a return would occur in proper order. Since Barbara doubted that this was the case, she and her councilors offered no greetings, warm or otherwise, but simply and immediately asked whether Margaret had in her possession any official documents granting her permission to leave Scherpenheuvel. All her hopes threatened in these first few moments, Margaret blurted the lie that Pastor Bouckaert would bring them in a day or two. But this was not good enough for the delegation: until the papers arrived, they informed Margaret, she was to remain in the guest house—outside the cloister, outside the dormitory of the nuns. At this point the shattered Margaret decided to tell the truth, hoping it would soften them: she had come of her own accord, she admitted, without the permission or knowledge of Pastor Bouckaert, but, she surely added, it was only because she was cured. Still it wasn't enough for the gathered sisters, and they again pointed Margaret to the guest house.

With Margaret put away, Mater prepared to dispatch two lay sisters the next morning to inform Archbishop Boonen in Mechelen of the news, and two more to visit Pastor Bouckaert in Scherpen-heuvel, from whom she hoped to get a fuller account of things. Following the customary three bells that rang in the convent's church after Compline, to remind all of the eternal virgin the Mother of God, Margaret must have passed a lonely, bitter night.

Bethlehem, November 1624 through January 1625. Margaret's arrival opened all the old wounds, plus a few more.

Joost Bouckaert wrote Archbishop Boonen on November 6 to tell him the news of Margaret's escape. Everyone, he lamely explained, had been caught completely by surprise. It was true that Margaret had recently pressed to return to Bethlehem, determined as ever to live in the convent where she had professed. Yet the very day before her flight, he thought he had convinced her to be patient and wait. Obviously her resolve was greater than he realized. Whether that resolve was born of God or the Devil or Margaret he dared not speculate, but since she contradicted the advice of her superiors he had a good hunch. Who would help her now to avoid her old infirmities? The Franciscan confessors of Bethlehem would not go near Margaret. Pastor Bouckaert pitied them all: the nuns who needed Archbishop Boonen's "singular paternal help," and of course Margaret, who needed help staying free of "malignant corporal infestations."

Sister Catharina Rijkeboer wrote Archbishop Boonen just as quickly and painted an even more dismal picture. Though Margaret's friend, she could not condone Margaret's actions, which displayed ingratitude toward the Archbishop, who had labored so long and at personal expense on her behalf, and toward Pastor Bouckaert: "she fled her shepherd and guide too soon." Still, Catharina pleaded that the Archbishop not desert Margaret, lest she again become desperate. After all, since Margaret got along with no one in the convent and would have no confessor there, the old troubles could easily begin anew. "The devil is not far from her." Margaret meant no harm: "it was a temptation she followed through her own fantasy." But because of her rashness there would now be much sinning on all sides.

After several days, Margaret herself wrote Archbishop Boonen as well, to plead for forgiveness and to explain. Though adamant that her intentions had been noble, she now bitterly regretted her deed. "I hope that with God's help I'll never do anything again without counsel. I've deceived myself very badly." Margaret proposed that she remain in the guest room through the rest of the winter, perhaps forever, or that the sisters build her a small, inexpensive house in the garden where she might live as a recluse. Obviously she had no hope of leaving: "If I see things clearly, it seems it will be no easy task to find a convent that will take me; besides it would cost much money, and everyone will say, 'why doesn't she stay in the convent where she professed?' If they don't want me here, how much less will another?" Moreover, she was not willing to leave under the present cloud of suspicion, for the sisters of Bethlehem "will never cease gossiping about me and passing it on to whoever comes and goes," so that those in any new house would know the stories about her anyway, and despise her just as much.

Most discouraging of all, Margaret continued, was her fear that even Joost Bouckaert had lost patience with her, for one condition of his care had been that she remain in Diest and away from Bethlehem: just because he believed her account of past events did not mean he thought she should return there. The two lay sisters assigned by Mater Barbara to go visit Pastor Bouckaert had upon their return even told Margaret, spitefully, that "by no means would he bear me any longer." Thus Margaret feared that she would "never find comfort there again. I don't know what else to do, it's finished and must remain finished. I wouldn't for my life dare come to him again." In the meantime, she pleaded, like Catharina, that the Archbishop not abandon her, for she could not endure the suffering alone. "I have such a horror of that suffering that I think death itself is approaching." Had she known in advance the extent of her pain, she would not have left the convent in the first place, "for my life."

In early December 1624, Archbishop Boonen sent Peter Lucius, Dean of Leuven, to question Mater Barbara and Sister Catharina whether, under the circumstances, it would be best for Margaret to stay put in Bethlehem's guest room or leave the convent immediately. He did not bother asking other nuns, for he knew their opinions already. That he asked Catharina, who held no office as yet in the convent, reflected both the growing esteem for her at the Archbishop's palace and a sense that she could be expected to answer in Margaret's best interest.

Catharina still felt that the best solution was to return Margaret to Diest and let her live in the hospital, to be near Pastor Bouckaert. Margaret's idea that she become a recluse within the convent was ridiculous, for when alone Margaret would "have even more opportunity to yield to her fantasies and temptations, for she is little experienced in spiritual exercises and hardly knows how to get God to help her." The solitary life was best suited to a white-haired, deeply spiritual nun with many great triumphs over the devil. The guest room was no solution either, for after the storics told by Barbara Beli, it was still too close to other nuns: they were so estranged from Margaret "that they quake at the thought of her someday taking up her old place." Margaret knew their enmity, and it caused her to sink into despair, which might revive her old troubles. In fact, Catharina had observed that those troubles were always preceded by Margaret's expressing angry feelings to one sister or another, "so that I've always had to struggle to get her to keep things to herself." This tendency in Margaret would never completely die.

The only hope, repeated Catharina, was Diest. The problem was, Margaret insisted on staying in Bethlehem, despite all the venom against her, for she feared the shame that attended any nun who left her convent. But such stubbornness was wrongheaded. "If

Sister Margaret keeps doing as she sees fit and holds to her desire to stay in the convent," wrote Catharina, "then I think her (though unawares) deceived by the whisperings of that crafty serpent from Hell who has long tried to trick her." The "sweetness" which inspired Margaret to return to Bethlehem was one such trick: Margaret was too unseasoned to realize that "the evil spirit often transforms himself into an angel of light." In fact, right after her return the sweetness disappeared and Margaret was "overrun by a multitude of temptations." She was even once again on the verge of doing that "which in the eternities she would have regretted"—a clear allusion to suicide.

Mater Barbara echoed Catharina in several letters during November and December of 1624. She lamented that Margaret was "so impatient and complains so much," demanding with such stridency to reenter the nuns' dormitory "that it eats away at those who must hear it." To Barbara, Margaret hardly seemed any different from the time "before she went to the hill." Margaret sat there daily "without comfort from God or sisters or confessor or Holy Sacrament." Joost Bouckaert was distant, no Franciscan confessor would speak with her, and a Jesuit who was asked to come insisted that she tell her story as he had already heard it—from Barbara Beli no less! And now other Jesuits knew the story, too, for "what one Pater knows, all know," claimed Mater Barbara. Mater did her best to "maintain peace and rest." She had once been willing to give Margaret another chance. And she still felt pity for Margaret. But she now wished, quite frankly, that Margaret "were so far from here that I would never have to speak to her again as long as I live, it would be a great comfort to me," she admitted. Others "say they would rather walk out the door of the convent" than live with her. "And I can't blame them, for if she reenters then our convent will be ruined, that is certain."

Perhaps because he heard of the tumult, perhaps because the Archbishop asked him to go, Joost Bouckaert made an unannounced visit to Bethlehem in mid-December 1624, to the delight of those who hoped he would take Margaret away with him, and to the astonishment of Margaret herself, who thought the Pastor had forsaken her. The visit began miserably. An ashamed Margaret had to be led almost forcibly from her upstairs room in the guest house to the parlor below. During their conversation she not only suffered the "usual quaking, movements, and other agitations of the body," which Pastor Bouckaert considered "of external cause," but also exhibited a horrible visage he had never before seen in her—so horrible that she seemed to be "threatened and embraced," and had to fight furiously to resist and escape the enemy. During "rebuking," a reference to further exorcisms, she displayed a "complete resignation to God and her superiors and opened her heart," but the lasting effects of this were impossible for the Pastor to measure. At last he persuaded Margaret to confess and commune, but she needed a nearby spiritual director immediately, and over the long run a place outside Bethlehem. Unfortunately, the obvious choice, the hospital of Diest, had at the moment no more openings and too many impressionable novices.

Margaret was "wounded in the depths of her heart" that Pastor Bouckaert had seen her in such an abysmal state, but overjoyed at his renewed attention, so that soon afterward she felt "restored." She even wrote the Archbishop that she lamented casting the Pastor "away so carelessly." Clearly the devil was using "all his deceit and lies" to separate her from Joost Bouckaert, for he was the only one now able to help her. "I still have very much to bear," but she was resolved to "give myself over, soul and body, to the will of God, and the will and good opinion of your reverence, to do with me what you please." And while his reverence cared for her soul, then would he be sure "to care for the rest" as well—or, in other words, the temporal. Here in the guest house she was cut off from a nun's common share of food and resources, and could not on her own support herself. Remember, she reminded the Archbishop, that "want of temporal things might bring me into error very easily once again." The Archbishop generously responded, for later documents would mention his long financial support of Margaret.

In the next weeks of December 1624, Margaret vacillated about leaving or staying. One day she wrote that thinking of leaving "buries me as if I were about to die; oh, if God would only take me from this world." Yet on another she wished only to be "away from here," for she suffered "unspeakable persecution and confusion at night, so that every day as evening falls I feel death itself approaching." Finally she yielded to the advice of Pastor Bouckaert, Mater Barbara, and Sister Catharina and agreed to leave Bethlehem if the Archbishop commanded it. Whether she suffered there or elsewhere, it didn't much matter, for "I know I've earned it, and much more." By late December the Archbishop was seeking a place for her in earnest: since Archbishop Hovius had found one for Lesken Nijns back in 1618, why wouldn't the influential, well-connected Jacob Boonen be able to find one for her as well? So confident was she that Margaret wrote in January 1625, "I expect any day to receive the command to leave."

If things looked somewhat brighter for Margaret by early 1625, they had become quite dim for Mater Barbara Noosen, who was beginning to long for the grave. Margaret's return, mountainous in and of itself, now converged in near-cosmic fashion with the convent's other problems: Barbara Beli, disappearing Franciscan confessors, and Mater Barbara's diminishing authority.

Since her revelations in late summer, Barbara Beli had continued to live uneasily within the convent, for most nuns still awaited opportunity to expel her. In October, that opportunity seemed to arise. It was discovered that Barbara suffered from a certain "accident"—probably a recurring illness—which did not afford her the physical strength necessary to endure the demands of a nun's life. And so, on the very day that Margaret returned, November 4, 1624, the convent began a debate whether to expel Barbara Beli immediately, or allow her to finish the full term of her novitiate. Days later, in the wake of the tumult caused by Margaret's return, a majority of nuns voted for immediate expulsion. This pleased Mater Barbara, who wanted to put the outcast novice in the guest house right away, in preparation for her departure.

There were just two problems. First, Margaret was now already there, and in the days since her return had learned of Barbara Beli's exploits in storytelling. If the two were in the same room, then Mater Barbara feared they "would have torn into each other, for Sister Margaret resents that Beli has said so much evil of her, that she still with tears in her eyes swears by her salvation that it never even entered her mind to do what the novice has accused her of doing."

The second problem was that Barbara Beli's patron, who had arranged for Beli's original entry into Bethlehem, was determined to protest and if possible reverse the decision to expel her protégée. This patron, a beguine* from Brussels named Barbara van Herssen, even rode immediately to Bethlehem upon hearing the news that Barbara Beli had been expelled, in order to complain to Mater Barbara Noosen. And thus began the War of the Three Barbaras.

There soon occurred between Mater Barbara and Barbara van Herssen a heated exchange. Van Herssen was suspicious that the novice's supposed illness was but a pretense to be rid of her, and so went straightaway to visit a doctor who had examined her. When questioned, this doctor laughed aloud at the notion that the illness was serious enough to prevent Beli from becoming a nun: he had never said that. When confronted with the doctor's words, and a demand from Barbara van Herssen to know the true reason behind Beli's expulsion, Mater Barbara spilled what many in the convent

---

*Beguines were women who were not quite nuns and not quite laity, for they took vows of chastity and obedience as long as they lived within the community, called a beguinage, but they were free to hold property and free to leave.

were thinking: that Beli was suspected of "dealing with the devil." Immediately Van Herssen protested to the Archbishop, writing that the Barbara Beli she knew was incapable of such evil, but that if she had in the meantime become infected with evil spirits then note well that it occurred within a convent run by Barbara Noosen. Mater Barbara of course defended herself to the Archbishop, saying the convent had enough on its hands to get one troublemaker out, so why should they risk accepting another? But the affair was hardly over.

Barbara van Herssen began to insist that in light of the statement by the doctor, the vote should be taken once more. When Mater Barbara refused, a number of sisters in Bethlehem took the opportunity to suggest to Van Herssen that she go over Mater's head to the current Franciscan confessor, plus a local canon named Michael Paludanus, a well-known theologian and poet. The sisters who suggested this did so not because they wanted Barbara Beli to remain—far from it. Rather, they sought to embarrass Barbara Noosen. The very act of revoting would be a political defeat for Mater, whatever the outcome of that vote. Mater understood this well, for when the confessor and the canon arrived in the convent to hear the votes she screamed that this affair did not concern them.

In the end, a slight majority predictably voted against Barbara Beli anyway: worldly clothes were soon prepared, and before Christmas of 1624 Barbara Beli left Bethlehem to live in Brussels with a still muttering Barbara van Herssen. Nevertheless, the goal of humiliating Mater Barbara was achieved, pleasing not only certain sisters but the convent's Franciscan confessor as well, who suggested to nuns that here was another piece of evidence that Mater Barbara was incompetent and that the nuns needed Franciscan control. But Mater Barbara had a different explanation for the turmoil in Bethlehem, besides her supposed ineptitude: the convent's troubles were the work of the "hangers-on of Henri Joos," who sought to be rid of the Archbishop and the leadership of Barbara Noosen all at once.

The "hangers-on" included five of the six lay sisters and assorted nuns, including "the youngest nun," who dared to "rebuke and talk back" to Mater. This youngest nun was Anna Vignarola, professed in June 1624, who along with "half the convent" sent yet another audacious petition to the Archbishop in early 1625, asking that Mater Barbara be replaced.

It wasn't unusual for Maters to resign or be dismissed from office as a result of conflicts, but it was always stressful—even when, as in this case, Mater Barbara herself supported the move. Wallowing in her troubles, she pleaded with Archbishop Boonen to be let go. "The unrest and tempest here are so great, the *fick-fackerie* so great, so many involved in it, that it's scandalous," she wrote. The supporters of Henri Joos, bolstered by laypeople outside the convent, "can't bear that I'm in charge, and are so rebellious against me that I pray you for the love of God and in all humility to release me from my office; your reverence will do me a great favor." Some nuns were insinuating that she ruled by sorcery herself, and thus was to blame in a direct way for Margaret's problems. "What greater misery is there than to be chained by the devil, and also to hear that I rule through the devil myself?" Once more she pleaded for release.

But criticism of Mater Barbara began to extend even to her own usually reliable supporters. She was indeed, they affirmed, partly to blame for the convent's troubles. Margaret, from her well-positioned perch in the guest room,* saw an endless line of outsiders besieging the grille in the parlor below her. If outsiders were therefore stirring up trouble inside the convent, it was because Mater Barbara let them. Dean Lucius confirmed that sisters were

---

*The sisters referred to the visitors' area in a number of ways: "guest room" and "parlor" were the most common, and interchangeable. Margaret's "guest room" was located upstairs from these areas and was a room where visitors had once lodged. The "guest room" where visitors came to talk was more properly the parlor, or *spreekkamer* (downstairs). I use the term "guest house" for the whole complex.

wearing out the tiles between the dormitory and the grille in order to greet and chat with friends. And even Catharina Rijkeboer, Mater Barbara's strongest ally, admitted that Mater was "very blunt and rustic in speech, most unmannered in things outward, uses little discretion, can't keep a secret, has little ability to rule, and doesn't understand the art of keeping sisters in peace or of going forward with a good example." Further, Mater did not help matters by speaking so critically to outsiders of certain nuns, referring to them as " 'the mob' and 'the faction,' and so on." In return for Mater's namecalling "many of the sisters, in her absence, poke fun and laugh about her with lay visitors" at the grille. "Even this very Wednesday past friends were entertained by stories of our contentions." And it surely didn't help that Mater often spoke "scandalously" of the Franciscan confessors, who served cheaply, and who reacted badly when they heard such ingratitude. Catharina longed for improvement, and even a new election, for "reformation and better adherence to our statutes."

In January 1625 Archbishop Boonen finally gave clear instructions to Dean Lucius on the house's myriad problems. First, the Dean was to inform the nuns that the Archbishop was earnestly searching for a place outside Bethlehem for Margaret, and was willing to provide her an allowance of one hundred florins per year. Second, the Archbishop promised the Dean that he would soon issue a set of new statutes for the convent, which he hoped would bring about greater discipline. Though he had not welcomed the sisters' petition for a new Mater, it did in fact seem to him that Mater Barbara was now "deficient in many things," and that she was certainly weary of her duties. Perhaps it was time to set her free from office, but if so, then discreetly, so as not to embarrass her.

The Archbishop's instructions regarding Margaret brought elation when the Dean repeated them to the nuns of Bethlehem, "resounding joyously" in the ears of most. Margaret herself was soon much improved, going to hear Mass on Sundays and feast days and regularly allowing pastoral visits by an "Augustinian confessor."

Catharina was "overjoyed to see Margaret in such spirits." And Mater herself hinted during a polite conversation with the Dean that she would not be "shamed" if the Archbishop decided to replace her.

Then, within days, Barbara's soul became an even more pressing problem than her shaky authority. By January 25, 1625, one year to the day since Margaret's miraculous recovery from attempted suicide, Barbara Noosen lay dying, of causes unknown. Her last written wish, composed a few days before, varied little from the goals that had consumed her these past years: to find Margaret a house, and the convent a permanent confessor. The Franciscans had finally, it seemed, abandoned them for good. "They won't serve us, nor set one foot in our convent." What if a sister should fall ill? Within two days of posing that scenario, Barbara Noosen faded herself. Fortunately, Joost Bouckaert happened to be in the convent that day and went in to attend her. He spent "a small hour" trying to lift her spirits, and she enjoyed some "moments" of clarity and light.

The days of Mater Barbara had been hard. Until the end she was unsure when the house would get its confessor, or where Margaret would go. She must have worried as well about who would succeed her, given the likely candidates and her longtime rivals within. But with Barbara Beli gone, with Margaret Smulders almost gone, and now nearly gone herself, Barbara Noosen had cause to imagine that this troubled community was on its way to being healed. And though the sisters had failed to show as much kindness to her in life as in death, she might have entertained the charitable thought that if her own rest could bring a modicum of peace to the place, then she would drink the bitter cup and give her life for Bethlehem.

Book Two

How Margaret Sought Her Revenge and Became
the Watchdog of Reform All at Once

9

The Burden of Bethlehem

Diminish not a word.

—Jeremiah 26:2

Back in the guest room at Bethlehem, May and June 1628. The nun continued as she had begun: confessing freely, in ink, the sins of her sisters. For days and weeks in the late spring of 1628 she shifted from her sewing to the small writing table and back—remembering the old, observing the new, jotting down, then to work again. And between prayers and choir and forgettable meals and discussions at the grille with Catharina, she watched and wrote still more, all in anticipation of the Archbishop's promised visitation. Her first entries were busiest, even furious, but the rest carried emotion as well, and the fervent hope that something would come of her labors. At the same time, she worried that the visitors might not believe her, because of her past, and because she surely wrote so much more than anyone else.

Still she kept writing anyway, constrained not only by a desire for improvement in the convent, not only by festering memories from her first two decades in Bethlehem, but several discouraging events that had occurred since the death of Mater Barbara Noosen in January 1625.

First, contrary to all expectations, Margaret did not leave Bethlehem or this suffocating guest room—not in 1625, or the next year, or ever. Since even the powerful Jacob Boonen failed in finding a place for her, it was doubtful that anyone else could. Unmovable, unreconciled with her sisters, unable to return to the cloister, with only dreaded, relentless sameness before her, she might have had a better future in Purgatory.

Second, the election of a replacement for Mater Barbara, around February 1625, turned out the way Margaret feared: power swung, as it often did even at the highest levels of the church, to the chief opponents of the previous regime. This time the Archbishop allowed the votes of the nuns to stand, rather than impose his own choice as Mater: the winner was Adriana Truis, perpetual thorn in the side of Mater Barbara Noosen while she lived, and loyalist of Henri Joos. But the Archbishop did make one important intervention of his own, in an attempt to reduce factionalism, or at least to placate both sides: he appointed Catharina Rijkeboer as the convent's first-ever Vicaress, a position Catharina herself had suggested was necessary for the convent. It was no small token, and no small sign of the Archbishop's trust in Catharina, since it made her, a mere thirty years of age, second only to Mater in authority.

To Margaret, Catharina's promotion meant little, for in practice Adriana wielded all power. Adriana was not only Mater but still Bursaress, responsible for distribution of the convent's goods, a task she had performed since 1613. Moreover, Adriana appointed to every other important office in the convent her chief allies, likewise friends of Henri Joos. These were Henri's sister Maria Joos, now Portress; her cousin Lesken Joos, a lay sister, now Infirmarian and the woman for whom Maria most often opened the convent's door; and worst of all to Margaret the pretentious Anna Vignarola, barely twenty-four years of age, now Sacristan (or caretaker) of the choir. All together, these women muffled whatever authority Catharina should have enjoyed. All together, they held Margaret in conspicuous contempt.

A third disappointment for Margaret came soon after the ascension of Adriana Truis as Mater. When Margaret complained to the Archbishop's right-hand man, Vicar-General Peter van der Wiel, about conditions in the convent generally and its new leaders in particular, and urged him to reform Bethlehem, the Vicar-General virtually ignored her. It was not that he opposed reform, for he was zealous, but rather he implied that the troublemaking Margaret was hardly the person to act as chief advocate: let her solve her personal troubles before she condemned others. He could easily have viewed Margaret as acting from hostile motives rather than pure, and as urging reform to cast aspersion on foes rather than out of sisterly love for their salvation. Neither was the Vicar-General sympathetic to Margaret's appeals to be removed from the guest room and returned to the community of nuns: since members of various communities were often separated on grounds of physical sickness, he reasoned, then why not on spiritual as well? The convent needed to convalesce, and it was more likely to do so without Margaret.

But a few small triumphs for Margaret had made these past several years in Bethlehem better than the first twenty. To her delight, Archbishop Boonen decided to retain jurisdiction over Bethlehem rather than hand it to the Franciscans. True, he managed to find no better confessors for the convent than those same Franciscans, whom he somehow persuaded to continue, but at least the Archbishop was ultimately in charge. Moreover, both Jacob Boonen and Joost Bouckaert seemed quite prepared to advocate the sorts of reforms for Bethlehem that Margaret had recently put forward to the unresponsive Vicar-General. The Archbishop had even visited Bethlehem personally in July 1625, remembered Margaret with unmistakable satisfaction, to address certain issues regarding the grille, and again in 1626, this time with the intent of bringing about reform in Bethlehem from top to bottom. On that blissful June day in 1626 he had not only called upon Mater Adriana, as expected of official visitors, but gone out of his way to speak with lowly Margaret in her guest room. Did he explain to her at this time that a move to another house was unlikely? Did she hold any resentment toward him for his failure? If so, it never surfaced. In fact, Margaret quickly became the strongest supporter of the Archbishop's plans for reform, which took clear shape in August 1626, when he sent to Bethlehem the long-promised set of brand new statutes. There in unilluminated but glorious manuscript were twenty-two chapters treating Worship, the Grille, Punishments, the Office of Mater, Profession, and on down the usual ladder of topics in conventual life. But there was nothing usual about the Archbishop's timing of the statutes: they were no less than a message of warning for Adriana. If Adriana held power in the convent, she also bore responsibility for its continued shortcomings and the need to redress them.

To what extent Margaret supported the Archbishop's reforms in order to have revenge on her enemies, or to serve God better than she had before, no one could say with precision. But whatever the mix, it was clear that Margaret's concern for her own plight and her zeal for reform became virtually one. Any criticism of the status quo not only implied the need for change but helped to soothe her scorched soul, for with chapter and verse she could show why her sisters were no more perfect than she—and, incidentally, if that were true, then why should she not have back her rightful place inside the convent?

The word "reform" had many meanings in Margaret's Catholic world. Thanks to the wide-ranging Council of Trent, she lived during a general age of reform in the church. But Trent was only one banner Margaret had in mind, especially since its basic requirements for female religious were quite traditional. She and her sisters could look as well to a venerable tradition of reform within monasticism itself. Here was reform in the sense of stricter adherence to existing monastic rules, such as at Cluny in tenth-century

The Black Sisters of Mons receive their statutes, 1543

Koninklijk Instituut voor het Kunstpatrimonium, Brussels, © IRPA-KIK Brussel

France, or stern "Observant" reforms in various monastic families during the fourteenth century. Here was reform in the sense of establishing brand new monastic orders, such as Franciscans and Dominicans in the thirteenth century, or Jesuits in the sixteenth. Here was also reform in the branching off of an existing order, such as the Franciscan-related Capuchins of the sixteenth century. And here was reform in a highly specific sense as well: reform of a single house, of behavior at a grille or a particular door, of communal property, of finances, and so on.

Clearly reform meant different things—from a desire to return to something pristine and undiluted, to a stricter observation of existing standards, to the establishment of something new and creative. For long, observers emphasized the first two, basically conservative sorts of reform in the church during the period after the Council of Trent, but over time the creative side became clear as well. Both were evident in Bethlehem, in the strict, old-fashioned monastic discipline promoted by Margaret and Archbishop Boonen, and in the lively debate over reforms that soon broke out in the convent—a debate not only of words but of deeds. Basic monastic standards, such as chastity and cloister, were certainly closed to debate, but the spirit and practice of particulars, such as how long and how often sisters should talk with outsiders at the grille, were argued worlds without end, including in Bethlehem. To complicate matters, debate was not merely about the intellectual or spiritual merits of this ideal or that, but involved personal relationships as well, and other terribly human considerations. It was a process that occurred, in different mixtures, in a thousand other communities as well—lay or religious—and the particular mixture in Bethlehem put Margaret clearly in the middle.

Besides the Archbishop's reforms, another reason for Margaret to seem so hopeful by 1628 was the continued improvement in her individual spiritual condition. Catharina, who knew her best, wrote in 1626 that Margaret gave no further cause for resentment, then in 1627 mentioned her "delight" with Margaret's "reasonable contentment." Even Mater Adriana spoke hopefully: "Margaret Smulders has been quiet; if it lasts long it will work to our salvation." Margaret had to admit that things had improved—even if her Augustinian confessor lasted only a couple of years, even if Johan Evangelista could not be re-enlisted to help her because he had after all finally moved away from Leuven, even if Joost Bouckaert could visit only occasionally from Diest, and even if she wrote in February 1628 that forgiveness was not for her and that her troubles at night threatened to reappear. Despite all these, in general Margaret was much better than before; and despite her recent worries, she never succumbed to demons again. She also ceased worrying to the point of incapacitation about the old events with Henri Joos. The reasons for such a recovery were unclear: further counseling with Pastor Bouckaert? New hard-earned resolve? Increased attention from Archbishop Boonen? Most likely it was connected to her new zeal for reform. No longer did discouragements and continued humiliations debilitate or render desperate. At worst Margaret now had a cause to preoccupy her; at best she had a cause she truly believed in.

An all-seeing Margaret had come to disagree mightily with how the sisters of Bethlehem, especially the leading faction, were interpreting the Archbishop's general reforms of 1626, or his more specific reforms of the grille in 1625 and 1627. There were no gross violations, but by early 1628 she saw more transgression in the convent "than ever before." In February, during a low point, she sent yet another warning letter to the Archbishop in Mechelen. What the convent needed, Margaret wrote, was another of the Archbishop's official visitations. In a mailed letter to him, sent by messenger, she could not reveal all, for if the Archbishop subsequently and suddenly responded to her letter by ordering Adriana to fix this problem or that, then Adriana would easily guess his source of information and unleash her wrath against likely suspects. An official visitation, on the other hand, offered a bit of anonymity, for all sisters were obliged to participate in a personal interview with the visitors and tell honestly what they knew of conditions in the convent. During that interview, sisters were also free to hand over more detailed written testimony. This universal participation and personal delivery made it difficult for Mater to determine who had revealed this or that shortcoming in the convent. Moreover, Mater was by statute forbidden to punish or threaten any sister who chose to speak her conscience during the visitation. It was true that Adriana still tried to identify the sources of negative information anyway, and often said ominously after visitors had left, "I know well whence this or that comes." But a visitation was relatively safer for disgruntled sisters and offered more hope for improvement than individual letters sent by visible messengers.

Perhaps because of Margaret's short letter of February 1628, or perhaps simply because it was time again (in theory each convent was supposed to be visited every other year, an ideal rarely adhered to), the machinery at the episcopal palace started up, in preparation for a full-scale visitation to Bethlehem in the spring. It was upon hearing this news that Margaret decided to begin her incomparable account of the convent and tell almost all. Since there was not enough time in a mere interview to tell everything she knew, she intended to be prepared in advance with a long letter as well.

After making as many as forty-three different entries during a period of composition that lasted from May well into June 1628, Margaret abruptly finished her letter, as if she had decided to write until the moment that the visitor arrived and called "stop." At some point as she worked or sipped her soup, or as she finished and realized for the first time the immensity of her thirty-two-page creation, she might have broken her usual somberness to chuckle at the irony that on first arriving in the convent she had been unable to write at all.

10
Favorites

Margaret's letter did not follow classical rules of composition. She fired a prolonged salvo once, twice, then even three times, with some variation, much passion, and excessive repetition. "I fear that on some matters I've repeated myself," she admitted in a rare understatement. Yet if her sins of style proved tedious for the Archbishop, they also revealed the intensity of her feelings, especially on three related themes: (1) Mater Adriana worried more about her power within the convent, (2) and pleasing those without, (3) than she did about good old monastic discipline—and her example in each moved many of the nuns to imitation.

None of these themes was, in the monastic world, unique to Bethlehem. But what Margaret did better than most was to convey the texture and detail of daily living in a cohesive picture, a picture more alive than one constructed from fragments of evidence in different convents. Instead of composite scenarios and personalities, drawn from dozens of convents, instead of treating issues in religious life as if they had a separate existence from the people who confronted them, Margaret offered a complete cast of full-bodied characters—including herself—who mixed together their personal biases with lofty spiritual ideals as easily and half-consciously as the nuns of Bethlehem prepared the batter for their famous waffles.

Excerpt from the first page of the visitation letter of
Margaret Smulders, 1628

Archive of the Archdiocese of Mechelen-Brussels

"Most Reverend Lord, if we had a Mater who was a lover of true religious life, observing and enforcing the praiseworthy statutes and wise ordinances of your reverence, given through the Holy Spirit, then there would be no need for any of us to trouble and burden your reverence with all these silly problems, for it's certainly within her power to improve things if she pleased to do so."

This opener set the stage for Margaret's entire letter: Mater Adriana was to blame for what ailed in Bethlehem. Of course any Mater was ultimately responsible for her convent, but Margaret meant more than this. Adriana consciously and pugnaciously ruled by her own passion rather than out of respect for law, custom, ecclesiastical authority, and the Holy Spirit. Indeed it was pointless for the Archbishop to issue decrees that ran contrary to her tastes, "as we see now in many matters decreed but not observed." Her willfulness developed long ago and would not easily bend, wrote Margaret, for Adriana rose to office when just "a child." From her earliest days as Bursaress, Adriana "lorded it over other Maters." They "were always having to dance to her tune, and couldn't have the smallest thing without being treated as if they were little children. I can't begin to count how many tears I saw those women shed because of her; she was a princess in the convent before most of us were here."

With these claims Margaret implied that sisters fulfilled the reverence owed to Mater. That when passing before Adriana they all bowed, that when she entered a room they stood or bowed, that when she commanded or punished they humbly inclined and thanked God, and that they regarded the house as Noah's ark, having but one captain and door. Adriana would have scoffed at the notion that such deference existed in Bethlehem, but her turn to accuse would come.

One of the damaging consequences of Adriana's passion-driven regime, continued Margaret, was her natural tendency to play favorites, and thus nonfavorites. She did not show a "common, motherly love for each," but instead sponsored "murmuring, factionalism, resentment, gossip, little respect, and much evil speaking." Here Margaret tapped into a precept of monastic life with deep roots and wide branches: special friendships in a convent hindered charity. Teresa had only recently worried about such friendships in her new convent in Avila. And while pregnancies and other occasional scandals were trumpeted louder than any other transgressions in convents, the most frequent and serious sin was, according to many observers, favoritism between nuns. In the archdiocese of Mechelen favoritism was denounced more strongly in visitation decrees than any other transgression, and considered "the source of much unrest, ill feeling, gossip, and other such faults." Archbishop Boonen and Vicar-General Van der Wiel both detested this "plague against sisterly love," while the statutes of Bethlehem required Mater to eschew partiality, and to rule "more through love than fear."

Despite these exhortations to truly equal sisterhood, special friendships developed anyway—and Maters were often at the center of them, wittingly or not. Some deliberately led a faction, while others became the target of critical nuns who banded together in common cause. These nuns often held up another nun as their leader, in many cases Mater's obvious and natural rival, the Vicaress. Sometimes division was simply one generation against another, or women of one social rank against another. But whatever the configuration, Mater was in the middle, whether she liked it or not.

The Outcast

According to Margaret, Adriana was no reluctant leader, no helpless target, but the heart and soul of factionalism. Mater "is as double-hearted as anyone I've ever seen walk the face of the earth." In fact, continued Margaret, "I say that there's no religious in this convent who is a greater respecter of persons, no one who is more full of passion." And, "Her heart is so full of bitterness toward some that it often spills out. It's all a want of love." Like the knights of medieval romance, Adriana was a scourge to her enemies and fiercely loyal to her friends.

The person Adriana happened to dislike most, besides Margaret, was Margaret's friend Catharina, who as Vicaress should have been Mater's closest adviser. When Vicaress tried mildly to exhort or pass along complaints from other sisters, Adriana responded in a manner that was "scandalous for a superior," and complained that Catharina "pays heed to marvelous gossip." Most of the time, in order to maintain peace, "Vicaress is compelled to silence and to allow Mater her own way, just as we have been compelled to silence." Indeed Catharina dared not offer any advice at all, for Adriana was "so proud that she listens to no one and asks advice of no one." Mater even said that Vicaress would not be content until she was Mater herself. To the contrary, alleged Margaret. Catharina had no taste for power, but instead a "very great desire to be set free from her office," for Mater could not bear her.

Given these sentiments, "it was vain to name a Vicaress here, for she may not begin the smallest thing, but instead must endure much from Mater, even behind her back, in ridicule. She isn't regarded well by the community, and that's Mater's fault." Without cause Adriana overruled Catharina in the presence of the entire convent, and looked ill upon anyone seen talking much with her. Adriana even worked to alienate from Catharina the convent's novices, "from the first day the young ones come to live here." This was especially serious because Catharina, as Vicaress, was also automatically Novice-Mistress, responsible for their training. But by leading the novices another way, Mater could assure herself of their loyalty and continue doing as she pleased forever. That, concluded Margaret, was precisely why Adriana often "speaks two hours long with the novices," and "if Vicaress commands or forbids them something, Mater will tell them the opposite."

Adriana worked to win the young ones not only directly but through her creatures. To diminish Catharina's authority, said Margaret, Adriana appointed Anna Vignarola "to teach the young ones" how to sing the Divine Office, notwithstanding that Anna was the "most unsuitable of all, and was appointed for no other reason than to pull the young ones to her." Mater told Catharina that Anna would perform this task for two weeks only, but it had lasted eighteen months already. Now, said Margaret, "Vignarola is much freer in calling and commanding the novices than Vicaress, thanks to the great blind love Mater bears for her. She thinks no one more able with the novices than Vignarola, though she is certainly the most unlearned and the most coarse of manner and as cliquish as it's possible to be in a convent." What a disgrace, thought Margaret, that Vicaress should be "snapped at by the youngest professed," or that behind Vicaress's back Anna dared to say that "Vicaress is but a marvelous fishhead." She had no reason to speak thus, for Vicaress "speaks ill of no one and does no one no evil." What Mater truly sought, suspected Margaret, was the removal of Catharina as Vicaress and the appointment of Anna Vignarola instead, but if that occurred then "it will become a sorry convent indeed."

Another object of Adriana's displeasure was Maria Coninxloo, whom Adriana thought in league with the despised Catharina. Before the whole community Mater heaped scorn and barbs upon both women, suspecting them to be the Archbishop's chief sources of negative information about the convent, and calling Maria a "wonderful Gabriel" since, like the angel, she was so keen to bear messages to others. In fact when Mater saw talking together any two sisters who were "not of her people," she suspected them of conspiring over what to tell during the Archbishop's next visitation. "She says straight out, 'what council is held here?' when the others had no such ill intent." It was difficult for Margaret to express how worried Adriana could get "about Sister Maria and still others." But suffice it to say that as a result of Adriana's open contempt, Maria and Catharina were now "hated by many others as well."

One of the most visible ways Mater expressed her dislike of Maria, explained Margaret, was in choir. Instead of seating the nuns there according to seniority of profession or age, as was customary, Adriana made Maria sit "on the same side of the choir with the young ones," or novices. After much complaining, Mater finally placed someone "beneath Maria, namely the youngest novice!" It appeared to Margaret that Mater thought she might "stifle Maria's passions in one fell swoop," yet Mater was greatly influenced by her own passions. "She's full of herself." As far as Margaret could tell, Adriana disliked Maria simply because Maria was "curious and observes everything, and occasionally writes it all to your reverence." Adriana knew Maria wrote letters to the Archbishop because those who carried letters from the convent, the lay sisters, told Mater so. There was also the time Anna Vignarola overheard Maria uttering a few indiscreet words, which Anna immediately passed on to Adriana and which remained "stuck in Mater's head." And now, said Margaret, Adriana warns all nuns to "beware of Sister Maria as of a serpent, that she passes everything along to the superiors."

A final manifestation of Mater's less than full heart was her toleration of old stories. Such were a cause of ill will and division within various religious communities, as in Bethanie in Brussels, where a Sister Elizabeth was said to have stoked up younger nuns by repeating to them the past misdeeds of the elders. In particular, Margaret condemned the telling of stories about "Sister Lesken Nijns, who is now in another convent"—stories that of course included Margaret as well. Sometimes, said Margaret, the nuns "start talking of things which of themselves are neither good nor bad," but soon nothing was kept back. "I say that this is the cause of many sins, even if they don't realize it. Mater herself is often the cause of such talk, and it would be more honest and salvational for her to keep silent, especially since she knows that some things used to be said about her as well." Adriana, tantalized Margaret, had a shady past of her own: "others say about her secretly, 'though she's now Mater, she's not the holier for it.' "

If Margaret expressed deep concern about Adriana's perceived rivals, she spent even more energy railing against Adriana's favorites. "All her little friends are in office," protested Margaret, and they were "together always, early and late, during Silence, confiding in each other. The smallest word cannot be said in private but that Sisters Maria Joos, Vignarola, and Lesken Joos run right to Mater and repeat it," especially if it was something "that displeases them," and the opinion of those three about another sister "is immediately the opinion of Mater as well." This kind of favoritism was alone repugnant, but it also caused Mater to allow these sisters great freedom. "They've become so bold that they lord it over everyone, and all they don't dare say they get across with their smirks." If Mater had learned something confidential about a sister, either through the confessor or other means, "we know it immediately by the smirks of those to whom Mater has complained."

Most offensive of all to Margaret was Anna Vignarola, who like Adriana had professed at a young age and quickly assumed important office in the convent. "Mater is so crazy" for Anna that "in my whole life I have never seen such great love between two like people," or, in other words, people of the same gender. "They're like love-struck suitors who can't bear to be apart; usually one party loves more than the other, but in this case they are both blind with love, so bowled over. It's no simple favoritism, if you ask me, and it goes beyond them to all they favor: who Vignarola attacks, Mater has by the neck, and so it goes with all the hangers-on." While Adriana lavished praise on Anna, Anna in turn claimed in public that there was "no more able Mater than ours," in regard to promoting common love, reconciling foes, and loving her enemies.

Among Anna's other privileges, claimed Margaret, was her freedom to visit the sick in the infirmary, even outside appointed hours. When Adriana lay ill, "then Vignarola must be there too or the scene is incomplete. And when they're not sick, they still aren't much outside the infirmary, at all times, early and late," for they could visit there with their ally Lesken Joos, the Infirmarian. The same was true if Maria Joos or Lesken Joos or "someone else from her brood" lay ill. And if Anna Vignarola was ailing, "then Mater is there with her, like the most anxious mother in the world with her dearest child, as if Mater and the Infirmarian had nothing else in the world to do." Mater's great compassion, Margaret continued, did not extend to all the sick, just as it did not extend to all the healthy. "Mater always says that she'll do for each what she does for one, but God forgive her that we see a different story with our eyes. If Sister Maria Coninxloo or many other sisters I could name were sick, you wouldn't see Mater running to and from the infirmary." Even when no one had told Margaret exactly who was sick, she could guess simply by the number of trips Mater made back and forth. And if it was someone Mater liked, then "the doctor, the druggist, the barber, 7 maids for one sister," were also "sent immediately to the infirmary, however small her affliction." And this while the unfavored were required almost to sneak in their medicines and cures. "Oh excessive foolish love!"

In short, "Anyone who wants to test Mater's feelings for Anna need merely say something good about Anna, and Mater will agree with you immediately; she'll transform herself into a loving soul, happiness evident in all her expressions; but say something ill and at once she transforms again, baring her teeth, the face marvelously angry, the words spiteful." To improve things, Margaret thought it a good idea that Anna and Adriana should have less to do with each other.

If Margaret resented Anna because she was privileged and young and able, Margaret disliked Lesken Joos because she was favored, a lay sister, and a relative of Henri Joos. Mater enjoyed the support of almost all lay sisters, but Lesken occupied a special place. Margaret could only wonder why: "It's a person who doesn't particularly look for work. If there's something to be fetched, some medicine for the sick or something else, she must have a maid do it for her, unless of course it's for Mater, Sister Maria Joos, or Vignarola, then someone else cannot be trusted." Worse, like Mater and Anna Vignarola, Lesken was partial, "a respectress of persons," paying little attention to the unfavored beyond their barest needs. To compound her sins, "She's also a big gossip, painting things as darkly as possible, and coming into the convent to announce all that the sick do or say. Those not in her good graces she hardly cares for or does little to help them relieve their sickness. Also, if anyone has an accident or requires medicine which might be embarrassing, then she does little else but ridicule that person," and by her actions urged others to do the same. "Everything stinks to her and makes her feel faint," which caused only more telling of embarrassing details. "I'm ashamed that I've had to listen to some of this talk, and if I were so afflicted I'd rather die than admit it," decided Margaret.

Not only Lesken but all the lay sisters bothered Margaret, because of their most-favored status. Mater allowed them to have the upper hand over the veiled nuns, and they concerned themselves with even the smallest things in the convent. "Their chirping, murmuring, and ranting have no end, and they dare reprove the nuns even in the presence of Mater, who actually encourages them." Vicaress was of course one of their favorite targets. "Before the whole community they rise up against the Vicaress like barking dogs, as if they'd tear her to pieces." But whoever their target, the lay sisters dared much. "I suppose there's not a convent in the world where the nuns are so snapped at as here." If the nuns asked a lay sister to run an errand outside the convent, "they snarl at us so that we wish we'd never asked them to begin with; and when they return home with less than we'd asked, we keep quiet, or they say to us 'go get it yourself,'" which for a veiled nun was of course out of the question. And they hardly did their best when outside. "They're such costly traders that it's amazing; we'd do as well if we sent children." If they did not like someone, "they're not choosy at all, no matter how bad the item." Sometimes the lay sisters even ridiculed the contemplative regime of the nuns. "They make fun of things pertaining to choir" and the Divine Office, saying that "nuns are but ladies, that they do nothing except hold a book in their hands." It would do no good to admonish Mater to order them to cease, for she would not do it. To Margaret, the only cure was for the Archbishop to speak with the lay sisters himself, in the presence of Mater and Vicaress, ordering them to refrain from matters "pertaining to the nuns alone," and to cease sitting together for the purpose of making "a gossip-house."

HAVES AND HAVE-NOTS

Adriana's favoritism not only inflicted emotional pain on nuns like Margaret, but it had tangible effects as well: unequal distribution of the convent's precious goods. It wasn't that Margaret craved wealth or even comfort: "We don't carry anything with us anyway" when we die. Rather, what disturbed her was Adriana's indifference toward the physical necessities of certain nuns and her exaggerated concern for that of others. Favorites prospered, while the rest suffered and watched in silence.

The root of the problem in Bethlehem was the same as in most convents: lack of a truly common fund that benefited nuns equally. Most houses tried to build a common endowment from donations, income from work, and annuities brought by nuns at entry. Ideally, all resources were pooled and evenly divided. But because donations and income were chronically insufficient in female convents, it was customary to allow an incoming sister to use her annuity for herself, assuring her family and herself that at least she would enjoy a predictable and modest standard of living. The nun's vow of poverty made it necessary for Mater to hold and administer those annuities in the nun's name, but in most cases the annuity was for the nun alone: thus the greater the annuity, the greater the potential for one sister to enjoy more comfort than another—and the greater the potential for there to prevail in the convent the same sort of material and social inequality that existed in the world. Even nuns in poorer convents found it hard to leave the distinctions of rank behind. If Lesken Nijns, Anna Vignarola, and Susanna Haechts all brought annuities of fifty florins per year, someone such as Margaret brought much less, and suffered the results, materially and socially.

And so Margaret accused Mater Adriana long and often of seeing to the wants of her own, while denying the wants and needs of other nuns: "Part of the convent flourishes, the other has to look like simpletons." The common portion provided to each nun by the convent included only meals—not clothing, and not bedding. "All that we need we must get ourselves," complained Margaret, "but those who've brought annuities have hose and shoes and even sometimes nice clothing, especially those who stand in the good graces." As for meals, they were meager, excessively so during Lent, when Mater would "rather burst" than give Vicaress the smallest extra crumb at table, though the two women sat right next to each other. Between Easter and Pentecost of 1628, Margaret maintained that three or four days a week nuns without annuities received at noon only "potage and an egg, and at night some milk. During the summer there were many days when we had nothing but some salad and potage at noon, and then again some milk at night." As for the sick, continued Margaret, why they had no more than the meager common portion, "unless each buys what she wishes to eat. In eating and drinking, we may not have so much as some white bread or a pint of good beer, even when it's on hand, unless we buy it ourselves." Perhaps Adriana should have tasted poverty herself, thought Margaret—then she would show more sympathy. But "she has carried the purse for so long she gets what her heart desires. Her followers don't know poverty either. Yet in all the years I've lived here, I don't think that I've ever seen the crust of a white loaf of bread, in sickness or health, nor have they ever sewn for me in the convent as much as a handkerchief, but that I've had to pay for it."

The high-living favorite who rankled Margaret most was no

surprise: Sister Anna Vignarola, who "has her own little heaven here." She would have a hard time dreaming up something new, for she already had all she could want, "all her heart desires, piles of things, in secret and in public. And Mater says she loves all of us the same, and that what she does for one she would do for another. Mater is blind. She sees through windows and doors of foolish love, so it should be forgiven her. Otherwise, I'd say with cause that she tells lies, hurtful lies." Margaret anticipated Adriana's response to any charges of temporal favoritism: as Mater it was her charge to administer goods as she saw fit, and also to kill desire for such goods. In other words, Adriana would claim she withheld from one and gave to another for spiritual reasons. But this was a ruse, said Margaret. For in killing the desires of others, Adriana merely fed her own, and those of her friends.

The most glaring example of this was the haggling that occurred when one of the nuns was about to die. Adriana, claimed Margaret, could "hardly wait until the soul has left the body to start handing out the goods, in the same way that lay people treat death so as to get the goods." Lesken Joos, the Infirmarian, didn't even wait until death, but started rummaging through the belongings around the patient's bed.

Another practice that drove the emotional and temporal divisions in the convent especially deep, since they were not routine but by invitation only, was the new custom of private parties. Ostensibly intended as work parties, these get-togethers soon turned into real parties. Anna Vignarola, Sacristan of the choir, one day enlisted four nuns to clean. The next day, six people went to clean, the entire day, "and the whole day with whooping, yelling, and ringing that you'd have to hear or see to believe. In the evening, some dishes were prepared for when they finished, an idea of Maria Joos, and then they can all carouse respectably." Running through Margaret's mind were no doubt the customary monastic rules that when talking nuns should be reverent and to the point, that sisters should show each other a common love, and that no one should eat outside of prescribed mealtimes, to promote discipline and community spirit. Yet certain nuns did not care. In fact, "I've noticed that each year the party gets bigger, each wants to show great liberality and good feeling, and through this the group of little friends, or better said the dear ones, increases in number." There were six dishes at the last party, by the way, but it sorrowed Margaret even to name them, so costly were these. And "there was no want of noise either. They sat there long and very late, like drunks on the beer-bench, and were so giddy that you'd hardly think them religious." As if such gatherings were not bothersome enough within the convent, Margaret was sure that outsiders heard the noise also, which disturbed their peace and their good opinion of the nuns.

Rather than stopping such occasions, Adriana actually promoted them. "These things are brought in more and more every day, for Mater comes alive with all this, she's always at the party too. Tuesday it was in the choir; then Wednesday five were reveling in the refectory, without as many dishes as last time, but with no less noise." Such precise information about the food prepared hints that Margaret got her information from Joanna Schoensetters, a lay sister who was also cook, with whom Margaret sometimes chatted, and the only lay sister of the convent's six to be out of favor with Adriana. "Thursday it was the workroom," then on "Friday, when Mater ought to give her community a good example in not breaking the fast without need, she took four sisters to clean her room, and in the evening she sponsored another get-together for them all, where the manners were as fine as at the others." What the nuns ate Margaret could not say this time, "but they were so tipsy that one of the sisters had to be helped out of the refectory, for she couldn't stand on her own."

What perturbed Margaret further was that "to all these parties are invited postulants and novices, when we have them." This was troublesome because if these "young ones" later decided to forgo the religious life and leave the convent, they would tell friends and family that religious women do nothing but "clean and shout."

When these same nuns were in the workroom they showed "all possible coarseness, from morn until eve, shouting, yelling, gossiping, clamoring, eating, and drinking." The chosen only occasionally dined with other nuns in the refectory during regular mealtimes, claimed Margaret, and sometimes even waited until the common meal was over so that they could then do and eat what "their little wills pleased." Again Margaret knew Adriana's response: the work parties cost the convent nothing, since the participants paid for them out of their own annuities. But even if the practice was technically licit, argued Margaret, it certainly wounded the spirit of monastic living. "Aren't these ugly customs for people in monasteries, that no common work can be done except with carousing? When we share as one, eating together, hushed, that is praiseworthy, but God help those who wish for such nowadays." Bethlehem's unfortunate fate was to be burdened with a Mater who "loves to hold frequent small tavern-parties." Margaret held dear "the common life. But I think there are few here who desire a common life. They're much too accustomed to buying all they want, needed or not."

Margaret's complaints help explain why in 1592 Archbishop Hovius had established in a convent called Thabor various laws designed to erase economic distinctions: he outlawed entry fees, and decreed that if anyone received food from outside it should be immediately divided among all, cut into as many small pieces as necessary. These rules were crucial to poor women such as Margaret Smulders, who supplemented her pathetic six florins a year with secret charity from Archbishop Boonen. Then again, perhaps Margaret desired the common life due to a genuine spiritual preference and truly wanted to think of food as medicine rather than as spice, as urged by many devotional writers, or believed with still others that there was no higher abstinence than controlling one's stomach at a table full of good food and drink. The problem was, she didn't have a chance to exercise such control because she had no choice—there was no virtue won through forced privation. The

Grey Sisters of Leuven were, like most nuns, not the elite medieval mystics who sought every possible way to avoid food. Nor were they wealthy nuns who required sumptuous fare or pampering. The women of Bethlehem were generally of a middling status, and found no contradiction between a decently stocked larder and good monastic discipline. But the blatant inequality of near-perpetual deprivation for some and plenty for others fell short of even that modest ideal, at least in the judgment of Margaret.

One of the greatest crosses of the monastic life was therefore to live harmoniously within an area of a few thousand square feet with a few dozen other people, in the realization that such an arrangement could last forever. It was difficult, but intentionally so, for it was the difficulty itself that helped to purify: communal living served as a fire in which virtue was forged. In close quarters, the chances for anger, envy, or indifference increased, but the refining fire of common sisterly love was also hottest and most effective. Some made it through the fire, some struggled along, some were hardly touched at all. The experienced religious must have recognized that truly common love, expressed in emotions and temporal care, was to be learned anew with each generation of nuns, even with each new individual.

11

Almsgetting

As offensive to Margaret as Adriana's favoritism within the convent was her excessive attention to friends without. Such attention was partly for fun, of course, but there was serious purpose as well: the convent's need for alms. Margaret preferred to provide for Bethlehem's material needs through the old-fashioned methods of common work, penny pinching, and belt tightening by nuns, in tandem with unsolicited alms granted spontaneously by pious benefactors. Adriana, on the other hand, sought temporal well-being largely through the aggressive courting of regular benefactors and their alms, pious or not: by pampering certain outsiders with food, drink, and other privileges, she hoped to stimulate gifts that were not only generous but predictable.

Hospitality toward guests was an established monastic custom, but in Margaret's eyes Adriana went too far: her efforts among outsiders cheated the nuns of time in devotion or work, turned minds to matters of the world, and plundered the convent's meager common goods, hurting poorer nuns most of all. In short, Adriana's plan was not only a spiritual travesty but an economic failure, for according to Margaret the indulging of outsiders ended up costing more than it brought in.

Most of the subtle soliciting of alms in Bethlehem occurred at that small area so often the object of controversy in convents: the grille through which sisters and visitors spoke to each other in the parlor.

Many of the best fireworks on the question of guests were shot off in Bethlehem even before the visitation of 1628. Between 1618 and 1624 Archbishops ordered the convent to cease the old practice of allowing outsiders to spend the night in the guest rooms. Then in 1626, and again in 1627, Archbishop Boonen even ordered nuns to cease serving food and drink at the grille, both to cut expense and to avoid the appearance of worldly feasting. If visitors came, they were merely to sit and chat briefly, without further ado. Margaret, Catharina, and Maria Coninxloo were overjoyed by these decrees—especially Margaret, who from her quarters in the guest room was plagued more than anyone by the fuss that attended such visits. But most nuns were mad as "snarling dogs" about the ban on refreshment.

Margaret explained that the lay sisters, upon learning of the ban, began "ranting and raving like they were out of their senses." But "captain of all" was Maria Joos, who spoke without reason "as if the community had been dealt the most unfair blow humanly possible. She went after the Vicaress like a snarling dog intent on the kill." Maria even said to Mater Adriana, "If I were you, I'd throw the keys at the Bishop's feet and say to him, 'do it yourself, I can't do it this way,' and I'd let him decree and command all day long, but I'd do as I saw fit and throw all his edicts in a pile, and let him pronounce and proclaim to his heart's content, but we will not do it; we'd rather rise up against him, rather leave the convent, than be ruled this way." Such rebellion was intolerable to Margaret. "God grant that the others weren't affected by such a display of disrespect for her superiors," Margaret prayed, for many thought that Maria "spoke under the influence of the spirit of God, because she appears to be more pious than the others, and she speaks so smoothly that no one is her equal."

Though Margaret conceded Maria's talents, this did not atone for temerity toward authority, nor liberality with goods. Before the new decrees were proclaimed, Maria had so many friends eating, drinking, and sleeping in the convent, that "we might as well have hung out a sign and called ourselves the 'Do Drop In,'" a common name for taverns, even borne by an establishment right around the corner from Bethlehem. And despite recent decrees, Maria still "gives food and drink to everyone, from high to low, whenever she may or can; she says that the Bishop supports us in this and will leave us in peace."

As vigorous as Maria Joos in opposition to the Archbishop's new decrees were the guests themselves. According to Maria Coninxloo and Catharina Rijkeboer, outsiders were adamant about continuing their frequent visits. In St. Teresa's Avila, lay women apparently expected nuns to act as confidantes in return for moral and financial support. The nuns of Bethlehem sensed similar expectations of their own friends and wished not to displease. They would not go as far in opposing their superiors as certain medieval English nuns, who were so angry with the Bishop of Lincoln's restrictions on their conversations with friends that they chased him from the convent and threw the official bull at his head. Still, the women of Bethlehem did not shy from "stoking up Mater" to change the mind of Archbishop Boonen.

Such adamance by nuns about the grille was not, however, merely about monastic custom or the chance to socialize. For poorer nuns, such as those in Bethlehem, it was also about getting alms. As they explained to their confessor, they were "paupers" and had more need than "fat abbeys" to seek alms and keep friends. In other words, to get alms, one had to treat friends well, and even give something first, and the best place to do that was at the grille. Some alms-bearing friends who visited were "rustics," obviously thirsty after a long journey: why should they not have a drink, on grounds

A view inside Leuven, from a book of sixteenth-century watercolors. No illustrations or paintings of Bethlehem have survived, but, like the religious complex depicted on the right, it was located next to the Dyle River, which meandered through Leuven.

© Royal Albert I Library, Brussels

of compassion and good relations? The Bishop of Gent, Antoon Triest, revealed a similar sentiment in a convent in Oudenaarde: the house confessor drank too much not by nature, said the Bishop, but because the nuns knew no better way to please their friends than by filling them with wine at the grille. Thus, to all other points the sisters of Bethlehem would submit, the confessor informed the Archbishop, but beer for their friends they would have.

Even Margaret would have had to agree with Bishop Triest that the getting of alms, and the politenesses it required, were venerable monastic traditions. Everyone recognized that even the most ascetic establishment required some kind of temporal footing or the establishment would not exist: the trick was to secure that footing without too much distraction from what was supposed to be the most important activity in convents, prayer. There were two basic approaches to meeting physical needs: ignore them as much as possible, or work to achieve a measure of security in the hope of then being able to focus on higher things. The first could be found in a few strict convents, but the second was the overwhelming favorite, including in Bethlehem.

The most basic means to attain that security included the annuities brought in by nuns, as well as the common work, another monastic tradition, which said that physical labor was good for the soul as well as the body. In spite of decrees that "handmaidens of the lord" should avoid "very heavy toil," this work could take on quite laborious and even undignified forms, among not only active religious but contemplative, according to what sisters thought would best engender spirituality and cash. These included hostelry, education, laundering, the renting of funeral palls and ornamentation, the usual sewing and handicrafts, child care, and the production and sale of wine, beer, and spirits, among others. That cloistered orders did these more for money than the discipline of work was reflected in their taking on, out of necessity, even the most unpleasant tasks, and their frequent complaints about them—such as when the White Ladies of Leuven barely stifled their protests against babysitting for longer than expected two children of a supposedly well-to-do Irish couple. But in light of chronically insufficient funds, and despite the ideals of Trent, even the unpleasant tasks continued.

Convents that truly wished to increase their temporal standing, however, went beyond annuities or the meager income of the common work and put greatest hopes in alms from friends. In return, these benefactors expected and received—in addition to various tangible benefits—the convent's prayers. But a serious problem for female convents was this: nuns could not say Mass for the living or the dead, the service most heavily funded and desired by almsgivers. In other words, male convents, full of Mass-saying priests, usually received more alms than female convents, whose sisters could merely pray or sing in return for gifts. Moreover, nuns had to hire priests to perform Mass for them, adding to a convent's expenses. And because nuns were forbidden to leave the cloister, they could neither go out in good Franciscan fashion and beg directly for alms, nor walk in processions and increase their visibility to potential donors—other moneymaking practices in which male religious often engaged. As a result, female convents tended to be poorer than their male counterparts.

Certainly some male houses were poor. And even the women of Bethlehem suffered less than most peasants in the world: scattered financial records from the 1640s and 1650s suggest that the house at least broke even at times, though to do so it surely depleted capital funds. But in general, wealth in female houses such as Bethlehem was comparatively and absolutely rare, and many nuns existed in a state of perpetual unsatisfaction. Margaret's response to indigence was to cut back even further on expenses and to suffer together in dignity. But Adriana's was to follow the road most traveled in the monastic world, one marked by the concise dictum in Isaiah 1:23, "Every one loveth gifts," including potential givers. Despite the Archbishop's warnings to leave friends dry, Mater Adriana and her kind continued to wait upon visitors as actively as ever, for both pleasure and profit.

THREE SPECIAL FRIENDS

The most popular friend to grace the grille of Bethlehem was, according to Margaret, still Henri Joos. Despite living in distant Mol, the ex-confessor not only remained the cornerstone of factionalism within Bethlehem, not only showed himself affable as ever at the grille, but was expensive.

Though all of Mater Adriana's creatures were of course devoted to Henri Joos, Anna Vignarola stood out. As Margaret told it, Anna felt "that there is nowhere to be found an equal" to the man, "nor will there ever be, in holiness, wisdom, discretion, love, mercy, and all virtues, that in our lives we have never enjoyed such an exceptional confessor and preacher as he, nor will we ever enjoy, and that we were the luckiest persons ever born when he served us." Further, said Margaret in her vivid prose, Anna believed that those who had said otherwise "deserve to have a red-hot iron through their tongues, and merit punishment now and hereafter." Anna was even so brazen as to wonder "what judgment" Archbishop Hovius and others "now dead" had earned for their past treatment of Henri Joos. Yet as Margaret pointed out, Anna was not even in the convent when the events in question had occurred: "she would do much better to keep quiet; if she had lived here during those years, then she'd have some right to speak."

For the first time since the unpleasant events of years past, Margaret expressed to the Archbishop her own feelings for the "Pastor of Mol," as she always called Henri Joos now. He was not devoid of goodness, "for he in fact shows much virtue and mercy, and his countenance and deeds are good; especially the last time (not the very last) that he was here, was I surprisingly edified." But in regard to his "past holiness, only they who experienced it as it actually was can say, and they're not all dead." Unfortunately, others who knew the ex-confessor's darker side too often remained silent, or praised him "highly so as to play the game and keep the peace."

If Margaret was right that some kept silent about Henri Joos, it was surely in part because of his temporal importance to the convent. Anna Vignarola "speaks alone with him regularly; it seems she can't miss him, whenever he comes. She sends him frills yearly; and in gratitude, and because she's the special one of Mater, he sends her money, and in this she also pleases Mater. Who wants to be friends with Mater speaks and gives to him; the more it is, the more she likes it, and not only to him but all his friends." Here Margaret linked explicitly inside and outside friendships, and their relationship to alms. Yet Henri Joos was a prime example that the policy of giving-to-get cost more than it brought in. It was still said in Bethlehem, claimed Margaret, that Maria Joos's "dear brother" served the convent for nothing, and that he gave one hundred florins a year for his meals. But it "would be to our ruin to have such a one again," for even if he gave two hundred florins a year it would not have been enough for all the sheets, napkins, towels, beds, and other such things he used up. Rarely was he without guests of his own, who stayed "for months" while the convent fed them as well. Then the "nuns in his fold were invited to dine with him twice every week, and stayed there the whole day banqueting, singing, and making noise." If any of the other nuns complained, his devotees "ran straight to him in disbelief, mouths gaping, and repeated it, for he made them gossips. And then he spoke very nastily about those not in his grace, which after all was very ugly for a confessor, for it brought great oppression of conscience. And people complain that we lost so much." To Margaret, it was good that he was lost, for economic reasons and otherwise. "Though he often gives us gifts, he still owes us. Even if he gave us half his goods, it wouldn't be enough to repair the damage in soul and body, he knows that well."

After Henri Joos, the house's biggest friend was someone Margaret identified as the "Woman *In Den Luypaert*," or In the Leopard, the name of a house around the corner, possibly a tavern or brewery. This woman happened to be (not surprisingly) friends as well with Henri Joos and the leading nuns in Bethlehem. Mater Adriana, claimed Margaret, was "more concerned for the people In the Leopard than for her own convent and religious." Every day the lay sisters "go there, sometimes two or three in a day, and not only while she's in childbed," when her appetite was especially keen, "but year out year in, never too early or late, whatever high feast day it may be or whatever we have to do ourselves." The woman was "very well cared for, and all that Mater and others can imagine or dream up, they make for her, whether something fancy to eat or some frill, all that they can invent to give her children. Nothing is too much for Mater if it's for that house." This disturbed Margaret not only because of the expense, but because all the giving "amazed" outsiders, "who say we're not so poor after all if Mater can give such gifts to the children." Margaret too worried about the convent's image with outsiders, but in a way different from Adriana: if people thought the convent rich, they would be less inclined to give it alms. Adriana, on the other hand, thought the way to get alms was to do favors first, among a group of select, reliable friends.

And so Adriana gave and gave. Yet Margaret concluded that, despite Mater's bragging about all the kindnesses received from the Woman In the Leopard, they amounted to very little. She "sometimes gives us portions of beer and meat and other things. But we do as much kindness for her as possible," yet had never received "any extraordinary gift" in return, small or large. In fact, "if it were all piled together they'd be more bound to us than we are to them." What did other convents do with overindulged patrons, wondered Margaret? "One or two or three times is nothing, but always cooking and smuggling for her, now some pork, then a tart, cottage cheese, flan made in the dish, an apple spiced with wine and sugar, and so many other things that I don't know how to write it all. I see it all prepared, more than the others. Mater would say that the woman provides the goods, but it's like the old saying, 'Who sets the table has the greatest expense.'" The woman had a bad spiritual influence as well. "It's a woman who's full of gossip and complaining, and brings in much back-stabbing concerning one's name and honor, in regard to her maids as otherwise."

A third and final best friend was the convent's steward. Every convent employed a worldly-wise person to represent it diligently in temporal affairs, "as a good faithful steward is obliged and ought to do." But the current steward of Bethlehem was, in Margaret's eyes, more a consumer of the convent's goods than a defender. Besides his high fees, explained Margaret, the man had a ravenous appetite. "When he comes he announces it well in advance, and the preparations commence as if he were a prince." He began with "the heel of a ham, a piece of spiced meat, seasoned mutton, all as costly as possible," and a bit of *Hutsepot,* a kind of stew with good beef. Then it was "anything else they can dream up or lay their hands on. He devours it all, and is so ill-mannered about it that they don't dare serve anyone else before him." When meat was served, he refused to eat it "unless it's been cut into very tiny pieces, and cooked and recooked at great expense." Then he usually stayed "long, five, six, eight days before leaving, and is so unspeakably delicious that nothing can be made for him that is too fine. He'd probably have to plead poverty if not for his acquaintance with us." Moreover, the man never ate alone and he had only recently married—which meant even larger parties to come.

If it were up to Margaret, the steward would board elsewhere when in Leuven, and be granted merely the usual fee for his services. Otherwise he would continue to visit three or four times a year, eating and drinking himself to sleep, "and if he's drunk as he often is, then he can't be put into bed at all. There's not a worse sight than seeing a religious up so late with a drunkard." Here was something to disturb Archbishop Boonen, for in the very year of his visitation to Bethlehem he unearthed similar stories in the convent of Jericho, near Brussels, and dismissed the steward, who among other things had entertained nuns in his rooms until four in the morning.

New Recruits

Clearly the kind of giving and catering to outsiders described by Margaret went far beyond the monastic tradition of hospitality. And it extended to others besides the big three.

As usual Anna and Adriana led the way, often together. Mater Adriana encouraged Anna to make acquaintance with outsiders, in the hope of gaining tangible favors. "Mater has no greater pleasure than providing the convent's guests with the company of such an agreeable religious." Anna was "an expert talker and could easily tempt someone. It's too bad she's so spoiled; she could have been a most able religious had she been well trained and exercised from the beginning, and made more respectable. Now there's nothing to be done about it, she has so much license." Whoever came, Anna was right alongside, sometimes visiting with "fourth-hand acquaintances," and chatting not only with those who had come to see her but those come to see other nuns.

Mater Adriana was equally adept at making friends. And she paid special attention, said Margaret, to wealthy families with daughters who might one day enter Bethlehem. Provided a young woman had money, Adriana was "content to accept anyone" as a nun, "even if crippled, half-blind, and dull-witted, all are welcome, though Mater doesn't stop to think whether the person is able. If Vicaress suggests they ought to consider health and ability, she gets no thanks; she is a true devotee of monastic principles, but Mater on the contrary is a spacious dish."

As proof, Margaret related the case of a postulant accepted two years before, whose curious medical history should have disqualified her. She had "an imperfection in one of her eyes, for when young she fell into the fire." As a result, she had to wear eyeglasses always, for if she did not, then she could hardly see. Moreover, said Margaret, "the eye also moves around, so that she can hardly bear the presence of light or fire." As if these physical afflictions weren't enough, the candidate had a "blow from nature" that prevented her from eating various foods lest she bleed more, which was a great inconvenience for the convent. And often, "when she comes into the choir, or workroom, or refectory, or whatever she's doing, blood suddenly starts streaming from her nose and soils all around her." Then there was the woman's unsuitable temperament: she complained about the common work, she chattered, was strong-willed, and spoke abruptly and rudely. Finally, this woman was too expensive, for though she had lived in the convent for two years her father had provided "not a single stiver" for her costs. Despite this plenitude of impediments, Adriana welcomed the woman into Bethlehem because she and Anna Vignarola were "crazy" about her, and because they expected abundant temporal fruit from her family.

Besides recruiting new families, Adriana spent much money on her own. Her nephew got his "meals from us almost every day for two years." Then there was another nephew, and a niece, both of whom cost more than they brought in. But whoever the guest, it was as if they "haven't been unless they've been seen into the guest room," wrote Margaret. If the situation continued, Margaret would lose her resolve to remain in the guest room, for she often felt that she lived "in a tavern, as they sit there and banquet, drinking beer and wine and eating different dishes, from noon until night, young beguines from outside and young religious from inside the city." Male and female "sit and carry on so that by evening they're so drunk they can't remember how to get back to their convents." Margaret knew what Mater would say: "No one eats here." But, volunteered Margaret, that was only true "as long as no one comes," for once guests were in the parlor, the serving commenced. Adriana and hers were perhaps foolish enough to think that Margaret could not see this, but Margaret wrote that "nothing can happen in the guest room, however secretly it's done, but that I see or hear. They certainly employ much finesse and deception, but unless I'm in the Divine Office, it's all in vain." When these private meals for friends were learned of by tattered nuns who just moments before had been told that the convent lacked money to buy "a few scraps of linen" with which they might mend their clothes, the pain only deepened.

Yet another way the nuns of Bethlehem lavished gifts upon friends was their "very ugly and harmful custom" of home delivering a favorite regional specialty: waffles. "Every year on Shrove Tuesday," told Margaret, "Mater insists on baking a great pile of waffles, from convent funds, to be taken to very many places. Two sisters need an entire day to bake enough, one after the other. Three, sometimes four sisters then do nothing but carry waffles to every corner. Mater would certainly answer, 'I didn't start this custom, it's been around since before my time,' and that's true, but never was it done to such excess." A waffle here and there for the convent's rightful friends, such as the Franciscan confessors or the Dean of Leuven, Margaret was willing to concede. But the nuns filled up even those persons from whom nothing could be expected. The labor was so offensive to less solvent nuns, and wood for the stoves "so scandalously expensive," that Margaret couldn't keep it in her heart "any longer." At the most recent Shrove Tuesday "it lasted fourteen days long, that baking and taking, one to her mother, to cousins, nieces, nephews, others their sister or brother. That's not so bad, but then some send off to a dear friend, another to a cleric, young theologian, an Augustinian, another young male or female religious, and here to the needy or to pigs! In sum, if this keeps on there won't be anyone left who hasn't tasted a waffle baked by the Grey Sisters."

Not surprisingly, a whole chestful of waffles had been sent recently to Mol—and thus Henri Joos. Yet Margaret received nothing of these treats herself. "I was present when the waffles were baked for the gift to Mol, but civility wasn't great enough to allow me to taste even the smallest crumb. In fact, I was sick at the time and right before my eyes I had to see the convent's goods given away." Once again Adriana justified it by claiming she gave with purpose, but Margaret countered that for every ten who received from the convent, one gave back in return. "If she's so devoted to baking waffles perhaps she should open a stall on the market and bake them on the spot for sale by the piece."

Since it cost so much to care for the twenty-six nuns who lived in Bethlehem, Margaret couldn't imagine how the convent could serve up so many meals, run a delivery service for waffles, and still survive. Yet she held out little hope for change. It was Adriana's "inclination, like a thief is inclined to steal."

Beyond Food and Drink

Though much of Margaret's criticism focused on victuals, she worried about other expenses as well. There was one sister "who for how many years I don't know has done nothing but make Agnus Dei's and Gospel books," all given away to friends as amulets. And this was not to mention the presents of flowers, bouquets, decorated flower branches, tree branches, and embroidered dresses for Our Lady. "I know that often one must give, but it must be done with prudence, according to ability and as the situation demands." Mater always claimed "she doesn't give without knowing where she's giving," but Margaret countered that most of the time the convent's efforts to get something in return were fruitless.

Anna was again the most guilty. "Vignarola is an expensive creature," Margaret began. Alone she gave away "100 times more than the whole community." And if someone outside gave something to Anna, then Anna insisted on giving something back, thus negating any advantage the convent might have won. Such largess was only possible, presumed a jealous Margaret, because as Sacristan Anna had greater access than others to the common purse. The nuns learned of a recent immoderate act after a slip by one of the convent's chaplains, who revealed that Anna had fashioned, from metal and silk, an expensive bouquet as a gift for her godfather. It was the sight of a few of those petals that caused the chaplain to wonder aloud to the other nuns how such a costly gift from such supposedly humble nuns could be justified. Margaret explained that Anna had offered this gift in the hope that the godfather would in return commission a painting for the choir. But what if the godfather didn't reciprocate as expected? "Oh he'll promise her, and she'll assume that he'll come through, but when reckoning day comes it will be holy garden-water, and who will pay for it all then? Probably Mater from the convent's funds."

Another favorite and costly practice of Adriana and Anna was the old custom, observed on St. Gregory's or St. Gertrude's day, of dressing small children as nuns and beguines. Mater thought the practice good for local relations, because parents loved to see their children so fussed over and dressed up, and because they enjoyed their conversations with Anna Vignarola, who was sent especially for the task. "There is at no time to be any nun-making or beguine-making" of children, quoted Margaret from the statutes. There was of course the time involved, for two or three religious had to neglect the Divine Office in order to attend the children. There was the threat of violating cloister, because much of the costuming of these children occurred before an open door in the guest house. Finally, the crowds of children were growing, since even strangers now brought their children to frolic for the day, strangers "from whom we receive nothing, and from whom we can expect nothing but idle hopes; just as in everything else we do this in the hope of getting something back." Yet when all was said and done, the convent's godly reward from most consisted of nothing but "dirty linens, and running after this, that, and the other."

A similar family-pleasing custom was allowing infants inside the cloister. Perhaps there were cultural or emotional reasons for nuns to dote over infants, or perhaps, as they did not present the same threat as adults, children were let in for a change of face and pace. It could even have been grounded in the Franciscan tradition of meditating upon the childhood of Christ, thus giving the Grey Sisters a special affinity for children. Most likely, however, it was tied, like nun making, to the desire for alms—to primp the children of potential and current benefactors. Margaret contended the practice had long ago been condemned. "Once again it's necessary expressly to prohibit Mater from allowing children to come inside or be carried inside, however many there are, old or young, daughter or servant; it was once again done, very recently, despite the last decree against it."

Then there was Adriana's willingness to store the goods of outsiders, including wine. This was not only inconvenient but raised legal problems as well, because monasteries were exempt from taxation and were not to extend that privilege to others. "In the first place, it brings no thanks from the debtor who seeks to hide his things here while he pretends to be bankrupt; it also brings no thanks from those who leave their things and then come back some time later and say, 'there was more than this,' or, 'this wasn't spoiled when I left it here,' and so on. We can't keep the rust off iron goods, we aren't responsible to clean them! And by doing the dirty work of others we place our convent in peril." Why should the nuns "make ourselves night and day the slaves of outside people, without need or profit to soul or body, or without any reward or thanks but only ingratitude, as I've seen too often?"

Finally, there was Adriana's still more burdensome custom of lending the convent's goods. "Mater has even lent grain from the attic to strangers, once a whole *mudde*" (three U.S. bushels), which the convent was repaid only three years later, and then "with much ingratitude and shock that it had to be repaid, and then when they pay us back we feed them." Adriana had loaned another half *mudde* four years before, an amount still not paid back: "It was to a stranger who's never done a thing for us. And afterward you can well imagine that we had to buy more grain, at the highest possible price." Mater also loaned movable goods to the extent that the house had become a kind of rent-all. "Beds, sheets, woolen blankets, pillows, tablecloths, napkins, tins, dishes, pots, pans, even by the dozen, chairs, benches, tables, even the beds and pillows of the infirmary! In short, all that we have is soiled or damaged or lost by the people who borrow it, and we don't even know sometimes who's borrowed. If some people are having a big dinner, or are in childbed, or it's kermis, then they all come to borrow these things, kitchen utensils and otherwise." But the borrowers often brought the goods back "looking like no utensils I've ever seen. We're forced to be the maids of strangers." Again, if the convent could expect any "kindnesses from these people, it would he different." But such was not the case. Instead, the convent only gave the impression it needed no kindnesses at all. "We are poor, and we want to be called poor, but by lending so we don't act poor. The richest abbeys would never be able to do this."

In short, concluded Margaret, "Mater is rich enough to give outside, but inside she gives nothing at all, for she doesn't have the will to. If she'd never in her life gotten her finger into the temporal pie, then we'd have our due." The problem was, "no one else may do anything, for she holds every office, though not well; she is Mater, Vicaress, Bursaress, Cellaress, Novice-Mistress, in short everything." To Adriana's argument that "who wishes benevolence or favors from people must do favors themselves," Margaret responded, "How many mugs of beer has she given in vain?"

Overflowing with memorable detail, Margaret's gloomy assessment illustrated the inevitably busy role of the convent in larger society, and vice versa. As the historian Roger Devos concluded about nuns in France, "In a sense a monastery can be considered a 'practical utopia,' an 'other' society, dominated by values at odds with the society around it." But "this 'anti-world' was situated squarely in the world. The endeavor to live separately and distinctly was very quickly limited."

12
Worldly Ways

Living "separately and distinctly" was a challenge not only temporally for convents, but spiritually. Here was the last and longest of Margaret's three blasts against the current regime in Bethlehem: the waning of monastic discipline and the flowering of worldly ways.

A Choirful of Posies

One manifestation of the world in Bethlehem was the tendency to waste. Although Margaret found it wrongheaded to invest in dubious outsiders, so as to provoke alms, she at least saw a purpose behind it. But when nuns wantonly threw away time and goods on activities that had no useful purpose at all, she was offended to the depths.

What good could possibly come, wondered Margaret, from gifts lavished upon other nuns and convents? Why did Mater Adriana allow sisters to waste money on fashions, some wearing white shoes, others black, according to taste? What example did it set for Adriana while in the workroom to use a silver thimble or sit in a Spanish chair, when previous Maters had been content with ordinary thimbles and chairs? And why were nuns allowed to waste so much on potions, pills, and plasters, "as they dream it up"? But what especially got Margaret's attention was the overdecoration of the nuns' choir, inside the church.

To what extent the choir was visible to the public would have depended on the size and design of the screen that usually divided nave from choir in convent churches. The choir was certainly at least partially visible, especially when the communion window within the screen was opened during Mass. Because the choir's sights and sounds were the two chief attractions for visitors attending Mass, decoration was there in part to please patrons, and thus could be regarded as an aspect of almsgetting. But to Margaret it was even more about waste, plain and simple.

The extravagance ate away at her. She expressed a desire, for instance, to halt the "ugly practice" that called for nuns to make regular donations toward the choir's adornment. Whenever a nun celebrated a birthday or feast day, Anna Vignarola, the Sacristan of the choir, handed a plate to Adriana, who then walked around the choir gathering money from the nuns. "It's a sight to behold," said Margaret, "and it's all wasted money, lost money," spent especially on Anna's handcrafted artificial flowers. "I say it's a sin that so much rubbish, which is no more necessary than it is for me to jump into the water, finds its way to the choir. Further, she damages as many things as is possible for someone in a convent."

Most of Anna's flowers were used to beautify the "little altars," or shrines, positioned all around the choir and dedicated to a particular saint. To Margaret, it was more "puppetry" than worship. Not, she was careful to say, that she was annoyed, as a Protestant might be, by a well-adorned image of a saint, "for that pleases me in the extreme." But the overabundance offended and embarrassed her: once again, it was important that outsiders see the convent as poor because most of its members were poor. What were people to think of "all those small shrines, those little altars, covered with silken flowers, extravagantly made so as to be lifelike?" First it was "plain flowers," after that "fancier colored flowers," made of fine

A sixteenth-century *hortus conclusus*. This one highlights Saints Ursula, Elizabeth, and Catherine.

OLV Ziekenhuis, Mechelen

linen, and then recently it was silk, in the shape of gillyflowers, roses, and other flowers. "By the time they're finished they'll cover the whole wall" of the church, feared Margaret. "The great shrine with Our Lady at the head of the Choir is covered from top to bottom with flowers, and on each occasion there's something new."

These little altars or shrines, so utterly condemned by Margaret, were among the most stylish items in Catholic devotion of the time. Developed in the fifteenth century, and perfected by nuns and beguines who often worked in tandem with lay painters and wood-carvers, such shrines came to the Low Countries by way of Brugge around 1500 and spread from there. Some were in the form of a triptych, as most altarpieces, but much smaller, perhaps thirty-nine inches high by fifty inches wide. The wings, usually painted by professionals, portrayed saints or benefactors of the house and order. But the central portion was the crucial and distinguishing part, for it was usually fashioned by the nuns themselves, and often stood alone. It consisted of a fairly shallow case full of meticulously carved figures—saints, angels, biblical characters, and so on—which were then adorned with a wagonful of carefully crafted artificial flowers, usually from silk or parchment or even metal. Situated behind a small fence that might stand amid imitation grass, here was the *hortus conclusus*, or enclosed garden, which was not only the usual symbol of Mary's virginity but also the place where the inspiring characters portrayed—and by implication the chaste viewer as well—could best work out salvation.

Besides the general artistic significance of the little altars, they likely reflected as well a distinctively female way of expressing religious feeling or artistic prowess in this time—for cloistered women inevitably restricted worship to their home convent, while the better-traveled male religious might worship in a multitude of places during his life and possess less motive or opportunity for the careful embellishment of his house. Indeed, a comparison of decoration in male and female convents, or for that matter between female convents and parish churches, may lead to the detection of genuinely different attitudes between the genders about form and manner of worship—just as Professors Rudolph Bell and Caroline Walker Bynum have detected differences between medieval men and women in attitudes toward food and the Eucharist. But despite critical acclaim over the generations for these absorbing objects, despite undeniable beauty, despite the recommendation of St. Teresa that the production of religious art was an ideal means to combat monastic melancholy, it was all lost on Margaret.

She went on for long about the subject more than once in her letter. Every Saturday, claimed Margaret, Anna Vignarola "spends the entire day in the choir. She begins in the morning with picking flowers in the garden; she then spends the whole day plucking and making bouquets. There's another who helps her with the bouquets, and then there's yet another who spends the whole time from noon until evening sweeping the choir and polishing the candelabra. That's three people for one poor, smoky choir. Sister Anna Vignarola goes neither to Vespers nor Compline nor to refectory, and this is every Saturday. In the evening until long after eight o'clock she's running from one side to the other like an unbound calf, calling out and chattering as if it were the middle of the day, and the same thing in the morning when she first arrives in the garden, oblivious to the time."

Margaret blamed Maria Joos for initiating the practice, but Anna had made it worse quite on her own. Instead of an occasional bouquet in the choir, there were now "every day, winter and summer," twelve pair of bouquets. Such required extensive planning and maintenance. "Every high day, whether Easter, Pentecost, or any other, she works three days straight in advance, one day to clean thoroughly, another to redo things, and the third to decorate, and don't forget all the hands that help her, not to mention all the special little shrines that each decorates for herself." All the images of Our Lady and other saints "have so many different robes that you'd think the sisters were clothing real people." Such expense and effort "on shrines that are so tiny—what a waste of money." Obviously Margaret liked her images to be not only few but big and visible: she had no appreciation for the patience and dexterity required in miniaturism.

Even as Margaret wrote, the decoration changed. For weeks, early in the morning and late at night, with the infirmary as their secret working place, Mater and Anna busied themselves sewing "a skirt for Our Lady, from excellent satin and very lavishly embroidered." There was money enough for such things, and "to buy velvet in Brussels for still more little altars, and there must be gold fringes, and Our Lady must have yet another robe of gold linen, even though she already has two satin robes, two or three of crimson, and a few others of still other material. But even that's not enough to satisfy them, because they don't have one of red velvet, and they lament it. There are still other images of Our Lady in the choir, and I couldn't begin to describe all their clothes." And yet, reminded Margaret, the convent had not yet even finished constructing one of the cloister walls, a far more essential element of monastic life in her view.

NOT-SO-DIVINE OFFICE AND OTHER DEVOTIONS

Another sign of worldliness in Bethlehem was the lack of reverence in choir, despite the abundance of pious objects all around.

Margaret found it difficult to be reverent herself in the presence of so much smoke from candles, which the sisters insisted on piling up around their beloved shrines and images. Candles were in part for light, in part a symbol of Christ the Light of the World, and also a symbol of personal devotion to a particular saint. But to Margaret the burning was excessive. "Unless it's halted, they'll soon burn a candle before each image." In times past only one or two candles were burned at a shrine, but now they were "around and in front of every shrine." During meals in the refectory "no more than two skinny candles" burned, so that nuns could barely see their food. But in choir there was always money for extra candles and frills, and so it overflowed, to her irritation. "The choir is very small and one can hardly bear the stink from all the candles. One must kneel right beneath many of these candles and their smoke is then overwhelming." Margaret would let the Archbishop "judge how healthy that can be, in such a small place." Moreover, "the humidity that rises from one's head is like steamed cooking." Then there was the grease. During early morning services in winter, when the choir was darker than usual, Margaret often knelt accidentally in the residue left by candles. "It seems a small matter, but it's most inconvenient," she decided. Several others were displeased as well by the candles, claimed Margaret, but no one dared speak up, because of Adriana. And so the excessive burning continued, almost daily, and even more on feast days. If someone was hoping for good weather, then candles were burned for a changing wind. If it was the feast day of a sister's patron saint, then the candles burned all day and night.

Add to the inconveniences of overdecoration the noise it brought into choir, continued Margaret. During services, assigned sisters sometimes made "four or five" noisy trips to trim the candles and keep them burning. More generally, there was "never any stillness in the choir, but always chattering and railing; long discourses are spoken and much visiting occurs there," engaged in by Mater Adriana as well as others. Upon entering and exiting "almost all the religious tramp and stamp across the choir as if they were shodden horses, so impious is it; it's a scandal that it's all heard in the church too," where laypeople sat to hear the services.

The nuns also showed irreverence by performing services sloppily, without careful attention to proper movements, or pausing between verses, a problem noted in many visitations of the time. This was "not observed in the least." Sister Anna Marcelis took to stamping "like a wharf-horse" if the pace of singing wasn't fast enough for her. Maria Joos and Anna Vignarola chattered away "as if that's why they're there." As in other convents, in Bethlehem "many words and phrases fall away" because nuns rushed through.

"In singing it's like a contest. Mater adds to her fame by boasting that her people can be done so quickly" with services. Margaret wished "that they would be so hasty in speaking at the grille or in their chattering and carrying-on at table." Surely Margaret wished as well that Bethlehem would require, as did the convent of Thabor, that those who couldn't sing well would make a place in the choir for those who could, or that nuns who disturbed the simplicity of the service should be forced to read in silence.

Margaret's concern reflected the central place in monasteries of prayer and singing to God. This was especially true in regard to the seven daily "hours" of the Divine Office (which in fact took closer to a total of three or four hours to perform). Also important were regular confession and communion, attendance at daily Mass and public sermons, and meditation, prayer, and self-discipline. All these activities began, ended, and filled the nun's day, and helped to distinguish her from lay women who could not afford the luxury of so much time for devotion, or even from active orders, in which sisters were sometimes too busy or tired from their worldly labors to perform all their prayers. But contemplative nuns were to order their lives around devotion, to represent the "best part" of the Holy Church—or, according to the Franciscan author De Soto, the Marys over the Marthas. Thoughts of the other, better world were to occupy their minds and hearts the whole day through, and especially during the Office.

The women of Bethlehem, like many nuns, were to arise promptly at 4 A.M. (except on feast days, when they rose at 3) and proceed to their humble church for Matins and Lauds together. Then from morning until eve they were recalled six times more by a signal, sounded by the youngest sisters, for Prime, Terce, Sext, Nones, Vespers, and Compline, each different from the others in the arrangement and selection of prayers, readings, and hymns (usually from the Psalms), and also different according to the time of the liturgical year. Entering the choir, they sprinkled themselves with holy water and fell on their knees to honor the Eucharist, then

A Hospital Sister at prayer, sixteenth century

moved to their seats, usually according to seniority, in the rows of stalls that faced each other across an aisle. During the Office, the sisters either read aloud or sang, according to the day and the ability of the convent (the Black Sisters of Leuven, for instance, didn't even read aloud, but each sister read quietly to herself). In cloistered houses, group singing or reading was ideally from the "Great Office," in other words the Latin, full version rather than the vernacular, abbreviated "Small Office" used by most laypeople and less-lettered female monasteries. The women of Bethlehem, though not all literate by 1628, seem to have been among the many nuns who recited or sang the Great Office but who probably did not understand it fully—many of Bethlehem's prescribed prayers, for instance, use the familiar Latin titles and phrases. Even if un-Latined, however, one could make that language's "completely religious sounds," which only enhanced the sense of mystery and power.

The sisters also attended Mass at least once per day, seated again in the choir. Almost every day meant a prayer for a different benefactor or saint or deceased sister, or a feast that required more elaborate services than usual, or general prayers for the success of Catholic or national armies or the conversion of sinners and heretics. The nuns of Bethlehem could not perform the Mass, but they could help sing or simply listen to it, as some benefactors requested. They didn't have the twenty-seven high Masses or twenty-six hundred low Masses per year of a St. Germain des Prés in Paris, but the convent church was home to hundreds of Masses per year, in most of which the nuns probably participated. Their biggest days of celebration, like other houses of Grey Sisters, were the Four High Seasons, Our Lady's Ascension, the Circumcision of Christ (New Year's), Three Kings, the Ascension of Our Lord, Holy Trinity Day, St. Francis's, St. Elizabeth's, and the feast of the dedication of their church (the Sunday after St. Francis's day, October 4). And there was of course St. Renildis's day, for the special patroness of the convent of Bethlehem, on July 16.

Margaret did not elaborate on other devotions in Bethlehem,

providing merely clues: the "discipline" of Barbara Beli or the use of hair shirts by certain nuns reflect common practices of the day, but to what extent were they used in Bethlehem? Did the sisters who participated in these devotions chastise themselves regularly, to the point of real pain? Pinelli, a devotional author for religious, reminded them that "if you don't mortify your flesh, it will be unchecked and become wild." On special occasions, did the sisters endure self-castigation with a "discipline" "until it bled," as prescribed for a penitent sister in the diocese of Brugge? Yet they should not "cut off the neck," wrote the Franciscan De Soto, but show moderation. In fact admonitions to moderation were perhaps even stronger than admonitions to extremes, for even moderate acts of devotion and self-denial were challenging enough. Were the sisters, for instance, silent from Compline until 7 A.M., and on Sundays and holy days until noon? When sitting around the fire, did they really contemplate the faithful souls of the next world and think of the Psalms De Profundis or Pater Noster? Did they really have much time for private prayer in the three half-hour periods allotted per day? When retiring at night did they lie in the manner they imagined they would look in the grave, and if they awoke from sleep because of "the enemy" did they run to a crucifix and pray to the sweet, mortified, wounded Lord, as recommended by the regionally famous reformer of the Grey Sisters, Peter Marchant? Could it be said of the sisters of Bethlehem, as it was of St. Francis, that his prayer was like thunder and his life like a bolt of lightning? Did they lard their souls with two kinds of spiritual fat, as suggested by the devotional author Guevera? When they worked, did they imagine that they helped the Lord to carry his cross, or when they ate that they were taking mouthfuls from the wounds of Jesus and drinking out of his heart, or when they suffered that they hung with their bridegroom on the cross, and when they slept that their pillow was the thorny crown of Jesus? When they heard the sermons of their Franciscan confessors did they imagine that they were with Mary Magdalene at the feet of Jesus? Did they hear preachers as colorful as the medieval master Jan Brugman, whose favorite allegory was heaven as a banquet with an abundance of Rhine wine? Did any of them pray like St. Angelina de Fouligny, whose tears burned her face and could only be put out with cold water, or like St. Mechline whose knees stuck in the ground for so long that they filled with worms? Did they confess humbly, never putting their head above the level of their confessor's, and take communion with the mouth reasonably wide open so that the priest wouldn't touch their teeth, but not too wide lest they be suspected of witchery? Did they then quickly swallow lest the host be disturbed by coughing, sneezing, wheezing, or otherwise? Did they think about the miracle of transubstantiation, but not too deeply, lest they become clouded, and merely ponder that if Christ could feed five thousand with a few fishes and loaves and provide the Old Testament widow and her son with unending oil and meal, he could certainly be present in hundreds and thousands of different wafers at once? If Margaret had little to say about such things, was it because they were assumed, or because they existed not at all in the convent?

PLAY

Margaret revealed much more about another worldly practice in Bethlehem: the overcelebration of recreation days.

Recreation in convents mirrored the two equal but opposite ways of observing feast days throughout Catholic Europe: fasting and merrymaking. Depending on the occasion, one mood or the other prevailed, but merrymaking was what concerned Margaret, especially the ever favorite theme of the world upside down. In Mechelen, for instance, on the popular Feast of Fools, soon after Christmas, people of low rank chose a humble person to serve as the day's "bishop": he was called Mule-pope, Mule-bishop, Fool-bishop, and even coarser names. This leader clothed himself in an outrageous way, often wearing mule ears. Then a mock Divine

Office was performed in the church, sung off key and including readings with comic (rather than pious) interludes and the splashing (rather than sprinkling) of unholy water on the audience. Depending on one's interpretation, this was all done to emphasize the proper order of things—through such blatant contrast with the ideal—or to allow venting of pent-up feelings, or a combination of both.

Though it was not unusual for convents to join the fun of such days—usually behind their own walls with private celebrations—Margaret believed her sisters should have been more subdued. True, they were less sophisticated than nuns in Italy who composed complex plays based on the writings of Petrarch or the Song of Songs, occasionally dressed as soldiers in tights and short pants, and often performed before outsiders, but the women of Bethlehem were at least as enthusiastic as their Italian cosisters. And in Margaret's judgment it simply was not right.

Adriana played more "wildly" than anyone else in the convent on play days. She also compelled "one and all to play as well, without ceasing, and without permission to quit the game until the very end. And if anyone happens to leave, she runs to get them or commands them to return, and gives a special order that everyone must play, and says they'll earn more merit through play than by going to do their devotions to God during that time." On such days there was no quiet, except perhaps during Mass, Margaret charged. But as soon as the Mass was over, "then it's back to yelling, light-mindedness, and ranting, which one can see or hear the whole day through, and which the worldly folk all stand around to hear."

Here was a major offense to Margaret: although the celebrations occurred behind walls, as they should have, the nuns through their racket and behavior joined the wider celebrations of the community—both figuratively and literally. More than once had Margaret found herself at the grille, speaking with "a distinguished man" (probably Joost Bouckaert), when the noise caused her heart to "sink with shame." It was Adriana who egged them on. "She never urges them to play in a proper conventual manner, but she who yells most Mater considers to be most virtuous. And she says that no one can dare call herself devout who doesn't play, and where pleasure in playing dies there dies devotion and love. That's a regrettable thing. Then where does that leave the Capuchins and other convents who never play? Playing itself doesn't bother me, but that hateful yelling and ranting!" Not one item in the convent's statutes was as carefully observed and so strictly enforced as this one, said Margaret. In fact, Adriana handed out penances more readily to those who failed to play up to her standards than for truly serious breaches of monastic protocol.

Some of those breaches occurred through play itself, Margaret demonstrated. On many recreation days, the nuns sat at the refectory table late into the night, "howling and banging the table like drunkards sitting on a beer-bench. That makes so much noise, with all the dishes, pots, and utensils on the table that one isn't sure where one is. Those who don't like to see or hear all this are then spoilsports, hardheads."

The biggest day of all in Bethlehem, as in the wider world, was Epiphany, or Three Kings Day (January 6). On this day the nuns of the convent turned the world upside down with zest. Following the pattern of lay festivities, nuns chose an upside-down queen for the day, probably from among the younger sisters, and called her "My Lady." But the most desirable role was that of the fool, a practice that offended Margaret deeply. The nuns were too eager for this role, she thought, drawing lots more than a month before, during Advent, for the chance to play the fool. On the glorious day the lucky one, called *henneken*, or "mother hen," was crowned and dressed. So troubling was her costume that Margaret described it in detail. It consisted of a special dress, embroidered in yellow and red and other colors uncharacteristic of nuns, a long white apron, a veil, a *paternoster* and other flourishes around her neck, a nightshirt with big needles stuck into it, a cap on her head, all kinds of sticks with bells on them, a doll in her arms, a ham on her side (a symbol of the excess food typical of such celebrations), and a large fool's fiddle—all in contrast to the dignity prescribed for nuns. "When it's time to eat," continued Margaret, each nun comes to lead the fool to the refectory, "singing and jumping along the way, the fool playing on her fiddle." Everyone then played upside-down music, hitting keys on kettles, lids, and anything else "they could lay their hands on." People outside the convent heard the racket and ran right to their attics, or climbed trees in their gardens to see. If there was good weather, then the nuns ran into the convent's garden, which, to Margaret's chagrin, was visible from a variety of vantage points around the neighborhood.

Besides the outrage of it all, one of the unfortunate consequences of exuberance was that under the guise of celebration nuns felt free to poke fun at rivals. As the widely published Franciscan author Guevera wrote, when the stomach was content, which it easily was on feast days, the mouth began to work in earnest. Many songs sung "in fun" were so pointed and piercing and "poison" that love was greatly damaged. "Through laughter, people are wounded to the heart," said Guevera.

Margaret explained that in Bethlehem "whoever is dressed as the fool supposes that she is free to do whatever she pleases, laughing at and ridiculing one and all, lay or religious, and spitting out anything that's been in her head." Some nuns were eager to play the fool precisely for this freedom to "say anything she's ever dreamed up before. Some know how to make jokes out of little thorns, with which they greatly puncture many hearts. Though it's supposed to be said in jest and laughter, they're too prepared with their lines." Adriana was one of the best at this, for she was an expert mimic: "you'd have to see and hear" how she mimicked some, in word and manner." Those "peasant-like, droll farces of hers" were scandalous, decided Margaret.

Still more perilous to Margaret than mere imitation of the world was the emotional bond that nuns might form with it. Any worldly contact upset discipline, but some forms of contact presented eternal dangers to the soul.

The classic and most basic symbol of separation from the world was cloister, especially for female religious. One early motivation to raise up walls around these women was physical protection from a brutal world. But it became ever more clear over the centuries that the walls were also there to protect society's notions of what a religious woman should be. A devout, roaming woman was long an oxymoron in European minds. Secular authorities in fifteenth-century Florence were not alone in expressing anxiety about ill-observed cloister among nuns, nor in their fear that want of cloister put nuns in peril of losing their virginity. Indeed, lack of strict *clausura* in a nunnery was often regarded around Catholic Europe as a sure sign of unchastity among the loosely bridled occupants. Then there was the related notion that a woman by nature needed protection against herself, an idea articulated by Idung of Prüfening, a twelfth-century Cistercian monk: since even vowed women were more susceptible to worldly delights than were men, he argued, it was in the eternal interest of female religious to remain shut up. He therefore advocated cloister to curb the "natural fickleness" of women and "also because of outside temptations which womanly weakness is not strong enough to resist." Idung did not invent this idea, nor did it die with him: by Margaret's time it was, in various degrees and forms, still alive and well.

More positive reasons for cloister were also rooted in ideas about purity. The Franciscan Ferraria agreed with Augustine that the conquest of all fleshly desires, implicit in the second monastic vow, was the severest battle any Christian, male or female, must fight. Cloister, he promised, was one of the best weapons with which to wage that fight. The Council of Trent also stressed the idea of cloister as an aid to maidenly chastity.

Despite its importance, cloister was long a problematic issue in convents, due to disagreements in interpretation, legal disputes, and the limits of enforcement. In plenty of convents nuns wished to observe cloister less than completely, or differently from how bishops preferred, such as at a convent in Zichem, near Scherpenheuvel, where in 1618 a Mater enjoyed the occasional late-night glass of wine with visiting priests, or at Bethanie in Brussels, where in 1592 two monks from nearby monasteries entered the convent's workroom, formally off limits to outsiders. Margaret herself showed how Bethlehem, though officially cloistered, nevertheless lacked a complete wall and often acted as if it were part of the world anyway. In many convents there were arguments and even lawsuits over attempts to impose cloister where it had long gone unobserved, such as at Groot Bijgaarden near Brussels, or at well-heeled German Cistercian nunneries where vowed sisters went in and out of cloister, took companions along with them on trips, and often lodged with laypeople. Overworked members of the ecclesiastical hierarchy could easily develop a sense of futility in dealing with one stubborn community after the next.

Yet it would be wrong to view the history of *clausura* as merely one of troubles, resistance, and sporadic enforcement. The tradition of laxity or local custom could be strong, but so was the power of the universal, heroic ideal: *clausura* was attractive to some precisely because it was difficult, a step above the natural human yearning for society. It was true that some convents after the Council of Trent had cloister forced upon them, but it was also true that some houses took the initiative and demanded *clausura* themselves. The fledgling Theatine nuns of Pescia were not the only ones to keep their internal troubles secret lest superiors decide not to award them cloister, the ultimate test of legitimacy for convents. Right in Mechelen the nuns of Blijdenberg pleaded with Archbishop Hovius in 1616 for the "privilege of cloister." Indeed, Netherlandish nuns possessed a special affinity for cloister, argued professors at local universities. With seventeenth-century medical logic, they maintained that while warm-blooded nuns in Spain or Italy required walls forty feet high to keep them inside, nuns in the Spanish Netherlands, where temperatures and bodily desires were cooler, required no such drastic measures—strict cloister was unnecessary, and walls of "only" fifteen feet would do. "Cloister is better protected here by a single grille," they explained, "with three, four, or five inch square grating, than over there with double grilles of two inch square grating surmounted by protruding spikes a foot long."

Hence, although the history of cloister was not a calm one, its prestige endured. Many debates in convents during Margaret's time, including in Margaret's own, were not about the formal acceptance of cloister, or even over whether cloister should continue to be the ideal. Rather, debate often was waged over the spirit of cloister, which usually meant the extent of contact with outsiders at the convent's points of potential vulnerability: doors, gates, and grilles. No sketch of Bethlehem has survived, but it apparently possessed four grilles, that famous invention of the twelfth century. Two were in the guest house, presumably so that more than one group of visitors at a time could be accommodated, and two were in the church: one between the altar and the choir, through which nuns could take communion, and one in the wall between hospital and infirmary, so that sick nuns could watch Mass. The debate in Bethlehem was not over whether nuns would accept cloister, but under what circumstances and for how long and on what subjects and with what feeling should conversations occur at the grille? The 1627 decrees reforming various grilles in Bethlehem had actually called for reducing the size of the holes in the grilles of the guest rooms, while doubling the amount of iron—quite in contrast to what defenders of Netherlandish nuns had maintained was necessary for women of cooler, northerly passions. And though the grilles in the guest rooms were used most heavily, those in the church presented special problems, since built into the bars of each grille were fairly large windows that could be opened, in theory for liturgical purposes only. Well aware of the old and new ideals, and worried about the abuses that she perceived, Margaret revealed to the Archbishop the multitude of ways in which she thought it possible for a nun to sin against grilles, doors, and the spirit of chastity.

THE PRICK OF THE FLESH

As in much else Adriana was, in Margaret's view, most to blame. "She comes alive when she can be around laypeople," Margaret wrote. "It would be the joy of her life to always have workmen, meals, and banquets; oh blessed statutes, what rest do we have now?" The biggest star in Adriana's galaxy of male friends was of course Henri Joos. But Margaret went beyond her complaints about the heaping of food and drink for the man: he was a threat not only to the convent's pantry but its purity. "That glow, and the unspeakable happiness shown by Mater at his arrival, and that frequent speaking alone doesn't edify some of the sisters. It can certainly happen without any evil," conceded Margaret, but she still thought it would be best "if she avoided this."

Adriana simply trusted him too much, thought Margaret. On the Monday before the most recent Pentecost, for instance, after Henri Joos had visited at the convent for four hours with Adriana and his sister, Maria, "Mater had four lay sisters accompany him so that they could all carouse on his way to Mechelen." Among the lay sisters, explained Margaret, was one who had previously been "hit" by Henri Joos—an idiom the Archbishop's Vicar-General would render as "suspicion of incontinence," a common way of referring to sexual misconduct. Whether this sin occurred when Henri Joos was confessor or afterward went unstated, but the situation caused Margaret "to wonder greatly at Mater's lack of judgment; that she allows such is to be lamented, for the same sister is most uncomfortable in his presence but doesn't dare contradict Mater; and as often as he comes to Leuven, and returns in the evening to his lodgings, Mater always sends that same sister with him." The sister in question even once approached Margaret about the matter, perhaps knowing the rumors of Margaret's own history with the man, but if the Archbishop were to raise it with Adriana, there would be such commotion in the convent that Margaret did not know what would be worse: calling a halt to the practice, or allowing it to continue. "And the sister would resent me greatly for saying anything, which is natural, for she doesn't know the whole story."

This "hit" sister was very possibly Joanna Schoensetters, the sole lay sister to dislike Mater Adriana, and the sole lay sister with whom Margaret was halfway friendly. But whoever it was, the whole subject put Margaret in a more indignant mood toward Henri Joos than she had showed earlier in her letter: "I wish he never would come to Leuven again as long as he lives, but it's to be feared that it will happen often, at least two or three times a year, and then he always comes to our church and reads the Mass and preaches; God knows how pleasant that is for me and still others." Yet others in the convent "get such unspeakable joy from this that they think themselves ready to be taken up to heaven," and so his visits were likely to continue.

When Henri Joos was absent, Mater's attentions turned to workmen, said Margaret. It wasn't that Adriana expected liberal alms from these workers, nor was she there to encourage them to do the best work possible. Rather, she simply seemed to enjoy their company. As with her other friends, Mater saw personally to the generous provision of food and drink for the men. "The joiner, carpenter, digger, woodcutter, five masons at once, the plaster-carriers," not only put away piles of food but "seem to have barrels for hands. What they call drinking! I think that when a man drinks 7 mugs in a day it's too much." But this was about more than Adriana's typical overgiving: in Margaret's eyes Adriana was overly attached to the men. And her example of fraternity emboldened other nuns, who went "to stand by the workmen and chat with them, and through all the chatter they don't work for hours. And in the evening at dusk the religious stay to prattle with the digger all alone, and the next day with someone else."

Just as serious to Margaret as the alarming popularity of Henri Joos or the excessive attention to workmen was the private conversations held between Anna Vignarola and the convent's chaplains. These occurred most often at the two grilles in the church, to be opened only for communion but which some sisters tried to open at other times as well. Disturbing about the windows in the church was that they were large enough for a religious so inclined to climb through. "It's a more dangerous matter than some would suppose," said Margaret, and threatened the salvation not just of "one or two." At the noble Benedictine convent of Vorst near Brussels, for instance, a Sister Barbara supposedly received gifts and spoke often with a male admirer through the open communion window in the choir grille, which she unlocked thanks to another sister who snuck her the key.

Both the choir grille and the infirmary grille were favorite places of Anna, contended Margaret. As choir Sacristan, Anna obviously had to prepare for services, but Margaret argued that Anna abused her position by lingering around the sacristy to chat with the attending priest. Though Anna's responsibilities required her to have some contact with priests—passing along information on the day's services and so forth—Margaret believed that Anna turned this contact into near intimacy. "Anna Vignarola, the youngest nun," descended every day from the choir to go "speak with the gentlemen" at the choir grille. "She's also spoken for a long time at the open door of the sacristy."

Anna liked not merely outsiders, but men in particular, alleged Margaret. She "speaks with the chaplain as often as she pleases" from inside the window of the infirmary grille, where Lesken Joos was of course in charge. There stood Anna, "with the window open, leaning on it with her elbows and sticking her head into the church." On Sundays and Holy Days, Anna often neglected singing the Office with the community, "even on the Holy day of Easter." Anna also entertained a chaplain at other grilles as well, in the guest room or at the choir grille, "talking an hour or two at a time, and even singing." On occasion she even hailed a chaplain to look through grilles and doors into the cloister on recreation days. Margaret had "nothing but praise for this gentleman's honor and virtue, for how he edifies us in all things," and for being "as accommodating as anyone we've ever had or could have. But I say it's perilous. She is much too attached to him and has many worldly ways about her, and she can gossip marvelously well. Thus it's better to put a stop to it now. We've seen higher mountains fall, which were better grounded and more wise than she."

Margaret again blamed Mater for Anna's freedom. "Mater trusts her too much, which amazes me, since she had a bad experience this way herself." Here was Margaret's second hint about Adriana's "bad experience" in the past. Was Margaret suggesting that Adriana herself had been compromised by a chaplain or confessor? Another sister would make the same hint during this visitation, and still others in the future, so that Margaret was not alone. "If it's true" that the rumored event happened, said Margaret, then Adriana had even more cause to be sure "that it doesn't happen" to Anna. If Adriana "was deceived, as she claims," then why did she not "show more concern" that Anna be not deceived? "Mater would say, 'who is evil thinks evil.' Nevertheless, it's plain to see that Vignarola runs to the gentleman too often without need. I've never seen such running in my life," decided Margaret. "She's crazy about that chaplain. If anyone shows any displeasure with him or suggests she speaks with him too much, I don't know who'd be able to make peace after that. She'd grumble and pout for a week, and Mater would say as usual 'Vignarola is done with all that.' "

The problem of affection for outsiders went beyond Mater and Anna. Most occurred with less peril to chastity, but were troublesome nonetheless. The sister of Anna Coninxloo had recently been in Leuven and called at the convent eleven days in a row. The mother of Anna Vignarola visited long at least annually, and Sister Anna Marcelis hosted "every one of her relatives." But the nun most guilty of grille sitting was Adriana's other staunch supporter, the Portress Maria Joos.

To Margaret, Maria was hardly the model Portress, a sentry who, according to the ideal, would watch the convent's doors and grilles "as if she were guarding the tomb of Christ." Rather, Maria embodied the Flemish proverb about hiring a poacher to guard the forest. For instance, though visitors were not allowed to spend the night in the guest room, Maria insisted they were allowed to sleep there during the day. "Thanks to this reasoning she let one of the religious bring in some strangers, soldiers no less, who were completely drunk, to lie on the beds." Outsiders saw all this and might have charitably concluded that the soldier had a sister in the convent. But when those outsiders saw three or four other soldiers going in and then coming out drunk, "lying in the barley-plain," they would certainly pass on news of the unedifying scene to others, feared Margaret. Such "would never be allowed in other convents."

Then there was the behavior of nuns at the grille between the infirmary and church. If the grille in the choir was the larger of the two, and offered more privacy than others, the window in the infirmary was the most popular. Some sisters, advised Margaret, would try to tell the Archbishop that they used this window solely to witness the elevation of the Host during Mass. But beware, she warned, for "that's not really the reason nor is such necessary. They gather there like it's a gossip school, so that it's a scandal in the presence of God." If the sisters were well enough to crowd around the infirmary window, then they were well enough to take up their places in the choir, Margaret reasoned, and quit the infirmary. If the grille remained in its present form, then "the gossiping will never cease, nor the gaping. Not one person comes into the church without the sisters peering through that window and looking in and reporting to their friends who is there, and what they're wearing, and what they're doing; even during the Benediction they chatter with each other, 'She is there, she's doing this, has that,' and laugh and make noise. It's like an egg market." Often eight or nine nuns gathered round, "making such noise that I'm ashamed, for the chaplain can hear it all from the altar."

It wasn't enough for these sisters to look through the bars of the grille, but they insisted on opening the whole window and spilling out arms, elbows, and chins. If they didn't feel like hearing Mass from choir, or if they simply wanted a better view, then they stayed in the infirmary and watched from there. Whenever weddings or other special occasions were celebrated in the church, "there is such running to the window and gaping that they trample one another. If the women In the Leopard come to church then it's talking for an hour; the chaplain also talks with them, without need. I pray you to cast all these stones away." Margaret grieved, "Oh unholy windows! If they had been closed many years ago, what problems could have been avoided!"

EXCURSIONS

The final violation of the spirit of cloister, at least as seen by Margaret, was the damage caused by trips outside.

It was an "ugly custom" in Bethlehem, said Margaret, to allow novices to make one last journey home before they professed. Perhaps this was part of the one-last-fling syndrome, or was intended to please the novice's generous family, or was granted to allow the novice a chance to arrange affairs. Whatever the reason, Margaret believed that these final journeys made for bad discipline in the convent. "Their playing they can do before." Margaret believed that a woman who intended to be a nun should come to the convent once only, for if they left even briefly they might "grow wild" before returning, and "that which they learned outside they might not forget." The trip also increased the temptation for them to return to "the world which they have left and bid adieu."

Margaret thought it should be stopped. In fact, certain novices themselves actually "protested against leaving on this trip," asserted Margaret, but Adriana forced them to go anyway, " 'because it's the custom.' " Once outside, they were deluged with invitations, "eating, drinking, nothing in moderation; moreover, they then have more opportunity to tell what goes on in the convent; this shames me deeply." Some novices were sent with a "play companion," which might have allayed the temptation to reveal details of life within Bethlehem, but if any went alone then there was no holding them back, lamented Margaret. They "tell everything that's happened in the past many years since they've been inside, things of great importance"—such as Henri Joos, Lesken Nijns, and Margaret Smulders, no doubt.

The second problem with trips was the behavior of lay sisters, especially Lesken Joos. By definition lay sisters were allowed such trips, and were to have more contacts than veiled nuns with outsiders. Yet they abused that responsibility, declared Margaret, by being too interested in worldly affairs rather than viewing their excursions as necessary evils. "The lay sisters have their beaks in the street too much, without need. In an hour's time, five or six lay sisters often leave the house, one before, the other after, one here, another there, each as she pleases, though not without permission." Here Margaret reminded the Archbishop that Adriana at least tacitly consented to all this. Then, rather than send out the lay sisters in pairs, as decreed by statute, Adriana sent them out individually. This, explained Margaret, was due to Adriana's claim that if every sister went out in pairs then all the work could not be accomplished. But Margaret was offended by this breach of tradition, which insisted that women go two by two, for the sake of appearances and for a measure of protection.

Besides their irreverent manner while outside, the lay sisters brought back to Bethlehem gossip. Margaret wanted Mater "to forbid the bringing home or recounting of all unprofitable news and tidings. I don't think there's anything that happens in the world, of engagements, weddings, how and what, and also what happens in other convents, in other cities as well as here," that the whole of Bethlehem did not know. "Sister Lesken Joos is the ringleader, the one who brings home news in abundance and chews on it." There were periods of as long as six months when no nun lay ill in the infirmary, which freed Lesken to spend "at least half her time in idle gossip or the whole day in the street learning all the news and wonders and stories." Mater encouraged the women, and "listens to all this like it were one of the Gospels, as do many others; sometimes they sit at the table for two hours to listen to all this." Indeed, trumpeted Margaret, "Often you hear nothing but everyone sitting around and gossiping, telling much, passing judgment and sentence, each according to her taste and affection for the person under consideration."

The lay sisters assembled most of this news while attending women in childbed. Margaret realized that certain orders of religious women regularly engaged in midwifery and sick care; but this was not the task of cloistered religious, and neither should it be the task of lay sisters who served cloistered religious, she argued. "How harmful that is, and how much trouble that brings to cloistered people can't be shouted too loudly." Yet Adriana defended the practice, said Margaret, alleging that "those who object are disturbed in the head and sanctimonious, and she is so amazed at others who disapprove that she doesn't know what name to give them." In Margaret's "humble opinion, I judge this to be very damaging to the convent, in soul and body. It doesn't concern us." In fact, "God knows how harmful such things are for cloistered religious, and what thoughts they conjure up. Many would never have imagined such matters their whole life long save for these discussions. I pray you for the love of God that the brides of Christ ought not be familiar with such things." What had they to do with such affairs? "We've left the world to serve God; these things don't concern our vocation. There's so much to learn about God and matters divine, so that our hearts can be moved to love and gratitude; with other things we ought not be concerned."

A New Regime

After all her criticism, Margaret urged the Archbishop to take two specific steps in Bethlehem.

First, strip Adriana of her direct hold on temporal power by appointing someone else as Bursaress. "Though no one seems capable of being Bursaress, try someone; if she doesn't work, then try another, until finally somebody catches on."

Second, consider removing Adriana as Mater as well. The trouble with this, explained Margaret, was the lack of suitable replacements. "I doubt there is a convent in the whole world where there is less capability," was her pessimistic assessment. Anna Marcelis, whom everyone knew wanted to be Mater, was no more capable now than she had been at the election of 1625. "She is a slacker of all good discipline; she's good only at pampering her body, doesn't come much to choir, sleeps late, never observes silence, is tied to too many worldly folk, too easily tells them all that goes on; the other things I could mention I'll omit, and will say only that once pants fit a certain way, they don't change." Margaret's conclusion about Anna was this: "God preserve us from such a plague."

Maria Joos was no better a choice. Though a "very devout, pious nun," she was also "very quick-tempered and fickle." More troubling was that under Maria nothing would change: just as Adriana never governed without Maria, Anna Vignarola, and Lesken Joos, so Maria would never govern without them. She also allowed too many plasters, and too much reveling and novelty. "But what I dislike most about her," Margaret wrote, "is that she too much enjoys the company of young men, although she doesn't have as much chance as she would like. She should give herself more to God."

And what of Catharina Rijkeboer as Mater? Margaret did not

think even her friend capable. The other nuns would never elect her, to begin with, claimed Margaret, because they didn't like her, because they feared she would allow Margaret to return to the nuns' dormitory, and because they supposed that Catharina "would be much stricter in all things than Mater." Being Mater would not suit Catharina's temperament and fragile health anyway. "Knowing her as I do, there would be no greater burden for her in the world. It would bring her to the grave." Catharina was "sincere" and "good-hearted" and would not have courage enough to perform the unpleasant deeds necessary "to put things here on a good footing. She who will be or remain Mater here must put on her harness, get a grip on courage, and hang on for dear life." Margaret also feared that Catharina had no knack for temporal matters, caring as she did for the things of the next world rather than this. "She wouldn't miss a step even if the front door of the convent were moved to the back."

If these were the best candidates to succeed Adriana as Mater, no wonder Margaret held out little hope for the convent. "The more I observe the behavior and personalities of all these, the less I can say who would be qualified." Thus there was no real solution but for the Archbishop to correct Adriana herself, if he could.

When the time of visitation finally arrived, Margaret took her thick narration and showed most of it to Catharina (holding back sections that discussed Catharina herself) for her approval. Then she prepared to deliver it to the visitor. To her disappointment, it would not be Archbishop Boonen himself, but his wary second-in-command, the Vicar-General Peter van der Wiel. Margaret was certainly self-conscious of her letter's length and the tendency any reader might have to think that she exaggerated. After all, why wouldn't other nuns, who lived inside the cloister, say as much, or point out as many problems as she? It was because, Margaret explained in advance, that some nuns were simply indifferent to problems, and some had less opportunity to write. And what of nuns who did write, but offered a completely different picture from

Margaret's? She could only trust that the visitor would have the gift of discernment. "I say with the Holy Apostle Paul that I lie not," promised Margaret. "May God the Lord grant you knowledge of His pleasure and what will promote His glory and the salvation of us all, to the peace and rest of the whole community, to the observance of all good monastic discipline, and the edification of all people."

13
The Visitors

If thou, Lord, shouldest mark iniquities, O Lord, who shall stand?

—Psalm 130:3

Bethlehem, June 19, 1628. There was very little about conventual life that Peter van der Wiel had not seen or heard before. In fact, as a former teacher of philosophy at the University of Leuven, as canon of the cathedral chapter in Mechelen since 1599, as longtime book censor of the archdiocese, and especially as the Archbishop's Vicar-General for the past decade, he had grown familiar with every sort of institution and person in the church, from the leanest of the flock to the fattest.

Even before arriving at Bethlehem today, for instance, Vicar-General Van der Wiel knew that during his private interviews with nuns there would be the usual variety of stories and motives at work. He knew that though all sisters would swear to him to reveal the truth about conditions inside the convent, some would see things as night and others day. He knew that among the tellers of unflattering tales some acted from a sincere desire to help offenders, while others merely hoped to humiliate rivals. He knew that among those who said all was well in the convent, some truly believed it, while others sought simply to protect the current regime. He knew that among certain sisters there would emerge an amazing correlation of views, either because they had coordinated responses in advance, or because they genuinely saw things the same. He knew that some sisters would withhold incriminating information about the convent, either because they assumed an outsider would not understand, or because they had been intimidated by cosisters or superiors into silence. He knew that each nun would likely be on her best behavior, unlike the German nuns who between 1440 and 1442 had so disliked a visitor that once they locked him in a cellar after he went to inspect it, and another time tried to kill him. And the Vicar-General knew that as in every convent some nuns in Bethlehem were indifferent toward visitation, some had pleaded for it, and still others had wished it into the North Sea.

The implicit purpose of visitation, after all, was not so much to commend as to improve, to highlight problems rather than virtues, and this made some uneasy. Certainly this focus on shortcomings meant that visitors developed a distorted picture of conditions in a convent: just because sisters mentioned a problem did not mean that the house was in turmoil or wholly bad. Yet it was also true that one serious scandal, or one chronic problem, could devastate a convent's morale or reputation. In other words, faults were both routine and irritating. Correction and improvement were part of the very purpose of monastic life and visitation, but some faults meant unwanted trouble. It was the task of diligent visitors to sift carefully through the diverse and bountiful harvest of stories produced during interviews, construct a picture of what they regarded as the truth, and decide what required attention most.

With such a complex task before him, Peter van der Wiel was surely grateful for the experience of hundreds of other visitations, in convents or elsewhere. From nuns alone he had recently heard of obvious violations of decorum, *clausura*, reverence, and even monastic vows. He regularly considered complicated cases neither black nor white, such as whether a confessor who had kissed a nun should be summarily dismissed. He suffered headaches from beguines, such as those at Vilvoorde who despised one of their mistresses because she was a "bumpkin," or who engaged in "dishonorable" kissing with monks and priests, especially on feast days. The beguine Angela Speyskens supposedly wiped her mouth with a napkin and said, " 'I must get it clean to go kiss all those gentlemen,' which deed she fulfilled." And one male visitor to the beguinage exclaimed, "how vigorously these beguines kiss, my wife won't kiss me so!" It would take much to surprise Peter van der Wiel.

For all his experience, then, it was remarkable that after three decades of visiting the Vicar-General's notes remained consistently fresh and detailed. He faithfully recorded the common as well as the scandalous in convents, the old as well as the new, while lesser visitors would have been worn down by the constant grind. The places might have begun to blur and look alike—from the Poor Clares and Black Sisters in Mechelen to the Augustinians of Kabeek in Tienen or the Leprosy house of Brussels. Yet he never tired of writing out the same formula during interviews with prospective nuns, or of noting the often repetitious responses of sisters during visitations.

With him for this particular visit to Bethlehem was the Dean of Leuven, the plodding but reliable Peter Lucius, an even greater devotee of record keeping than the Vicar-General. For while Peter van der Wiel kept records as a means to an end, Dean Lucius seemed to delight in the record for its own sake. His annual reports on the state of his Deanery were brutally consistent in length, regularity of submission, and even topics. In fact his greatest strength was his tolerance for tedium, for he could report the same thing year after year—decorations in a church, number of altars, number and value of pious foundations—as if a new and unusual discovery. Among his visits was one to St. Gertrude's parish in 1621, where he found the Vice Pastor, Henri Joos, absent on account of attending a profession feast across the street for a beguine. But he did nothing to try to punish the Vice Pastor, or compel him to return, for Peter Lucius was no more forceful than he was imaginative.

If not the most interesting personality in the world, the Dean could be counted on to do such things as assist with the interviewing of nuns in Bethlehem. He did not have as much experience as Vicar-General Van der Wiel, but he had seen enough to become unruffled, including a recent visit to a convent called Florival, where four sisters had been accused of engaging in sexual relations with men. Thus the learned, intelligent Peter van der Wiel and the trustworthy Peter Lucius brought deep background to their visitation of Bethlehem.

They knew this house about as well as any other. The Vicar-General had visited five or six times before, in addition to letters received. His visits, and those of other officials, occurred less frequently than the ideal of once yearly, but in a diocese with nearly five hundred parishes and dozens of convents this was about as good as it got. The Dean, of course, lived in Leuven itself and so witnessed personally some events in Bethlehem. Both men therefore understood the issues likely to arise.

They knew about Margaret, and the incident with Barbara Beli, but they apparently did not know about the past of Henri Joos. They knew that the Archbishop's 1626 statutes had been meant to usher in a new era of reform in Bethlehem, but that within a year there already had been arguing over the grilles. And they knew that Archbishop Boonen had done as much as could be expected for this convent, not only visiting personally, not only providing upkeep for Margaret, but recently fashioning for each nun, as a gift, a special ring, twenty-three in all. The nuns had thanked the Archbishop for his "fatherly affection," but the visitors surely wondered why the nuns did not show thanks through their behavior instead.

This and still more were on the minds and souls of Vicar-General and Dean as they presented their credentials to the community during a ceremony in the church, then retired to the parlor to speak with each sister at the grille. The entire process usually took a day or two. The Vicar-General would question and prompt, while Dean Lucius was there for his skill at recording. This meant there were at least three filters to getting at what the sisters thought of conditions in Bethlehem: what those sisters chose to reveal; what Dean Lucius decided should be written down, or not; and what Vicar-General Van der Wiel, whose task it would be at the end to pull everything together and issue concluding official documents, most thought needed fixing, for not all could be fixed at once.

The interviews began with Mater Adriana. Even before taking the customary oath to speak truthfully, so as to unburden her conscience and improve her convent, Adriana asked to be released as Mater. To show her serious intent she handed the convent's keys to the Vicar-General. No doubt he eyed Adriana to see whether this was bravado, then calmly refused the request. Dean Lucius diligently wrote down the scene in his thick black letters and straight up-and-down hand. Finally Adriana began answering the Vicar-General's questions.

The scene was repeated almost exactly in the second interview, with Catharina Rijkeboer, who asked to be let go as Vicaress because Mater did not trust her. Again the Vicar-General refused and went ahead. Then it was on to the veiled sisters in order of seniority, from eighty-one-year-old Anna van den Broek to twenty-four-year-old Anna Vignarola. Given her status outside the community, Margaret Smulders was interviewed almost as an afterthought, even after young Anna. Last of all came interviews with the seven lay sisters, who like the nuns were asked about the general state of the house and the usual questions about *clausura*, outside friends, services, and so on.

In Bethlehem as in most convents, nuns who wished to bend the ears of visitors even further offered not only oral responses but letters prepared in advance. These, promised sisters, were just as truthful as their spoken words. They were also fuller, for good as Dean Lucius was at recording, his notes could not contain every detail sisters wished to convey. Six sisters presented letters: Mater Adriana, Maria Joos, Anna Vignarola, Catharina Rijkeboer, Maria Coninxloo, and of course Margaret—precisely the women who seemed the biggest rivals in the convent.

The testimony of most nuns was recorded in a page or two, whether in Dean Lucius's notes or in a letter. Hence, Maria Coninxloo's letter of eight pages certainly stood out, and even Catharina Rijkeboer's of four. But these and all others were positively dwarfed by the incomparable treatise of Sister Margaret Smulders. It was so large that Dean Lucius hardly bothered to make any notes at all during Margaret's interview, for most of what she wished to say was already written down. Here at last was one of those rare moments during visitation when Peter van der Wiel experienced something entirely new: he had never seen anything like this. Margaret's thirty-two-page letter was longer than the letters of all other nuns and Dean Lucius's interview summaries together, which came to a mere twenty-four pages.

When the interviews were over, the Vicar-General gathered up the Dean's summaries and the nuns' letters and took all with him back to Mechelen for the first step in the process after visitation: to read everything at his leisure, as if he ever had any.

OTHER VOICES

Eventually the Vicar-General would see that a few nuns agreed almost wholly with Margaret, many agreed with her on certain points, and another few disagreed with her completely.

Leading the way among other critics of Adriana were Catharina Rijkeboer and Maria Coninxloo, who cited many of the same examples as Margaret but with far less detail and rancor. Indeed, Catharina went out of her way to appear the reluctant reporter, acknowledging Adriana's many gifts even as she criticized: there was "no one among all the sisters" more suited to the office of Mater than Adriana. If some complained about Adriana then the Archbishop should remember that complainers had faults of their own. If some pointed out that Adriana did not treat Catharina well it "may be that the blame lies more with me." And if it was true that some said Adriana's past was hardly spotless, Catharina herself knew nothing that might lessen Adriana's "good name and honor."*

Yet for all Catharina's large-heartedness, she could not keep back her frustration. Neither could Maria Coninxloo, who did not even feign hesitation in attacking Adriana. Both Catharina and Maria, and a variety of other nuns, confirmed Margaret's accusations of favoritism, of unevenhanded temporal administration, of Adriana's tendency to rule through fear rather than love, of her efforts to recruit novices to her side, of her unbounded efforts to find alms, of her waffle baking, of her unbridled enthusiasm for recreation, of her toleration for busy grilles, of her love for lavish decorations in choir, of her own irreverence and even nap taking

---

*Catharina's phrase regarding Adriana's past is tricky. It reads: "Ick en hebben haer noyt geblameert bij de oversten als mijn Doorl: Heere, oft bij den Eerw: heere sijen Vicarius, veel min bij yemant anders, want ick inder waerheyt van haer niet en wete te seggen dat strecken souden tot verminderinge van haeren goeden naem oft eere; heeft sij beclapt geweest, dat heeft connen sonder schult wesen, ick en drage mij dat niet aen." The first lines say that Catharina had never said anything to Archbishop or Vicar-General blaming Adriana for past misdeeds, and that she knew nothing that would lessen Adriana's name or honor. The next clause, "heeft sij beclapt geweest," is the critical one: "clap" often referred to gossip, and thus it might read "if she were gossiped about." But such a connotation doesn't explain the next clause, "dat heeft connen sonder schult wesen," or "that might have occurred without guilt." Given this clause, the references to honor in this passage, Margaret's special usage of "clap" (or "hit") in 1628 in a very similar context, and later events in the visitation of 1637, the word "beclapt" here likely had the same sense that Margaret (and the ecclesiastical visitor who translated her phrase) gave it: as a sexual assault. Together, the last clauses therefore read, if Adriana were "hit," it wasn't necessarily her fault.

during the Divine Office, and of her ill treatment of Catharina, whom Adriana acknowledged in refectory with a bow so stiff and reluctant that she seemed to have "a kink in her neck."

But some nuns presented to the visitors an entirely different picture of conditions in Bethlehem than that offered by Margaret, Maria, and Catharina—as if they were speaking of another convent altogether. Among them were those who said simply that discipline was good, or those who said very little at all and thus implied satisfaction with the status quo. A few, however, went beyond implicit contentment and defended Adriana's regime with teeth bared.

If there was factionalism in the convent, argued Adriana's defenders, then it was the fault of Catharina Rijkeboer and Maria Coninxloo. Mater Adriana said straight out that Catharina was partial, listened to too many tales, was the source of "much contention, murmuring, and bad feelings," and spread gossip about "confessor, superior, and cosister." Catharina would do well, believed Adriana, to learn "a common love" for all, rather than "passing her time with two or three persons only," especially persons who had "not yet killed their passions," a reference no doubt to Maria Coninxloo and Margaret Smulders. Maria Joos went so far as to say that Catharina was despised in the convent precisely because she favored the obnoxious Maria Coninxloo. Anna Vignarola, exhibiting the polish condemned by Margaret, contended in her stylish script and short, tactful letter that Catharina simply indulged Maria too much: "not that she follows her in her evil, I trust, for she is pious, but she doesn't tell her she's wrong, or doesn't guide such persons to safe, humble ground, as the holy Father of our order, Francis, taught. I've experienced much this way myself; she says much but does little, I'll leave it there."

But Anna did not leave it there. She and most other nuns pointed out as well Catharina's painfully obvious inability to instruct the precious novices to sing: Catharina simply had an awful voice, said Anna, plus an irritating way of "drawing out the last syllables" when singing the Divine Office. When Catharina finally acknowledged that she needed help in training the novices, it was her idea to appoint Anna. Though reluctant to accept, because she "feared the gossip" and resentment that might proceed from Maria Coninxloo and others, Anna finally did so, after Catharina promised "that she would soothe" Maria and even ask the Archbishop to forbid anyone in the convent from speaking ill of Anna's selection. In the end, however, "it was all human promises," concluded Anna. For before a month had gone by, Catharina decided that she did not like the arrangement after all, and hence took the lead in spreading gossip about Anna's ambitions. Catharina, said Anna, "burdened me with assorted lies which no one knows except God and my confessor, whose counsel I sought, and which no one will know if it pleases God." Inspired by the vengeful Catharina, the silent reproaches of the other nuns "almost killed me," lamented Anna. "My conscience couldn't bear any more all the evil they heaped upon me, through hate, because I was the youngest nun and was to teach the young ones to sing." Anna's desire was not for office, but only to serve God: "that's the reason I left the world."

Want of a fine voice was hardly Catharina's only fault, in the eyes of some. They pointed as well to her chronic "tardiness" to the common workroom, supposedly because she lingered in her private devotions, or her skipping of the Divine Office to speak with Margaret at the grille. But always the criticism returned to Catharina's supposed affection for Maria Coninxloo. Catharina denied this, and claimed that Maria simply loved to talk and there was little anyone could do to stop her. But Catharina's rivals inferred from her reluctance to stop Maria that the two conspired with each other against the current regime. Adriana wished that Maria would be more modest and "reverent toward her superiors," and stop trying to recruit novices to her side. Maria supposedly tried to persuade one novice not to speak with Adriana at all, so that Adriana had been compelled to lead the novice through a kind of deprogramming session. As for Anna Vignarola, she characterized Maria in a way sure to get the attention of any obedience-loving clergyman:

Maria was "growing so stubborn that she will soon be ungovernable, I fear, for she may not be admonished in the least; if the confessor admonishes her, then she announces to everyone that he is restricting her conscience; if she is admonished by our reverend Mater, well this does more harm than good, for she then complains that Mater acts out of hate or that she doesn't like her; but in truth she isn't worthy of Mater's care and all the love she shows her, and how she so humbly tries to win her over as she does." In general, it was as if "Maria had made a vow to stir unrest," even stirring up sisters who had been assigned penance by telling them that Mater acted out of passion rather than judgment. "Let us hope that God will not judge her too severely."

One of the most serious accusations leveled against both Catharina and Maria Coninxloo was that they used ecclesiastical visitations as weapons against other sisters. This was strictly forbidden in statutes of all convents, as a breach of charity, but it was hard to stop, given the emphasis on fault finding that marked official visitations during this latest Age of Zeal. Catharina, Maria, and Maria's cousin Anna Coninxloo, according to Adriana, loved to boast about their contributions to the most recent visitation. Whenever the Archbishop's decrees were read aloud to all nuns afterward, Sister Maria Coninxloo "counts on her fingers the points she supposes were made at her behest, and shows by her expression and manner that those persons who are wanting in any of these points are to know with certainty that it was she who revealed it and who sought correction. And that isn't enough for her, for she chatters and goes on for so long until she is sure that they have heard it, and then she boasts that she was heard on every point she requested." She spoke loudly enough for all to hear, continued Anna, and would claim that in the next visitation she'd certainly have a few more choice bits of information to pass along. Anna warned the visitor that Maria was adept at framing her words and requests in such a way that it was impossible for an outsider to realize that she was motivated by passion alone, not love. Naturally Anna had tried "every means to win her over, to show I have compassion for her soul, but without profit. Thus I don't know what else to do except pray, and have patience."

This was the extent of the faults seen in the convent by Mater Adriana, Anna Vignarola, Maria Joos, and Lesken Joos. Adriana and hers admitted the occasional lapse in *clausura*, but nothing serious, and made no mention at all of any illicit almsgetting, improper devotion, or waste. Any problems in the convent were restricted to a few troublesome, unreliable persons. Even the style of Anna Vignarola's letter—short, graceful, and to the point—conveyed a message that Margaret and other rivals, whose letters were verbose, unrefined, and nose-to-nose, were hardly to be trusted. Anna's conclusion illustrated that well enough: what she knew she wrote in truth, but action she would leave to the discretion of Archbishop Boonen, "for my heart wishes nothing but peace; we must bear one another's crankiness, that's why we live together." Hoping that the Holy Spirit would guide the visitor to a good decision, she signed, "worms for lunch if God wills it."

DETERMINATIO

Mechelen, the Archbishop's Palace, late summer 1628. After reading Dean Lucius's interview summary and the letters of the sisters, Vicar-General Van der Wiel proceeded to the three remaining steps of the process: organizing the sisters' comments, drafting a set of necessary decrees for the Archbishop's perusal, and composing the final *determinatio,* or set of decrees, for the Archbishop's signature. These decrees should, like all other decrees issued after visitations, then supplement the convent's statutes, and, like those statutes, be read aloud in community four times per year.

The Vicar-General did not proceed immediately, given the crush of his other responsibilities, but by the end of the summer he was ready to begin weighing competing claims. First he made notes of the interviews and letters in Bethlehem, and arranged them by topic. Ordinarily he made only one set, but given Margaret's "prolixic" letter he decided, like Moses, to divide the sea in two: one set of notes for Margaret (three pages long) and one set for everybody else (one and a half pages long). He did not particularly like Margaret, but neither did he necessarily prefer the faction that surrounded Adriana. In fact his faithful summaries of testimony from both sides revealed his effort to remain as impartial as possible.

Next the Vicar-General composed, on the basis of his notes, a memorandum for the Archbishop. This listed the points he judged most in need of attention. Here Peter van der Wiel revealed best whom he trusted most among the nuns, for in this memo he picked out those bits of testimony which seemed most serious and believable to him—and clearly his favored source of intelligence was Catharina Rijkeboer. In fact, the decrees the Vicar-General sketched out for Bethlehem reflected especially Catharina's view of conditions there, and her vision of how things ought to be.

Though Catharina came in for some criticism herself in this memo (she deserved correction, noted the Vicar-General, for failing to reach out in love to novices, and for too easily hearing complaints against Mater), virtually every decree was a blemish on the regime of Adriana. She should stop gathering in the infirmary with her friends. Cease cultivating partiality with Maria Joos, Anna Vignarola, and Lesken Joos—"a lay sister," noted the Vicar-General, as if to say "no less." Cut back gift giving. Beware of feeding the steward. Eliminate the specter of private property. Use gifts to the convent for the sick in the infirmary and not merely among "the partial ones." Finish constructing the last segment of the cloister wall. Take seven other steps to improve cloister and behavior at the grille. Allow a personal inspection of the decoration in the choir and of the communion windows in the church. Seat by seniority of profession in choir. Stop allowing nuns to wear white shoes. Find a compromise on play. And stop dressing a nun as the fool on recreation days.

The recommendations Vicar-General Van der Wiel had in mind were therefore a triumph for Catharina (she never would have put it in such political terms), and by extension for Margaret and Maria Coninxloo as well. The Vicar-General was reluctant to rely upon or even name Margaret in his summaries, and loathe to agree with her. But despite this, despite his caution, and despite the real possibility of partisan motives among the nuns, Peter van der Wiel decided, like Margaret, that the root of problems in Bethlehem was Adriana herself. He even wrote a note to himself at the end of this memorandum to think about an "election of a new Mater." This was no mere formality, either, for everyone knew that if Mater were doing her job well, the subject would never be raised.

After completing the memorandum, the Vicar-General handed it to Archbishop Boonen for his comments and instruction. The Archbishop then noted in the margins which points were to be included in the written *determinatio* for the entire convent, and which were to be discussed in private with Adriana: visitors recognized that inflicting too much embarrassment on any nun, but especially Mater, might do more to promote discord than uproot it. Still, however tactfully it occurred, the rebuke of Adriana Truis and her allies appeared imminent. All that remained were the final steps, which usually occurred within weeks of the visitation: composition of the *determinatio*, its delivery to the convent, and the public reading before all the nuns. There was just one problem: not weeks, or months, or even years later did the Archbishop ever send any sort of official document to Bethlehem to conclude the hard-fought visitation of June 1628. In fact it was likely that no final *determinatio* was even composed.

In the autumn of that year and then through the spring of 1629, the nuns with the biggest stake in visitation worried that all the good evidence against Adriana was being wasted, and so they pleaded with the Archbishop in Mechelen and Joost Bouckaert in Scherpenheuvel for a conclusion. Maria Coninxloo was especially eager to see a *determinatio*, for she was confident that her revelations would compel visitors to action. Meanwhile, Margaret, Catharina, and Dean Lucius wrote additional letters to Archbishop Boonen to say that the romping in the guest room showed no signs of diminishment, that there was still no finished cloister wall in sight, and that there was great peril to chastity in Bethlehem: would the Archbishop therefore please send his decrees? Margaret even volunteered to apply the allowance he gave her toward the cost of building the wall. Joost Bouckaert took up the cry as well, and pressed the Archbishop for an end to visitation, peppering his letter with reports of new and alarming misdeeds in Bethlehem: some nuns were now "warming themselves" in a most "filthy" manner, by stripping their clothing conspicuously around a common fire, which in many persons might be an instigator "to movements of the flesh," and which was so offensive that even "cheap whores" would have refused to tolerate the indecency of it all. Moreover, Henri Joos was still visiting the convent, bringing gifts, and receiving presents from nuns, and still bothering Margaret by his very presence: "It may be that this fellow has changed his flesh and soul, may not have any evil intention, but I am unconvinced." Needless to say, the ex-confessor's presence bothered Margaret greatly, so that the Pastor could not care for her properly.

Despite these pleas, the waiting in Bethlehem dragged on, perplexing everyone who knew the Archbishop's reputation as a loyal, diligent shepherd. No one could say why he moved so slowly, but there were clues. In the first place, Jacob Boonen was as busy as ever. His agenda between 1627 and 1633 showed that he rarely stayed more than two weeks in any single location, and that his concerns were crushing: endless letters of recommendation, repeated decrees against eating sausages on unlawful days, the endowment of Masses for the soul of his sister, responding to circulars from Archduchess Isabella or criticisms of a priest whom even parishioners mocked with the title "preacher à la mode," because of such extemporaneous sermons as his recent one on the fundamental nudity of humans, for which the Archbishop had a Dean warn the man of the hazard this imagery could cause in weaker minds.

A second and better explanation for the delay, however, was the volatility of the situation in Bethlehem, and the need for some kind of balance there. However carefully he worded the planned *determinatio,* the Archbishop could, in light of the testimony on which it was based, hardly avoid the appearance of excessively chastising— which might cause even more trouble than existed now. To paraphrase old Mater Barbara Noosen, the visitors could pronounce to their hearts' content and then walk away, but the nuns had to live with Adriana daily. Should the visitors humiliate her, life in the convent could grow harder still for her subjects. Both the Archbishop and Peter van der Wiel were too zealous to ignore the ideals of monastic life, but they were also astute enough to recognize the political perils of drastic and rapid change—either in their treatment of Adriana or in removing her altogether. Their favorite (and perhaps only) candidate to replace her, Catharina Rijkeboer, would if promoted to Mater suffer mercilessly under the critical eyes and forceful personalities of her foes. Hence it was best to cope with the current regime as well as possible.

And so the Archbishop and his visitors decided to leave much in Bethlehem as it was, and to be content with a few strict-sounding decrees. To satisfy the demands of zeal and discipline, Archbishop Jacob Boonen wrote brief letters to Bethlehem to condemn eating and drinking at the grille, and sometime between April 1630 and the end of 1632 he even visited in person to deliver a belated oral *determinatio.* This would show certain zealous nuns that he had not forgotten them, or conventual ideals. But he would not turn Bethlehem upside down, or admonish Adriana in public, or even leave a written document condemning her explicitly, for these would surely worsen things. He knew after all the old Dutch idiom, "the spoken word flees, but the written remains."

In the end, the Archbishop would insist on only two tangible changes in Bethlehem as a result of the visitation of 1628—both of them consolations to nuns who had expected more. In August 1629 he ordered the election of a separate Bursaress, someone besides Adriana. The outcome was a severe disappointment to Margaret and others, for the winner, with a plurality of votes, was Adriana's friend Maria Joos.

The second change was much more hopeful for Margaret: a slight improvement in her personal living conditions. In September 1630 the Archbishop sent a delegation to Bethlehem to look into the question of Margaret's status. They decided the following: Margaret was to remain in her guest room, but only as long as Adriana kept the room immediately below free of outsiders. When ill, Margaret was to enjoy the same treatment as other nuns, but in her cell. When the convent received an important guest, Margaret was free to join in. When there was a distribution of alms to the convent, Margaret was to have her share. Though Margaret was still outside the convent, and though no one knew how seriously Adriana would observe these points, here at least was some official recognition of Margaret's letters.

It would have been much easier, and much less revealing for future generations, had the visitors of 1628 been able to come to that rare simple conclusion arrived at by Bishop Triest of Gent, in a visitation he made to a house of Black Sisters at about this same time: all things there were in good order, tranquil, and exemplary, so that nothing more need be said.

Book Three

How Margaret's Hard-Won Triumphs
Partly Fizzled Out

14
Justification

Bethlehem, October 14 and 15, 1633. In the year that the Archduchess Isabella died, and Leuven was besieged by the Dutch, and the moneyed convents left town to wait out the warring season in elegant refuges built elsewhere for this very contingency, the Archbishop's men visited the plain, housebound Grey Sisters of Bethlehem once again. Though the last visitation had ended with a whimper, it was past time for another—especially in the hearts, eyes, and souls of sisters whose genuine hope for reform, or desire to see adversaries chastened, sprang almost eternal.

Once more did Peter van der Wiel lead the visitation, and call the sisters to the parlor in order of their date of profession. Once more did Margaret bring along to her interview a monumental letter, which at a pithy sixteen pages still far surpassed the contributions of other nuns. Once more did she offer the usual disclaimer that despite her letter's length the visitors could trust the truth of what she wrote. Once more did she complain sorely that Adriana Truis, Anna Vignarola, and Maria Joos were overly familiar with one another, that Anna Vignarola "looks as if she'd like to kick me far away," that the "dreadful children" of the Woman In the

Leopard threatened the stability of every chair in the guest house, that illicit feasting with guests at the grille (including Henri Joos) continued unabated, that the convent was still used by outsiders for storage, that the lay sisters were as uppity and enamored of silver spoons as ever, and that Adriana still led the unruly celebrations of feast days. And once more did Adriana's defenders allege that Catharina Rijkeboer was the source of all factionalism in the convent, and that her voice was worse than ever (though they dared not rebuke her because of her ever withering health).

There were of course new themes as well in the visitation of 1633. This time around Margaret's favorite target was not Henri Joos but the tightfisted new Bursaress, Maria Joos, who, though "shortest in the convent," was master of them all and could hardly bear to give nuns even a "poor egg," a drop of beer, or even the "smallest rag" except with a "wooden face," so "impolite and doglike is she": if she had "gone to school all her life to learn the art of miserliness she couldn't have learned it better." This time Margaret had a new piece of evidence to demonstrate what she perceived as the self-aggrandizement of Anna Vignarola: a new organ, sure to deepen inequality in the convent, for it diverted resources from poor nuns, and increased the glory of certain sisters rather than God. This time Adriana's defenders added to their list of bad singers, by contending that Maria Coninxloo sang like a crow. This time Adriana's defenders condemned explicitly Margaret Smulders and the lay sister Joanna Schoensetters for sticking their noses into everything in the convent, then chatting about it together in the kitchen, "from morn until eve": whoever dared enter the kitchen when Joanna was there, said one nun, "takes up her cross, believe you me." This time Adriana's defenders wondered why Sister Margaret Smulders made such a great clamor upstairs when guests came to visit in the rooms below, and why she went to stand near the wagon-gate when workmen entered the convent, watching everything with "hands on her hips," and causing workmen to ask what "kind of a creature she is," so that nuns standing nearby "don't know what to say, for they must preserve the convent's honor." This time Adriana's defenders were perturbed that certain sisters wounded the convent's honor by telling novices "stories that supposedly happened earlier, about our secular confessor," Henri Joos. And finally, this time almost every sister, on whatever side, bemoaned the new moneymaker dreamed up by Maria Joos: washing the church linens of the Jesuits, which not only occupied sisters four times a year, three weeks at a time, but required long hours of ironing and drying in the attic, from where nuns could "gape" into the streets below.

Despite changes in details, it was clear that passions in Bethlehem were hot and familiar, so that in the end this visitation looked much like the last. There was one other strong resemblance between this latest visitation and that of 1628: a lack of conclusiveness. True, this time Vicar-General Van der Wiel managed to compose a draft of the final *determinatio* while still at Bethlehem, and a mere five days later actually sent the nuns a finished version. Moreover, the decrees reflected not only the latest problems but virtually all the points raised at the visitation of 1628 as well: perhaps past efforts would not be wasted after all. But this hope proved false, for the ordinary sisters of Bethlehem never even heard the *determinatio* of 1633. The convent's leadership, Adriana, Catharina, and Maria Joos, did have a chance to read it through quickly among themselves, but they sent it back immediately to Mechelen with a request for slight revisions. And that was the last anyone ever saw of the document.

Perhaps the *determinatio* was lost along the road, or in the Archbishop's mountain of papers. More likely, however, was that Jacob Boonen and his men were too busy, or once again recognized the greater turmoil that could come through strict reform. It was even possible that the Archbishop's men sought to repay the temerity of the revision-seeking nuns of Bethlehem, by refusing to respond at all. Whatever the reason, the *determinatio* was gone. Here, to the frustration of Margaret and others, was yet another visitation of the short duration.

The Return of Sister Margaret

1636. In the year after the plague that followed the siege of Leuven, and while some nuns of the city were still burning pitch to purify their convents, heartening developments unseen by most of the brooding world occurred in the life of Sister Margaret Smulders: Archbishop Boonen was ready to return her to the dormitory of the nuns.

Though the visitation of 1633 turned out to be as toothless as the last, like the last it at least resulted in betterment of Margaret's personal situation. She must have felt that her letters were having some effect after all, at least with the Archbishop, if not with the cautious Peter van der Wiel.

It was Margaret herself who initiated the process of her return by writing to Archbishop Boonen with a simple request: might His Most Illustrious Grace condescend to consider her petition regarding her reinstatement among the nuns of the convent, for she had long been separated from the other sisters, and in her old age (having recently turned fifty) she wished to enjoy the fruits of community? Margaret took care to enlist in her cause Pastor Bouckaert and yet another new Dean of Leuven, named Mannarts, whom she asked to intervene with the Archbishop on her behalf.

This was not Margaret's first such request, but this time the Archbishop, perhaps in compensation for his recent unwillingness to push through strict reforms in Bethlehem, or perhaps because Adriana had violated the terms of the 1630 agreement by allowing guests into the room just below Margaret's, was prepared to grant it—despite opposition from every side. The Franciscans in Leuven, who still served Bethlehem as confessors, vehemently contested Margaret's return, and they recruited an impressive array of dignitaries to say the same. Together with the distinguished Franciscan Bishop and diplomatic envoy Joseph Bergaigne, they warned that if "that one" returned, the effects would be clear in the convent "within an hour." Mater Adriana and the entire community had good cause, said these men, to "fear and lament the restoration of that person." Moreover, the Franciscans could not be sure that anyone in their friary would minister to Margaret if she returned.

The nuns of Bethlehem, as in years past, also pleaded, with all their souls, that Margaret remain in the guest house. In this they were supported by Vicar-General Van der Wiel, not because he felt any great alliance with Mater Adriana, but because he foresaw a great "cloud of dissension" ready to burst open if Margaret returned. Based on "the knowledge I have of the person of Sister Margaret, gathered over many years," and based on the "mournful" letters sent to him by many nuns of the convent, her return would ruin the community, said the Vicar-General.

Still Archbishop Boonen pushed on. At the Archbishop's request, Joost Bouckaert willingly drew up a list of principles for Margaret's return, to be reviewed secretly with Adriana. Margaret could no longer be barred from the dormitory, and was to have her choice of vacant cells. She was not to be expelled again, unless with the permission of Archbishop Boonen. Adriana was to persuade the Franciscans to minister to Margaret, so that she had a regular confessor. And Adriana was to encourage other sisters to bear Margaret in love as well.

Pastor Bouckaert also drafted a second and public document, for the entire convent of Bethlehem, explaining more fully why the Archbishop had decided to reinstate Margaret in the community. Jacob by the Grace of God and the See of Rome, Archbishop of Mechelen, and so on, had deliberated ripely upon the long pleas heard from Sister Margaret Smulders to reenter the community, from which she had been forcibly separated these past twelve years. She had agreed to this separation, it continued, not for any cause but by her own free, uncompelled will, for the sake of peace in the convent. If she once had infirmities, they were bodily in nature, a statement meant to mitigate Margaret's culpability in the old matter of the demons. Besides, thanks to various spiritual remedies, Margaret had been free of those infirmities for some time. No one could ever be sure in such matters, the document admitted, but "we willingly believe her," especially given her resolve, and given her long freedom from them. "We must be content that she is redeemed, unburdened, and free of them, and the community will have nothing to suffer from her." Hence, there was no reason she should not return.

Surely Archbishop and Pastor knew that most sisters would hardly share this interpretation of old events, and that Margaret's trouble with demons was only one of the things resented about her. But all that really mattered was that at some point in 1636, Margaret, for the third time in her life, moved herself into the dormitory of the nuns, a full-fledged member of the community once more. On this at least, the Archbishop would have his way.

The return of Sister Margaret of course brought complications and problems with it. Pastor Bouckaert was soon complaining of her treatment by other sisters. Her best friend, Catharina Rijkeboer, was no longer there to support her, having died in early 1635, at age forty—perhaps of the plague that hit Leuven that year, perhaps of the oft-mentioned but never-specified illness that afflicted her for long, or perhaps of a broken spirit caused by perpetual alienation from Adriana and deplorable treatment from Maria Joos, who brazenly laid claim on one of Catharina's petticoats and her fire-kettle before Catharina was even dead. Also vexing to Margaret was the election of Catharina's replacement as Vicaress: the winner was none other than Margaret's old nemesis, thirty-one-year-old Anna Vignarola, chosen on St. Valentine's day of 1635, on the strength of half of the twenty votes in the convent (including four of the six lay sisters). Anna's triumph meant that she, Adriana, and Maria Joos now filled all the chief offices of Bethlehem, which hardly boded well for Margaret.

But at least Margaret was back inside the convent, and would spend the rest of her life there: she had returned for the last time. In fact, emboldened by her personal victory, she ignored for the moment the sentiments that prevailed against her and nurtured greater hopes than ever for her long-sought reforms in Bethlehem. Now, back inside the convent, she could gather even more firsthand knowledge than in previous years, speak with more credibility to visitors, and work more aggressively to salvage her long-lost reputation. The news she had been awaiting came at last in early 1637: Bethlehem would very shortly receive another official visitation. And best of all for Margaret, the man designated to lead it was none other than her own special patron and protector, Pastor Joost Bouckaert. Surely he would do more than Peter van der Wiel had done, in either 1628 or 1633, to set things right.

THE SHAMING OF ADRIANA

Mol, March 11, 1637. Henri Joos busied himself with the usual priestly duties on this late winter's day: recording the final testament of a parishioner, baptizing or burying (here in the middle of Lent there was no marrying), saying Mass, counseling local magistrates, or fighting off the latest threat to his benefices. He worried as well about tremors of war: the Dutch, never far to begin with, were edging ever closer to Mol. In the midst of his concerns, there arrived a letter bearing the seal of the Archbishop of Mechelen. Here was something to arouse curiosity, for the Pastor's parish belonged to the diocese of Den Bosch, outside the jurisdiction of Mechelen. But here was cause for apprehension as well, since news from unexpected sources is seldom routine.

This was no exception. The Pastor was informed that henceforth he was barred from preaching or from hearing confession within the boundaries of the archdiocese of Mechelen. Was any explanation attached? If not, he could guess the reason, thanks to another letter from his sister Maria and Mater Adriana, of Bethlehem.

The women were enraged over a recent visitation to their convent, conducted the previous month by the indelicate Joost Bouckaert. During his two-day stay, Pastor Bouckaert had not only asked sisters the usual questions about the current state of the convent but insisted on raising the matter of Henri Joos's expulsion as confessor two decades before.

It was enough to humiliate anyone. Surely the resurrection of these old tales was what had prompted Archbishop Boonen to issue the most recent ban on Pastor Joos's preaching and confessing, duties the Pastor still liked to perform during his twice- or thrice-yearly visits to Bethlehem. Surely the ban was designed to embarrass him before the nuns, and to discourage him from visiting the convent at all.

The Pastor dashed off a response to Adriana and Maria, telling them of the new restrictions upon him, no doubt condemning those nuns who had spoken ill of him during the visitation, and marveling at ecclesiastical visitors who were so intent on finding trouble. One last thing. He would accept the invitation of the nuns to attend the convent's upcoming novice-clothing, on March 22. It would give him a chance to learn all the details of the events of recent weeks.

Bethlehem, Lent 1637. The visitation of Bethlehem in February 1637 was as bad as Pastor Joos feared, and as wonderful as Margaret had hoped. Here was Margaret's moment in the sun, the culmination of all her past emotions and struggles in the convent, for it was nothing less than the humiliation of Adriana Truis and Henri Joos together.

The key was of course Joost Bouckaert, who was surely chosen to lead the visitation this year as a way of protecting the recently returned and still vulnerable Margaret. But the choice had even bigger consequences than Archbishop Boonen had bargained for.

The visit began quite as usual. Accompanied by Dean Mannarts, Pastor Bouckaert arrived in Bethlehem in late February and began interviewing nuns on the typical subjects of conventual life. Soon, however, whether at Pastor Bouckaert's instigation or that of certain nuns, the "old, sordid tales" of the young Henri Joos became the center of attention. Would this man never go away? A confessor at a convent in the town of Bree dominated the factional dynamics within that house for seventeen years, but Henri Joos had been *removed* as confessor in Bethlehem twenty years before! And still he was at the center of controversy.

How the interviews with the sisters proceeded and exactly what they said were not preserved—the summaries and letters were all too sensitive, no doubt, and destroyed. Still, it was clear enough from other documents what caused the fuss in 1637: these stories were not only old, and not only about Henri Joos, but about Adriana Truis as well. For the first time, Adriana was semi-publicly implicated in the ancient scandal. Again the specifics were not recorded: that a young Adriana, before her days as Mater, had been intimate with Henri Joos? Or with someone else? There were after all longstanding if vague rumors of Adriana's past indiscretions. Whatever the details, the stories told during interviews certainly linked Adriana to the scandal of 1618, and thus caused her to be "greatly disgraced"—so greatly that there was almost immediately talk in the convent of an election for a new Mater.

It was likely that Joost Bouckaert, during his long association with Margaret, had already heard these stories about Adriana Truis and Henri Joos. What he apparently wanted was for the Archbishop and Vicar-General Van der Wiel to hear them as well, in part to show how unfairly Margaret had been accused and treated over the years. The Vicar-General himself did not know the details: when Margaret had the chance to tell him during previous visitations, she was less than specific, merely dropping hints about Adriana's strong feelings for Henri Joos, requesting that Joos visit less often, and casting a few vague aspersions on both his and Adriana's past holiness. And when Archbishop Hovius mentioned the affair to the Vicar-General years before, he had spoken in broad terms

A Grey Sister of Leuven, ca. 1650. If the description of this painting is correct, then the nun portrayed is almost certainly Adriana Truis, Mother Superior of Bethlehem.

Stedelijk museum Vander Kelen-Mertens, Leuven

only, "thus preserving the honor of the place." Even Jacob Boonen gave the appearance of having little more than this general sense of things, though certainly he remembered Margaret's side of the story from the old reports of Johan Evangelista. In any event, now that Pastor Bouckaert was acting as official visitor to the convent, and not merely as Margaret's private confessor, he felt free to explore unseemly events with other nuns and report what he heard to Archbishop Boonen: he did not have to keep things locked in his heart.

Even before Pastor Bouckaert finished his visit to Bethlehem, the convent was in turmoil over his interviews. After he left, happy nuns wrote letters of thanks to Joost Bouckaert, while distressed nuns complained tactfully to Archbishop Boonen and angrily to Vicar-General Van der Wiel. Obviously these women had grasped an old lesson about bureaucracies: if one official will not listen, another of roughly equal influence might. Those who rejoiced in the visitation put their hopes in Pastor Bouckaert, while those who regretted it turned to Peter van der Wiel.

Nuns displeased with Pastor Bouckaert were quite right that Vicar-General Van der Wiel would sympathize with them. He regretted the events of the recent visitation as much as they, not because the stories were right or wrong but because of the strife they produced. This was precisely why he had refused in the past to push vigorously for change in Bethlehem: any serious remedy there was sure to be worse than the ailment. Like many nuns, the Vicar-General blamed Joost Bouckaert, for tolerating such tales at all, and for trying to have Adriana dismissed because of them: the events were old and memories largely faded. No doubt, continued the Vicar-General, this was the Pastor's way of defending Sister Margaret, but it was a dubious goal, since for years she had been the cause of so much trouble in the place "and will continue to be," whoever was in charge. It was not worth standing the convent on end merely to give her satisfaction.

Despite such disparaging sentiments, momentum in Bethlehem was for a brief, glorious time clearly with Joost Bouckaert, and thus Margaret Smulders. For it was almost immediately after Pastor Bouckaert passed along his report to Mechelen that Archbishop Boonen sent to Mol the notice that Henri Joos was banned from preaching and confessing. And as much as the Vicar-General lamented the chaos of the visitation, he shared Pastor Bouckaert's low opinion of Henri Joos: not only should Pastor Joos be banned from preaching and confessing, he suggested to the Archbishop, but from calling at Bethlehem altogether.

And so, in the midst of the complaints, Pastor Bouckaert pushed on. He promised the Archbishop that he had carried out his commission with goodwill, and by "the grace of God," without any concession "to passion or vicious inclination." He had not, he insisted, initiated the questions about Henri Joos during the visitation, but neither had he silenced willing nuns who wished to talk about it. Those who chose to talk certainly did not act out of vengeance, as some sisters were claiming. He knew for a fact that "she," meaning Margaret, could "not have deposed in revenge regarding that most scandalous act and other things," or that she had stirred up others. His only intent, and by implication Margaret's too, was the betterment of the convent.

Satisfied that the Archbishop was still behind him, Pastor Bouckaert at last composed a *determinatio* that would conclude his visitation. Unlike visitors in years past, he was not about to neglect this crucial step. He sent a draft of it to Archbishop Boonen, who approved it almost without change and then issued it to the convent under his own name on May 20, 1637.

Here was the document Margaret had awaited so long, an even harsher document than the *determinatios* planned by Peter van der Wiel in 1628 or 1633 but never proclaimed. This one was not lost, not misplaced, not indecisive, not mere words in the wind, but an excoriation inked forever in parchment. Unlike most *determinatios,* which left out names and specifics and merely implied that Mater was responsible for shortcomings, the thirty points in this version put the blame squarely on her. Adriana was to appoint two new council sisters chosen by the Archbishop, and heed their advice. She was to care much better for sick and well from the common income of the convent, halt abuses at the grille, cease the practice of letting novices leave the convent one last time, remind the Dean to visit annually, stop giving away to friends more than eighteen florins of items per year, and account more carefully for alms. She was even instructed to remind the Archbishop every three years, starting next year, that it was time to hold elections for a new Mater!

Unlike Peter van der Wiel, whose chief intent in Bethlehem had always been to maintain some semblance of harmony among the nuns rather than force through ideals, Joost Bouckaert had fashioned a *determinatio* so one-sided that those who heard it must have wondered how, if every decree were observed, Adriana could possibly maintain her dignity and respect. The very first reading in community would have been enough to humiliate her, or any Mater. That this one was not only to be read aloud regularly, as usual, but even put into print for each sister, not usual at all, would have deepened the agony. The hard line of Joost Bouckaert had won this time around.

And of Margaret too, for the whole document, and the arrangement for its frequent proclamation, could as easily have come from her mind and hand. For at least a fleeting moment, or during the initial reading of the *determinatio*, she was surely more content than she could ever remember having been in Bethlehem.

The same could not be said for Adriana. The new decrees stung sharply enough, as did the limitations put on Henri Joos: worse still, however, was the Archbishop's agreement with Joost Bouckaert and even Peter van der Wiel that Henri Joos should be banned not only from preaching and confessing in Bethlehem but from visiting altogether. The Archbishop assigned Vicar-General Van der Wiel to tell Adriana, who in turn was very probably assigned to inform Henri Joos himself. The most likely occasion for Adriana to do so was the novice-clothing of March 22, to which the Pastor had already been invited, and to which he no doubt rode up full of questions, but still expecting merriment. Or did she wait until after the ceremony? And what sentiments occupied their hearts before he rode away? They may well have always regarded each other merely as kindly benefactor and pious nun, who enjoyed each other's company. Or were they linked more intimately, as some suggested, by an old event? No record remained of this scene, which was likely their last together. But whatever the exact nature of their relationship, it was a very bad forty-seventh year for Adriana Truis.

15

Capitulation

1638 to 1640. Neither Margaret's contentment nor the precariousness of Adriana's position as Mater lasted long. The harsh, seemingly unbreachable decrees of 1637 would prove to be just as flimsy and inconsequential as those of earlier visitations, and Margaret would be just as despised as before. The same old chronic problems conspired against their implementation.

Although the Archbishop seemed more willing in 1637 to go along with a stricter program of reform in Bethlehem, who would enforce it? It was undesirable for him or his agents to check on the convent day and night, or even weekly and monthly, since compulsion should ideally have played little role in monastic life. But even had the Archbishop tried, it was impossible to visit often enough to ensure conformity: he simply did not have the time or the bureaucracy to do so.

How many bishops or deans or other delegates could make, war or no war, the required annual or biennial visits to all convents and parishes, much less compel conformity to the Bishop's version of religious life? Bishop Malderus of Antwerp could report to Rome in 1615 that he had visited a monastery called Sion every year, but not most others—and Antwerp had only 150 parishes, plus convents, while Mechelen had nearly 500 parishes and some 75 convents subject to the Archbishop. Centuries later a fictional country priest in France was still saying, "We can barely manage our ordinary parochial round." How much more difficult was it for a bishop?

Even the energetic Jacob Boonen was far from perfect. He was surprised that the Grey Sisters of Diest had no statutes of their own, despite numerous requests over the years from the nuns to be granted some. After thirty-five years of exemplary labor and leadership among the female religious, he observed with "sorrow" that the statutes of the beguinage of Tienen were still "grossly or wholly neglected," and that women there had "trampled underfoot" respect for authority, and replaced simpleness of clothing with "novelty, high-mindedness, and wasteful excess." His efforts in Bethlehem alone showed how difficult it was just to get visitation decrees onto paper, much less enforce them. And he did not even have to contend with the steep mountains that confronted Bishop Jean d'Aranthon of Grenoble, who made the precarious tour of his diocese a heroic (but mere) three times.

Besides physical limitations, there was a limit to what visitors *would* do. They were influenced not only by political forces that existed in convents but by certain attitudes toward women religious. In 1640 Prior Benedictus Van Haeften of Affligem offered one reason for what appeared to be inaction by superiors: difficult nunneries did not need new statutes, more visits, and mountains of decrees, for an abundance of laws was "disadvantageous" when dealing with women, who "by their nature" were not easy to reason with, and more rules only aggravated what he regarded as their inherent stubbornness. None of the visitors to Bethlehem expressed this view out loud, but based on other, similar evidence it was likely hovering about in the hierarchy of Mechelen as well.

What visitors did or did not do was also influenced by rivalries among themselves, as between Joost Bouckaert and Peter van der Wiel. Ideally, a Bishop should have been able to send any visitor at any time and receive back a dispassionate, reliable account of conditions in a given establishment. But temperament and other earthly considerations did matter and led different visitors to different conclusions and actions. Joost Bouckaert saw Bethlehem in crisis in 1637 and took drastic action, while Peter van der Wiel, seeing the same conditions, thought it best to intervene as little as possible lest it upset things more.

As stipulated by the *determinatio* of 1637, Archbishop Boonen sent a visitor to Bethlehem in the spring of 1638. This time, however, he chose Vicar-General Van der Wiel, who would produce an entirely different result from the year before. Surely the Archbishop knew this, and surely it reflected his own persistent double feeling toward Bethlehem: Margaret needed protecting and the convent needed reforming, but both goals had to be balanced by the realities of politics within the convent. The decision also reflected the Archbishop's respect for his two very different ecclesiastical confidantes: each man was right and each was wrong about how to proceed. By sending one after the other, he could be sure that Pastor Bouckaert would protect Margaret and sound the trumpet of reform, but that Vicar-General Van der Wiel would prevent anything too drastic. Thus neither side within the convent would attain a complete victory, and all could maintain a certain amount of dignity and respect.

Indeed, when Peter van der Wiel traveled to Bethlehem in 1638, he was so eager to undo the effects of the previous visitation that after his interviews with the nuns he showed no intention at all of issuing any decrees, and certainly not of holding an election to replace Adriana. He even heeded a request from several nuns that various portions of the *determinatio* of 1637 be transferred to a private document, for Mater's eyes alone, in order to mitigate some of the public humiliation heaped upon her by that judgment. And rather than drawing up any memos or new decrees he merely offered an informal report to the Archbishop on his visit to the convent. There was, he admitted, "not a little dissension" among the nuns, but it was not the fault of Adriana. Instead it was Joanna

Schoensetters and three or four veiled nuns (surely including Margaret) who "conspired" to unseat Adriana. When the Vicar-General rebuked Joanna, and commanded her to respect and obey her Mater promptly, Joanna simply replied that she would pay no heed to Vicar-General Van der Wiel but only to Joost Bouckaert, whom she expected to visit any day, and whom she intended to inform about the Vicar-General's "thoughtless judgments." Surely this raised the eyebrows of the Vicar-General, as did a statement by the house confessor that Pastor Bouckaert's influence in the convent "was not particularly healthy." Peter van der Wiel was beginning to feel the same way. But obviously the question of what to do with Bethlehem, and what most needed fixing, was in the eye of the beholder.

One final element also helped undo the visitation of 1637: the stubbornness of the nuns themselves. Though Adriana and other nuns took seriously their duty to obey superiors and decrees, ultimately they did so as they pleased: they played as great a role as ecclesiastical leaders in establishing the standard of the "good nun." This stubbornness was evident in past years in Bethlehem, as it was in hundreds of other convents, but it was especially plain now, in the face of continued pressure from Joost Bouckaert. In August 1639 Pastor Bouckaert visited Bethlehem once more, albeit unofficially: still, he demanded to see the *determinatio* he had left behind two years before. Adriana responded that this was impossible, because Peter van der Wiel had taken it away with him in 1638, to see about revisions. Once again, fumed the Pastor, a *determinatio* in Bethlehem had gone missing. Angered, he promised Adriana that he would return to the convent soon and reconclude his visitation of 1637.

Adriana wrote the Archbishop to tell him of these events, and to say she found the Pastor's promise strange, for the visitation of 1637 had been concluded two years before and was thus rather old news. Such behavior, she decided, revealed the Pastor's desire to exert his own brand of control over the house, and to disregard the more recent actions (or inactions) of Peter van der Wiel. Joost Bouckaert heard about Adriana's letter, and sent a report of his own to Archbishop Boonen. He had merely, he explained, been passing through Leuven to seek advice from doctors there about whether he should continue to drink the waters of Spa, which so far had produced dubious results in his health. Thus it was not as if he went to Leuven solely to scold Adriana, as she made it seem. More important was Adriana's claim about the missing *determinatio:* "under the shrubbery are plenty of falsehoods," feared the Pastor. For he knew that Vicar-General Van der Wiel had taken from the convent only a copy of the 1637 decrees, and not the original, which had been left with the nuns. Pastor Bouckaert therefore suspected that Adriana had "mutilated," if not "destroyed," the original. Certainly she or Anna Vignarola, speculated the Pastor, possessed a "raging enough soul" to commit such a deed. The only way to get to the truth was for the Archbishop himself to ask Adriana to hand it over.

Understandably, Jacob Boonen was growing weary of Bethlehem, and so it was not surprising that instead of delving further into the mystery of missing *determinatios* he decided to consider a more radical approach: give up the convent altogether, and hand it to the Franciscans at last. The nuns had of course suggested the idea before, but when they suggested it again in 1638 the Archbishop seemed far more willing to listen. Here was yet another means Adriana saw to be rid of the *determinatio* of 1637 and even Joost Bouckaert himself. It wasn't long before the Archbishop was exchanging letters with Franciscan headquarters in Rome, to discuss details of the switch, while the nuns of Bethlehem themselves sent long pleas to the Pope, explaining how badly they needed to be under Franciscan control. By February of 1639 enough details had been ironed out that papal bulls ratifying and proclaiming the transfer were dispatched from Rome.

But just as in 1618, when Archbishop Hovius had tried to relinquish control of Bethlehem, the cathedral chapter of Mechelen decided to oppose it. Archbishop Boonen had warned Adriana this might happen: if the chapter was against the switch, "you will have great difficulties." That was why he instructed her to keep the negotiations secret: the chapter must find out about it only at the right moment. That was why Adriana said nothing about the imminent change to Joost Bouckaert when he came in August 1639 looking for his *determinatio*. And that was also why she could not produce the *determinatio:* believing that the convent's days under Archbishop Boonen and his undesirable agent, Pastor Bouckaert, were done, Adriana had very likely torn it up, delighted that it was no longer necessary.

In the end, the Archbishop was right: the cathedral chapter could not be persuaded to let Bethlehem go. Throughout 1640 the chapter threw up one obstacle after the next, and the transfer of jurisdiction was blocked. Bethlehem therefore stayed under the Archbishop, and his team of visitors, after all. The leadership of Bethlehem did manage to reap one great benefit from the crisis of jurisdiction, however: it complicated and even shoved to the background the now almost trivial dispute over the visitation of 1637. The strict *determinatio* of Joost Bouckaert was practically sent into oblivion.

Margaret was as disappointed as her protector by the demise of the visitation of 1637, for it effectively meant the end of her complaining. If change did not come about as a result of the scandals and petty sins she had revealed over the years, then it never would. And thus the targets of her criticism were freer than ever to run things as they pleased, and to despise her.

After his frustrating visit to Bethlehem in August 1639, Joost Bouckaert lamented to Archbishop Boonen that the nuns were bullying "the innocent Sister M," for which he now believed himself partly to blame. Many nuns acted as if she "were the cause" of his *determinatio* of 1637, or the final expulsion of Henri Joos. Anna

Vignarola, for instance, had recently sent a scathing letter about Margaret to the Dean of Leuven, so scathing that Pastor Bouckaert did not dare repeat Anna's claims. In the meantime, the Pastor tried to soothe the "afflicted Ma. (the name I omit)," to greater and more frequent exercise of faith. In fact, there did not seem to him "a more commodious and stronger means to conquer infirmities, temptations, and so forth," than such exercise. He also urged Margaret to recite frequently the profession of faith prescribed by Pope Pius V. For a time Margaret was so discouraged she refused to do so, but with "the benevolence of God," she finally agreed, "with exorcism having first been dispatched. I write this to the consolation of your Illustrious Grace."

If Margaret had temporarily gained some satisfaction from the decrees of 1637, now she was the one suffering most for them—and for her perceived role in the final expulsion of Henri Joos as well. It was an old dynamic alluded to by nuns, and perceived by certain visitors as well: despite the promise of anonymity during visitations, Mater Adriana usually knew anyway who said what, just by the contents of the subsequent *determinatio*.

Hence it was likely that at the end Margaret's position in Bethlehem was in many ways the same as it had been before 1624, or even during the years of exile in the guest house. True, her fortitude and resolve had certainly swelled over the decades, she was back inside as a full-fledged nun, and it was no small thing that Henri Joos was gone. But did she again require exorcizing, as Joost Bouckaert hinted? Even if not, she was faced daily with the hard fact that Adriana remained Mater until the end, with Anna Vignarola her loyal, eternal Vicaress. That Mater and Anna endured the storms was not to say that reform failed and laxity triumphed. It was rather that there were other matters to consider besides a single version of reform—matters such as jurisdiction, the reality of sincerely different opinions on what mattered most in monastic life, personal taste in relationships, and ecclesiastical and conventual politics.

Even with the closer, surer presence of Margaret, the leading sisters were under the circumstances quite free to shape religious life and reform quite as they saw fit. As Margaret once said on another occasion: "It's not enough, visitation, for they do what they please." Or, Mater "takes no regard for anything as soon as the visitors are gone. She goes her old ways then."

16
Finis

The Infirmary of Bethlehem, December 17, 1648. This year would be remembered best in European history for the Treaty of Westphalia, an accord so important that it not only ended long hostilities around Europe but from then on became a starting and stopping point for innumerable history courses and books. But in the saga of Bethlehem, 1648 stood out for another reason: it marked the demise of a nun who for decades had toiled, in her own irascible way, to carve out a niche for herself in the world of female monasticism.

The illness that preceded Margaret's death was "long," according to the only brief account of it, which could have meant weeks or months or even years, since the last word about her before this came in 1639. If her care went according to statute (which Margaret surely feared would not be the case), then Mater Adriana should have visited her daily in the infirmary, provided for her needs from the common resources of the house, and exhorted her lovingly to penance, reminding her of the inevitability of death and the strictness of divine judgments. In Mater's absence, the Infirmarian Lesken Joos, in the spirit of loving God and not herself, was to serve the patient faithfully, all the while keeping the infirmary spotless. Like Mater, she should have urged the sufferer to bear her illness with courage, should have spoken softly and briefly, and should have encouraged any visitors in the place to do the same. Perhaps this all happened. Perhaps the sick Margaret was finally conceded, at no cost, the fresh butter, white bread, and nice draft of beer or glass of wine she had so long desired. Or perhaps her nightmare of loneliness and absolute poverty came to pass.

If the patient heeded all the exhortations, which she was conscious enough to have done—for the Dean of Leuven wrote that her mind and spirit were sound to the end—she would certainly have taken care to confess her sins, which she knew were many. Unlikely was Margaret as heroic as the patron saint of her order, Saint Elisabeth of Hungary, who kicked everyone out of her room three days before death to refresh her memory for confession and to contemplate the terrible judgment that awaited her, who sang like a swan with the many angels around her, who fought off the devil's last-ditch attempt to grab her soul, and who died with words about the birth of Jesus on her lips. Though probably less dramatic, Margaret's last hours were undoubtedly just as anxious.

Fortunately she could take advantage of the recent proliferation of books that offered tips for dying well. A Franciscan named Leutbrewer put out a convenient, popular handbook, the *Golden Art of How to Prepare in Less Than Two Hours for a General Confession of One's Whole Life, with the Guarantee That No Deadly Sins Will Be Forgotten*. A basic general principle, reminded the author, was to confess regularly during one's life, something that at least by monastic standards this sister had not always done. Another goal was to ensure that confession was complete, for too often people were sloppy about confessing, especially at the end. In considering one's whole life, one should include a list of all the people known and possible sins against them, a list of all possible sins against the Ten Commandments, and a list of sins common to one's station. For each list the author generously provided a string of typical sins to jar the memory. Van Gorcum's *Comfort of the Sick* not only offered techniques to prepare for one's last breath but explained why the devil was especially busy at the time of death, a crucial topic given the history of this nun: this was the moment when the final choice was made. Fight him, exhorted the author, call on God and the saints that holy angels may come to drive out the demons around you. Use the crucifix for a comfort, just as Moses raised the serpent. See the Lamb of God, think that the cross drives Satan away, that it's the tree of life. Hold a candle, to remember who is the light of the world.

Who knew what last thoughts, or temptations, or scenes from her past, or snatches of joy flashed in and out of Margaret's mind as she pondered her life and death? And what did those standing around her feel? Were they relieved? Did they feel at least a moment of pity, even Anna Vignarola, who in the long run would forever hold a grudge against Margaret? No one bothered to say, but all sisters were supposed to be present when the Infirmarian gave the sign that the sick one was about to expire. Then they read the Pater Noster, Credo, seven psalms with Litanies and prayers, and one sister read aloud the Passion of Our Lord. These were some of the most fundamental statements in the Christian tradition, chosen as if to reemphasize what it was that united them even if much else might divide them. In the meantime, the confessor, or a sister, sat near the dying Margaret and urged her to give no quarter to the enemy, to call out with her mouth or heart the most holy name of Jesus. Given Margaret's poverty, few sisters were likely to have been thinking of how they would divide up her meager goods, a practice she had always found so tasteless anyway.

When death was near, two nuns left to recite the long Commendations, outlined in the breviary. When death finally came, the other sisters all disciplined themselves with a rod, to remind them of their sins and that death would befall them as well. Soon after these came the Vigils with nine readings, the placing of the body in the ground, and the funeral Mass. Reminders of death would continue for weeks. Mater Adriana was to ensure that the death was announced in all other convents of Leuven and the archdiocese, so

Finis

that the deceased's soul might be faithfully prayed for, out of love. Adriana did not announce herself, however, Margaret's death to Archbishop Boonen, but merely told the Dean, who in turn wrote to a canon at the Archbishop's palace. At the bottom of a letter full of other business, the Dean asked whether the canon wouldn't mind going to the trouble of informing the Archbishop that on December 17, in the Monastery of the Grey Sisters of Leuven, "Sister Margaret Smulders, known well enough to him, had passed from this life, after a grave and lengthy illness, but with optimum disposition of spirit and full senses until the end."

If the Dean was right about her good spirits and sound mind, then here at last was an immutable victory for her.

Epilogue

No one mentioned whether Margaret, around sixty-five at the time of her death, had succumbed to new and recent physical ailments or old and familiar ones. No one recorded the reaction of Archbishop Boonen, but the words of the Dean reflected the Archbishop's long concern for Margaret: in fact not one other such letter for any nun of Bethlehem survived among the Archbishop's papers, though many were written. Jacob Boonen would have readily admitted that Margaret caused him frustration, but given recent and looming troubles with the Jesuits, the news of her death must have taken him back to what seemed simpler days. If he never acted fully on Margaret's complaints and suggestions, neither did he fully disbelieve her, or dismiss her as merely a disturbed or "hysterical" nun, as Peter van der Wiel was inclined to do. Probably thanks to Jacob Boonen were the unusual letters of Margaret Smulders preserved. He may have saved them with no clear purpose, but for the same reason that many people save things: because it is hard to part even with seemingly trivial objects that remind one of the past, especially the emotional past, and even the unhappy past.

Since Margaret died within the bosom of the church and her calling, the best theology of the day would have concluded that her life was scarcely in vain. In the less exalted sphere of historical worth, this was even more sure: thanks to her there survived a vibrant image of life inside the convent. This did not mean her story or convent were universal. True, plenty of other places and personalities bore striking resemblance. A Sister Maria of the Black Sisters in Leuven told Peter van der Wiel that there was peace in the house, save for the "difficulties caused by Sister Barbara, who isn't well in her senses." A sister in Bethanie of Brussels was accused in 1590 of stealing two hats, of committing "44 crimes" against two cats that she owned, of throwing a key at the head of one of the other sisters (a serious act in a day of large keys), of stating one day in choir, "please read a Pater Noster and an Ave for our Mater, lest she lose her soul in how she treats me," of yelling at the confessor when admonished for this, and then screaming at Mater, "You're my enemy to the death, I'd rather see the devil than you." Bishop Triest noted that there were "two rebellious sisters" among the Black Sisters of Pamele, that new sisters Anna and Jacoba were insolent libertines, that Sister Anna in the hospital of Hulst was "greatly rebellious, turbulent, and irreverent," that Mater was too "morose and choleric" and indiscreet in chastisement, and that Sister Coleta among the Brigittines of Dendermonde was "greatly rebellious." Even in the later decades of the history of Bethlehem, Anna Vignarola was burdened by a certain Sister Regina, who wrote letters to the Archbishop that Anna termed "utter fantasy." How many other sisters might have built paper trails as long and colorful as Margaret's, only for them to be destroyed and their stories lost?

But beyond her particular story, Margaret demonstrated as well, however unwittingly, that the Age of Reform involved more than ecclesiastical visitors expunging and proclaiming: among other things, her story showed the intricacies of personal relationships and the limits of enforcement. Thanks to these, Margaret, Adriana, and other nuns, though unquestionably influenced by the official style of reform, had the last word in the shaping of religious ideals and practice. And this, one suspects, was how most people of the time, in whatever type of community, experienced their religion.

As for other members of the cast . . .

While Pastor of Mol, Henri Joos kept wonderfully neat accounts of endowed Masses and major gifts to his church. To the end he also remained a champion of ecclesiastical tithes. Perhaps he was not a bad Pastor either, for the magistrates of Mol would say at his death that he had "served the community well and faithfully." After the controversy stirred in Bethlehem by the visitation of 1637, Henri Joos would live but one more year. And an unhappy year it was. In early 1638 he, with many others, fled Mol because of war, and took refuge with one of his sisters, who lived in the beguinage of Diest. He died there on September 14. In his will he left gifts to various people and institutions but nothing to the nuns of Bethlehem: not even any clue that he had ever known them. Was he wounded by the final expulsion of 1637, or did the nuns never mean quite as much to him as he did to some of them—or as much as Margaret said he did? His burial marker next to the ironstoned church of the beguinage of Diest contained an epitaph that in 1900 was still partly legible but said nothing significant. Most of the symbols and words had by that time worn almost smooth, probably because the marker lay under the corner of the roof and for centuries was constantly pelted by all the water that ran off, as if Margaret herself were trying to erase his memory. The tombstone no longer exists, probably destroyed during the world wars of the twentieth century.

Because of old age, Peter van der Wiel concluded his days as the Archbishop's Vicar-General in 1641, a few years after his last visitation to Bethlehem. He asked that when the end came he might be buried before a "privileged altar" or at least a "suitable place" in the choir of the cathedral, preferably near the stall where he had sung the Office for so many years. And he saw to it that alms would descend upon a wide range of people and institutions, especially male and female religious houses, even outside Mechelen. But he did not think the Grey Sisters of Leuven merited or needed his aid, for they were not among the many names listed in his will. Nor was there anything else to suggest that he had ever been anxious about the convent. He died in January 1643 and was buried as he requested, his grave marked by a stone that told of his strenuous labor for God. The grave was demolished on May 21, 1810, during the reign of Napoleon. As late as the twentieth century, the anniversary of his death was still sung every June 18.

Joost Bouckaert was nominated to the see of Ieper (in the western Spanish Netherlands) in 1639, around the time of his squabbles with Mater Adriana. Thus he departed his dear Scherpenheuvel and the Deanery of Diest, where he had been Pastor thirty-two years and Dean twenty-two years. Did he ever see Margaret again? Probably so, but there remained no record of such, nor of his ever serving again as official visitor to Bethlehem. He died in 1646 on All Souls Day, at age sixty-three—quite an achievement for a body wracked by so much affliction during his lifetime. His tombstone praised him as a true Pastor of his flock, who desired neither filthy money nor honors, but only to love God and his neighbors. Indeed for all his distinction, he was never too proud to ignore Margaret Smulders. Like Archbishop Boonen, perhaps even more so, he took her seriously.

Jacob Boonen remained as busy and generous as ever, donating 10,000 florins over the years to the local Mont de Piété, 8,000 to the "Repentants," 30,000 to "introduce reforms," and so on. His expenses for 1636 alone totaled 43,277 florins (a staggering amount even for the great), including many gifts to individuals and convents—but no word in account books or will about his dependent Margaret, or the Grey Sisters of Bethlehem. He continued to promote strict living in the archdiocese generally, calling in August 1644 for renewal and rededication and wondering how God would hear people's prayers to stop wars and plagues as long as they continued to wear "shameless clothes" and engaged in drunkenness. It was precisely his preference for strictness that made the Archbishop sympathetic to the so-called Jansenists, who during the 1640s were opposed strenuously by Jesuits, in the latest controversy within Catholicism over the roles of grace and works. When anti-Jansenists got the upper hand in Rome, the Archbishop's good reputation there eroded, until absolute ruin came in 1652: in that year the Pope suspended Archbishop Boonen and Bishop Triest of Gent from office for refusing to condemn Jansenism. Though both men submitted and were restored by August 1653, the last years of Jacob Boonen were sad. For he was forced to proclaim and enforce measures from Rome that he neither believed in nor liked. Some in Brussels, Madrid, and Rome labored to pay him a final indignity by trying to remove him from his seat, but before they could succeed he died, in June 1655, age eighty-three. For decades, even centuries, he remained suspicious to many, and his name, which may some-day be great, has always been clouded by the taint of Jansenism.

The nuns of Bethlehem were long regarded by fellow Franciscans and the ecclesiastical hierarchy as yet another plain, obscure convent. A Guardian in Leuven glibly commented in 1646 that "the monastery is well regarded (I think) among the people of Leuven, God be praised." In 1659 an official visitor noted the "abundant praise of great unity there," that it was a good community, and "full of sweetness," and left it at that. A loose document from around 1670 asserted that the sisters in Leuven lived long in "good order, both spiritually and temporally," but nothing more. And the Franciscan historian Carolo van Coudenhove wrote in 1680 that "little was known of this house." But of course there was much more to the nuns of Bethlehem.

True, the fate of some sisters was uncertain. There was no record of Lesken Nijns, who had been sent to Den Bosch but who in 1629 was, with her cosisters, run out of town by soldiers of the Dutch Republic. There was no record of Barbara Beli's days in the beguinage of Brussels, where she surely sat spinning tales of Bethlehem, just as the nuns of that convent feared she would. There was no record of when Maria Joos passed on, or Lesken Joos, but they certainly were gone by 1669, for Maria Coninxloo was then the eldest sister in the house.

More clear was that in Sister Coninxloo's old age some of her zeal flagged, for during a 1669 visitation the recently jubileed nun had "nothing to say," except that she did what she was able and that Mater mingled too rarely with the community. Clearest of all was that the period after 1639 was the heyday of Adriana Truis and Anna Vignarola. All the foundation laying they had done to control Bethlehem was now secure, and remained so for three decades. Adriana continued as Mater to her death around 1668, when she was replaced by Anna, longtime Vicaress. Together and separately these women met the challenges of the place as they thought necessary, displeasing as ever some along the way. An ecclesiastical visitor of 1663 concluded that the convent's old statutes were ignored on many points, including sisterly love, *clausura,* the grille, silence, and the rightful place of lay sisters. A visitation in 1669, when Anna Vignarola was Mater, yielded some praise, but criticism prevailed. Several nuns disliked their new fund-raiser, the school for girls. Others said that Anna was too familiar with certain sisters, that poor nuns were treated badly, that choir services were wretched, and that lay sisters were incorrigible. Old Joanna Schoensetters said simply that Mater Anna "does as she pleases." In the most damning assertions of all, Sister Regina noted that Anna hadn't been to Matins in three months and that the noon meal sometimes lasted from ten to three, while Sister Els Caussmans claimed that when Anna was present in choir, she ignored the services and counted money instead.

Anna and Adriana continued to vacillate on the age-old problem of jurisdiction, preferring either the Franciscans or the Archbishop according to the current interests of the convent. In 1672, in the midst of one debate on the subject, an elderly Anna composed a very brief history of the convent's confessors, in order to argue her current preference for jurisdiction. She reserved particular praise in this history for one Henri Joos, who had served in Bethlehem more than half a century before: it explained his unfortunate removal, and expressed such anguished resentment at his "unfair" treatment that it was as if the event had happened just weeks before. The troubles over confessors and jurisdiction were not solved by the time of Anna's death, but only in 1693, when the house, hoping to attract new members and escape its poverty, decided to adopt the strict reforms of the Franciscan Penitents, a branch that absolutely required the jurisdiction of the friars. And so at long last Bethlehem's ties with the archbishops of Mechelen ended.

The convent survived the political onslaughts of 1773, when Joseph II, new sovereign of the once Spanish (now Austrian) Netherlands, insisted that only "useful," active convents be allowed to continue. But the convent did not survive the military ravages of the French Revolution. In 1796 French soldiers came twice to Bethlehem, first to demand the convent's tax and property records (some of which the sisters refused to hand over), and then to expel the sisters and demolish the buildings. In the midst of destruction, someone took care to preserve the records kept back from the French, plus a solitary portrait, completed around 1650 and most probably the likeness of Adriana Truis. Like many nuns displaced by Revolution, some of those who fled the convent of Bethlehem left the religious life altogether and survived on pensions from the new Revolutionary government. Others traveled north and accepted yet another monastic reform, the so-called Reform of Limburg, from which grew the convents of Dongen (1801), Etten (1820), and Roosendaal (1835). Cousins of the old Grey Sisters of Leuven, they survived into the twentieth century.

But again, Bethlehem itself is gone, its buildings, grounds, and cemetery vanished. The space it once occupied, on the corner of the Penitentienenstraat and Mechelsestraat, has since become home to a brewery, government housing projects, and a café named Oh!

Champs Elysées! There you can go sip on a Spa or a Stella and wonder just exactly where a couple of nuns named Margaret Smulders and Adriana Truis waged battles of life and death, or what a confessor named Joos looked like coming around the corner from St. Gertrude's to visit.

Bibliographical Notes

Works that influenced my approach, and provide general background to monasticism and the Age of Reformation, are noted under "Approaches to Early Modern Religion and Culture" and "To the Curious Reader." The remaining notes are organized by chapter and shadow the structure of each. I have not attempted systematically to update the bibliography that appeared in the first edition, but have kept the focus on those works that most influenced my telling of Margaret's story.

Archives Consulted, with Abbreviations

AAM   Archive of the Archdiocese of Mechelen-Brussels
       FK   Fonds Kloosters
       FA   Fonds Archiepiscopalia
       FM   Fonds Mechliniensia
       FV   Fonds Vicariaat
ARA   State Archives of Belgium
       GR   Geheime Raad
       KAB   Kerkarchief Brabant
       RSA   Raad van State en Audiëntie
BAA   Archive of the Diocese of Antwerp, Fonds Parochialia, Parochie Mol
GZ   Archive of the Archdiocese of Mechelen-Brussels, Fonds Kloosters, Grey Sisters of Leuven

KAM   Archive of the Chapter of St. Rombout's in Mechelen (housed at
       the AAM)
       FA   Fonds Archiepiscopalia
KB   Royal Albert I Library, Brussels, Handschriften
RAA   State Archive of Antwerp, Fonds Kerkarchieven
RAG   State Archive of Gent
       B   Bisdom Mechelen
SAL   Municipal Archive of Leuven
ST   Provincial Archive of the Franciscans, St. Truiden

Abbreviations of Periodicals and Reference Works

AHEB   *Analectes pour servir à l'histoire ecclésiastique de la Belgique*
ARG   *Archive for Reformation History/Archiv für Reformationsge-
        schichte*
CHR   *Catholic Historical Review*
DS   *Dictionnaire de Spiritualité*
FL   *Franciscaans Leven*
FR   *Franciscana*
HKKM   *Handelingen van de Koninklijke Kring voor Oudheidkunde, Let-
        teren en Kunst van Mechelen*
NBW   *Nationaal Biografisch Woordenboek*
NF   *Neerlandia Franciscana*
OGE   *Ons Geestelijk Erf*
SCJ   *Sixteenth Century Journal*

Approaches to Early Modern Religion and Culture

P. Burke, *The Historical Anthropology of Early Modern Italy* (Cambridge,
1987).

R. Chartier, *Cultural History* (Ithaca, N.Y., 1988).

P. Mack Crew, *Calvinist Preaching and Iconoclasm in the Netherlands,
1544–1569* (Cambridge, 1978).

R. Darnton, *The Great Cat Massacre* (New York, 1984).

N. Davis, *Fiction in the Archives* (Stanford, 1987); "From 'Popular Religion' to Religious Cultures," in *Reformation Europe: A Guide to Re-*

search, ed. S. Ozment (St. Louis, 1982); and *Society and Culture in Early Modern France* (Stanford, 1975).

C. Ginzburg, *The Cheese and the Worms* (Baltimore, 1980).

L. Hunt, ed., *The New Cultural History* (Berkeley, 1989).

J. Obelkevich, ed., *Religion and the People, 800–1700* (Chapel Hill, 1979).

E. Muir and G. Ruggiero, eds., *Microhistory and the Lost Peoples of Europe* (Baltimore, 1991), and *Sex and Gender in Historical Perspective* (Baltimore, 1990).

S. Ozment, ed., *Religion and Culture in the Renaissance and Reformation* (Kirksville, Mo., 1989).

D. Sabean, *Power in the Blood* (Cambridge, 1984).

C. Trinkaus and H. Oberman, eds., *The Pursuit of Holiness in Late Medieval and Renaissance Religion* (Leiden, 1974).

To the Curious Reader

Medieval Female Religious: Some general background works are C. H. Lawrence, *Medieval Monasticism* (New York, 1984); L. Eckenstein, *Women Under Monasticism* (New York, 1963); E. Power, *Medieval English Nunneries, c. 1275 to 1535* (Cambridge, 1922); L. T. Shank and J. A. Nichols, eds., *Medieval Religious Women. II. Peaceweavers* (Kalamazoo, 1987); and P. D. Johnson, *Equal in Monastic Profession: Religious Women in Medieval France* (Chicago, 1991); plus a host of specialized studies, such as R. Bell, *Holy Anorexia* (Chicago, 1985), and C. W. Bynum, *Holy Feast and Holy Fast* (Berkeley, 1987).

General Works on Early Modern Female Religious: I consulted J. Irwin, "Society and the Sexes," in *Reformation Europe,* ed. Ozment; K. Norberg, "The Counter-Reformation and Women, Religious and Lay," in *Catholicism in Early Modern History: A Guide to Research,* ed. John O'Malley (St. Louis, 1988), 133–46; F. E. Weaver, "Women and Religion in Early Modern France: A Bibliographical Essay on the State of the Question," *CHR* 67 (1981): 50–59, plus journals and histories of individual orders, such as *Franciscana,* M.-C. Gueudre, *Histoire de l'ordre des Ursulines en France,* 2 vols. (Paris, 1963), J. Moorman, *A History of the Franciscan Order . . . to the Year 1517* (Oxford, 1968), W. A. Hinnebusch, *The History of the Dominican Order: Origins and Growth to 1500* (New York, 1966), L. J. Lekai, *The*

Cistercians: Ideals and Reality (Kent State, 1977), *Monasticon Belge,* 7 vols. so far (Maredsous and Liège, 1890–1984), F. Hervé-Bazin, *Les grands ordres et congrégations des femmes* (Paris, 1889), K. Beloch, *Bevölkerungsgeschichte Italiens* (Berlin, 1939, 1961), and G. Pellicia, G. Rocca, et al., *Dizionario degli instituti di Perfezione* (Rome, 1974–   ).

Specialized Works on Early Modern Female Religious (by region): I profited from J. Brown, *Immodest Acts: The Life of a Lesbian Nun in Renaissance Italy* (Oxford, 1986); G. A. Brucker, "Monasteries, Friaries, and Nunneries in Quattrocento Florence," in *Christianity and the Renaissance: Image and Religious Imagination in the Quattrocento,* ed. T. Verdon and J. Henderson (Syracuse, 1990), 41–62; N. Rubinstein, "Lay Patronage and Observant Reform in Fifteenth-Century Florence," in *Christianity and the Renaissance,* ed. Verdon and Henderson, 63–82; Fulvio Tomizza, *Heavenly Supper: The Story of Maria Janis* (Chicago, 1991); E. Weaver, "Spiritual Fun: A Study of Sixteenth-Century Tuscan Convent Theater," in *Women in the Middle Ages and the Renaissance,* ed. M. B. Rose (Syracuse, 1986), 173–206; J. Bilinkoff, *The Avila of St. Teresa* (Ithaca, N.Y., 1989); R. E. Surtz, *The Guitar of God: Gender, Power, and Authority in the Visionary World of Mother Juana de la Cruz, 1481–1534* (Philadelphia, 1990); R. Devos, *Vie religieuse féminine et société: L'origine sociale des Visitandines d'Annecy aux XVIIe et XVIIIe siècles* (Annecy, 1973); C. Dolan, *Entre Tours et Clochers: Les gens d'église à Aix-en-Provence au XVIe siècle* (Sherbrooke, 1981); W. Gibson, *Women in Seventeenth-Century France* (New York, 1989); E. Rapley, *The Dévotes* (Montreal, 1990); especially G. Reynes, *Couvents de femmes: La vie des religieuses contemplatives dans la France des XVIIe et XVIIIe siècles* (Paris, 1987); and F. E. Weaver, *The Evolution of the Reform of Port-Royal* (Paris, 1978).

Active Female Religious: H. O. Evenett, *The Spirit of the Counter-Reformation* (Cambridge, 1968); C. Jones, *The Charitable Imperative: Hospitals and Nursing in Ancien Régime and Revolutionary France* (New York, 1988); R. P. Liebowitz, "Virgins in the Service of Christ: The Dispute over an Active Apostolate for Women During the Counter Reformation," in *Women of Spirit,* ed. R. Ruether and E. McLaughlin (New York, 1979), 131–52.

Female Religious of the Spanish Netherlands: E. Persoons, "Panorama van de reguliere clerus in de 17de eeuw," in *(Nieuwe) Algemene Geschiedenis der Nederlanden* 8 (1980): 383–92, is an informed short survey with a good bibliography. E. de Moreau, *Histoire de l'église en Belgique,* 5 vols. (Brussels, 1952), 5 (1559–1633), and A. Pasture, *La Restauration Religieuse aux Pays-Bas sous les Archiducs Albert et Isabelle, 1596–1633* (Leuven, 1925), include valuable information on religious.

More specialized titles (by language and religious order) include J. Ramsey, ed., *English Benedictine Nuns in Flanders, 1598–1687: Annals of Their Five Communities* (London, 1909); J. M. Canivez, *L'Ordre de Cîteaux en Belgique des origines (1132) au XXe siècle* (Forges les-Chimay, 1926); T. Ploegaerts, *Les moniales de l'ordre de Cîteaux dans les Pays-Bas méridionaux, depuis le XVIe siècle jusqu'à la révolution française, 1550–1800* (Westmalle, 1936–37); M. Sabbe et al., *Bernardus en de Cisterciënzerfamilie in Belgie, 1090–1990* (Leuven, 1990); P. Hildebrand, *De Capucijnen in de Nederlanden en het prinsbisdom Luik,* 11 vols. (Antwerp, 1945–56); Ph. Schmitz, *Histoire de l'ordre de Saint-Benoît* (Maredsous, 1948); M.-J. Juvyns, "La communauté des Riches-Claires de Bruxelles de 1585 à 1796," *Cahiers Bruxellois* 10 (1965): 181–239; J. Corstjens, "De Franciscanessen van het klooster OLVrouw-Ter-Rivieren te Bree, 1464–1797" (Licentiaatsverhandeling, Leuven, 1984); F. van der Berghe, J. van den Heuvel, G. Verhelst, *De Zwartzusters van Brugge, Diksmuide, Oostende, Veurne, en Brazilië* (Brugge, 1986); K. Baert and J. Dauwe, *Zwarte Zusters van Sint-Augustinus te Aalst* (Aalst, 1975); J. Okeley, *De Gasthuiszusters en hun ziekenzorg in het Aartsbisdom Mechelen,* 2 vols. (Brussels, 1992); D. Laureys, "Het Elzenklooster te Zichem: Een Slotklooster van Reguliere Kanunnikessen van Sint-Augustinus, 1660–1797" (Licentiaatsverhandeling, Leuven, 1987); H. de Backer, "Het Arme Clarenklooster te Mechelen, vanaf 1500 tot de Opheffing in 1966" (Licentiaatsverhandeling, Leuven, 1977); C. van de Wiel, "Bibliotheekinventaris van de Priorij Blijdenberg te Mechelen in 1743," *OGE* 47 (1973): 170–202, and "De begijnhoven en de vrouwelijke kloostergemeenschappen in het aartsbisdom Mechelen, 1716–1801," *OGE* 44 (1970): 152–212, 241–327; 45 (1971): 179–214; 46 (1972): 278–344, 369–428; E. Persoons, "De bewoners van de kloosters Bethlehem te Herent en Ten Troon te Grobbendonk," *Arca Lovaniensis* (1976): 221–40. For Grey Sisters specifically, see the notes to chapter 1.

The Meaning of Catholic Reform After Trent: I began with John O'Malley, *Catholicism in Early Modern History: A Guide to Research* (St. Louis, 1988); Ozment, ed., *Reformation Europe;* J. Bossy, *Christianity in the West, 1400–1700* (Oxford, 1985), and "The Counter-Reformation and the People of Catholic Europe," *Past and Present* 47 (1970): 51–70; Evennett, *The Spirit of the Counter-Reformation*. Also Jean Delumeau, *Catholicism Between Luther and Voltaire* (London and Philadelphia, 1977; first French edition, Paris, 1971); R. Muchembled, *Popular Culture and Elite Culture in France, 1400–1750* (Baton Rouge and London, 1985; first French edition, Paris, 1978); J. Wirth, "Against the Acculturation Thesis," in *Religion and Society in Early Modern Europe, 1500–1800*, ed. K. von Greyerz (London, 1984), 66–78; C. Harline, "Official Religion—Popular Religion in Recent Historiography of the Catholic Reformation," *ARG* 81 (1990): 239–62; R. Po-Chia Hsia, *Social Discipline in the Reformation* (New York, 1990); W. Reinhard, "Gegenreformation als Modernisierung? Prolegomena zu einer theorie des konfessionellen Zeitalters," *ARG* 68 (1977): 226–52, and "Zwang zur Konfessionalisierung? Prolegomena zu einer theorie des konfessionellen Zeitalters," *Zeitschrift für historische Forschung* 10 (1983): 257–77; E. Cochrane, *Florence in the Forgotten Centuries, 1527–1800* (Chicago, 1973), and "New Light on Post-Tridentine Italy: A Note on Recent Counter-Reformation Scholarship," *CHR* 56 (1970): 291–319; John O'Malley, "Was Ignatius Loyola a Church Reformer? How to Look at Early Modern Catholicism," *CHR* 77/2 (1991): 177–93. Both O'Malley, ed., *Catholicism in Early Modern Europe*, and Ozment, ed., *Reformation Europe*, contain excellent bibliographies of specific works that illustrate the complexity of Catholic Reform.

Catholic Reform in the Spanish Netherlands: Numerous studies are discussed in two most useful introductions: James D. Tracy, "With and Without the Counter-Reformation: The Catholic Church in the Spanish Netherlands and the Dutch Republic, 1580–1650," *CHR* 71 (1985): 547–75, and M. Cloet and F. Daelemans, eds., *Godsdienst, Mentaliteit en Dagelijks Leven: Religieuze geschiedenis in Belgie sinds 1970* (Brussels, 1988).

PROLOGUE: REMEMBERING

How Margaret Composed Her Letter, How Long It Took, What the Nuns Had to Eat, Where Margaret Was Allowed in the Convent, and Various Foibles of Other Nuns: GZ/3, Margaret's long letter for the visitation of 1628. Because Catharina was Margaret's liaison with the convent, I've assumed that it was Catharina who brought the meal, and also that it was at this time of day that Catharina broke the news about visitation.

GZ/8, "Heymelijcke Instructie" (dated July 10, 1636), "Secreta Instructio Matris," and "Jacob byder gratie Godts," also suggest where Margaret was allowed within the convent during the years she was exiled to the guest house.

Margaret's Lack of Hope for Forgiveness, Her Delinquent Jesuit Confessor, Her Request for a Relic and a Picture of St. Joseph: GZ/8, February 3, 1628, to Bouckaert. Various sisters also mention, in letters between 1626 and 1628, the house confessor's refusal to comfort Margaret.

Maria Petyt and the Sparrow: A. Deblaere, *De mystieke schrijfster Maria Petyt* (Gent, 1962), and Psalms 102:7, part of the fifth penitential Psalm.

CHAPTER 1: BEGINNING

Entry, Profession, and the Geographical Origins of Sisters: AAM, FK, Generalia, "Catalogus virginum quae in regione Lovaniensi examinata sunt ad professionem anno 1605" (which in fact goes beyond 1605); Margaret's interview for profession was on April 13, 1606. Of sisters who entered between 1605 and 1640 one was from Stalle, one from Chamont, five from Brussels, two from Tienen, two from Balen, four from Leuven, and one from Schiedam.

Margaret's Income: GZ/8, March 27, 1624, Margaret to Boonen.

Forced and "Romantic" Entries of Nuns: E. Power, *Medieval People* (London, 1924); Power, *English Medieval Nunneries;* Gibson, *Women in Seventeenth-Century France.*

Gifts and Dowries to Convents: Brown, *Immodest Acts;* Corstjens, "De Franciscanessen van OLV-Ter-Rivieren," 50, 51, 72; Juvyns, "La communauté des Riches-Claires," 206–7; P. Hildebrand, "Le couvent des Soeurs Grises à Iseghem, d'avant 1486 jusqu'en 1796," *NF* 2 (1919): 8–55; ARA, Fonds Notariaat Leuven, 13023; SAL, 4279; L. van Buyten, "Kwantitatieve bijdrage tot de studie van de 'Kloosterdemografie' in het Leuvense: De priorij 's-Hertogeneiland te Gempe, het zwartzustersklooster en de communauteit van het Groot-Ziekengasthuis te Leuven, 16de–18de eeuw," *Arca Lovaniensis* (1976): 241–76; Schmitz, *Histoire de l'ordre de Saint-Benoît*, 246–47.

Number of Women Seeking Entry: Brown, *Immodest Acts*, 32–37; Weaver, "Spiritual Fun."

Patronage in Convents: GZ/6, 1587 letter to Archbishop Hauchinus from an heir of one of the founders of Bethlehem; and GZ/8, Barbara van Herssen to Boonen, reveal some assumptions about patronage.

Origins of the Grey Sisters of Leuven: "Le couvent des Soeurs Grises de Louvain," *AHEB* 7 (1870): 213–17, on the convent's early days; also E. van Even, *Louvain dans le passé et dans le présent* (Leuven, 1895); R. van Uytven, ed., *Leuven: "de beste stad van Brabant"* (Leuven, 1980), 1, "De geschiedenis van het stadsgewest Leuven tot omstreeks 1600"; Van de Wiel, "Franciscaanse Archiefbronnen"; and assorted manuscripts in GZ, to 1605.

Physical Growth of Convents: SAL, 4262–63, on the Clares. Numerous letters give clues to the physical layout of Bethlehem: ARA, GR, 1125, August 10, 1594, and its response, September 10, plus documents dated between 1665 and 1669; SAL, 4278, in 1666.

The Third Order and Grey Sisters: Moorman, *History of the Franciscan Order;* Hinnebusch, *History of the Dominican Order;* and Lekai, *The Cistercians.* On Grey Sisters, J. de Cuyper, "Het 'Susterhuys' van Kortrijk: Het klooster van de Grauwe Zusters in de 15de en 16de eeuw," *De Leiegouw* 24 (1982): 3–15; G. van de Castele, "Grauwe Zusters of Penitenten-Rekollektinen te Nevele: 1502–1784," *Het Land van Nevele* 9 (1978): 155–247; J. Grauwels, "Een lijkbaarkleed der Grauwzusters," *Limburg* 62 (1983): 189; L.-L. Gruart, "Les Soeurs Grises de Comines," *Bulletin de la Comité Flamand de France* 14 (1951): 53–87; Hildebrand, "Le couvent des Soeurs Grises à Iseghem"; H. Lemaître, "Les soins hospitaliers à domicile, donnés dès le XIVe siècle par des Religieuses Franciscaines, les Soeurs Noires et les Soeurs Grises," *Revue d'histoire Franciscaine* 1 (1924): 180–208, and "Statuts des Religieuses du Tiers Ordre Franciscain dites Soeurs Grises Hospitalières," *Archivum Franciscanum Historicum* 4 (1911): 713–31; A. Roeykens, "Het Onstaan van het Klooster der Grauwzusters te Edingen in het begin van de 16de eeuw," *FR* 27 (1972): 51–90; H. Roggen, "Le Tiers Ordre Séculier et Régulier," in *Dictionnaire d'histoire et de géographie ecclésiastiques* 18 (Paris, 1977): cols. 965–71; G. Schoonaert, "Onderwijsstructuren in de 16e eeuw te Poperinge: de graeuwe susteren alleenelyck dochterkens leerende," *Aan de Schreve* 14 (1984): 28–31. The rule of Leo X, in GZ/1.

The City of Leuven: Van Even, *Louvain;* Van Uytven, *Leuven: "de beste* stad"; A. Meulemans, *Atlas van Oud-Leuven* (Leuven, 1981); H. van der Wee, ed., *The Rise and Decline of Urban Industries in Italy and in the Low Countries, Late Middle Ages–Early Modern Times* (Leuven, 1988).

St. Renildis and Other Relics: GZ/7, September 26, 1603; Pétin, ed., *Dictionnaire Hagiographique* 2 (Paris, 1850): col. 872; O. Wimmer and H. Melzer, *Lexicon der Namen und Heiligen* (Innsbruck, n.d.), 705; Anna Vignarola to the archdiocesan hierarchy, GZ/10, February 25, 1661; Gruart, "Les Soeurs Grises de Comines," on the famous relics there.

Bethlehem's Obscurity: P. Carolo van Coudenhove, OFM, *Provinciae Germaniae Inferioris Compendiosa Descriptio* (1680); information about Hertogendaal and Beaupré from J. de Brouwer, *Bijdrage tot de Geschiedenis van het Godsdienstig Leven . . . in het Land van Aalst tussen 1550 en 1621 . . .* (Aalst, 1961), 256; Fra Angelico in W. Hood, "Fra Angelico at San Marco: Art and the Liturgy of Cloistered Life," in *Christianity and the Renaissance*, ed. Verdon and Henderson; traffic on the Dyle from SAL, 3825–27, Dyle, and Margaret's visitation letters of 1628 and 1633, in GZ/1 and 3.

Procedures and Ceremonies for New Postulants and Novices: For Bethlehem see the rule of Leo X, and the house statutes of 1626, in GZ/1; also P. F. X. de Ram, *Synodicon belgicum, sive acta omnium ecclesiarum belgii a celebrato concilio tridentino usque ad concordatum anni 1801*, 4 vols. (Mechelen and Leuven, 1828–58), 2:492; and the "Catalogus virginum," op. cit., in AAM; Van Buyten, "Kloosterdemografie," on the length of probation for postulants and novices; specifics of the ceremonies are not in the statutes for Bethlehem, but see Petrus Marchant, *Den Reghel der Derder Orden van S. Fransoys* (Gent, 1626), and *Af-beeldinghe Des waerachtigh Christen Mensch, Naer het voor-beelt vanden Reghel der derder Ordre Van den Godt-salighen Vader S. Franchois* (Gent, 1639).

Training and Retention of Postulants and Novices: The house statutes for Bethlehem, in GZ/1; AAM, FM, Hospital Ninove/8, statutes; Bonaventure's *Spieghel der Goeder Manieren veur de Novitie, dat is, Proef-ionghers der Minder-broeders Ordene* (Antwerp, 1605); Cartusianus, *De Leere der Religieusen* (Brussel, 1626); Reynes, *Couvents de femmes*, 41–45, 50–51; Moorman, *History of the Franciscan Order*, 33.

Profession Ceremony: Not all details of the ceremony are in Bethlehem's statutes; I have supplemented these with GZ/11, letter by General Caraffa, January 19, 1647; M. Hereswitha, "Reguliere Kanunnikessen van het Heilig-

Graf," *OGE* 50/4 (December 1976): 401–2; Marchant, *Af-beeldinghe;* RAG, B, M242/22, "Forma vestitionis et professionis monialium in hospitali Gerardimonten/"; and De Ram, *Synodicon belgicum,* 1:322.

Chapter 2: Demons

Visitation of 1616: GZ/3. Anna Vignarola wrote in GZ/8, December 29, 1672, that Margaret's troubles started "soon" after profession, which occurred in 1606—but there is no clue of precisely when Margaret was forced to leave.

Witchery and Animals: F. Vanhemelryck, *Heksenprocessen in de Neder-landen* (Leuven, 1982), 110; J. Sumption, *Pilgrimage: An Image of Medi-aeval Religion* (Totowa, N.J., 1975), 16; K. Thomas, *Religion and the De-cline of Magic* (New York, 1971), 481; and J. Klaits, *Servants of Satan: The Age of the Witch Hunts* (Bloomington, 1985), 110.

Witchcraft Generally: P. Bange, ed., *Tussen Heks en Heilige* (Nijmegen, 1985); M. Caron, ed., *Helse en Hemelse Vrouwen* (Utrecht, 1988); Thomas, *Religion and the Decline of Magic;* Vanhemelryck, *Heksenprocessen;* Christian, *Local Religion;* Klaits, *Servants of Satan;* Th. Penneman, "Processen en Moeilijkheden wegens Toveren en Onttoveren in het Land van Waas tijdens de XVIde en XVIIde eeuw," *Handelingen van het XLIe Congres, Federatie van de Kringen voor Oudheidkunde en Geschiedenis van Belgie* 2 (1971): 221–40; L. T. Maes, "Un procès de sorcellerie en 1642, évalué à la lumière de récentes études européennes et d'après la législation et la théorie du droit du XVIIe siècle," *HKKM* 79 (1975): 243–68; R. Muchembled, "The Witches of the Cambrésis: The Acculturation of the Rural World in the Sixteenth and Seventeenth Centuries," in *Religion and the People,* ed. Obelkevich.

Possession: H. C. Erik Midelfort, "The Devil and the German People: Reflections on the Popularity of Demon Possession in Sixteenth-Century Germany," in *Religion and Culture,* ed. Ozment; D. P. Walker, *Unclean Spirits: Possession and Exorcism in France and England in the Late Sixteenth and Early Seventeenth Centuries* (Philadelphia, 1981); A. Lottin, *Lille: Cit-adelle de la Contre-Réforme? 1598–1668* (Paris, 1984), 177; Vanhemlryck, *Heksenprocessen,* 57. See also notes to chapters 4 and 5.

Marie Everaerts: Maes, "Un procès de sorcellerie en 1642," and *Vijf eeuwen stedelijk strafrecht: Bijdrage tot de rechts- en cultuurgeschiedenis der*

Nederlanden (Antwerp and The Hague, 1947), 211; R. Foncke, "Mechelsche Folklore: Een heksenproces ten jare 1602," *Mechlinia* 4 (1925): 121–32; AAM, FV, V/11, undated, identifies Marie as a Grey Sister; also AAM, FM, 3/fols. 253–55, and 6/fol. 58vo., 174vo.; GZ/5, 1597, testament of Marie Switten. Mater Barbara Noosen's comment on past witches in GZ/8, March 28, 1624, unsigned letter (in her hand) to Boonen. That sisters were corrupted during the exile to Cologne is from Anna Vignarola's short history of Bethlehem's confessors, December 29, 1672, GZ/8.

Chapter 3: Confessors

Women, Priesthood, and Confessors: D. Herlihy, *Opera Muliebria: Women and Work in Medieval Europe* (New York, 1990), 118–19; Norberg, "The Counter-Reformation and Women"; J. Bilinkoff, "Confessors, Penitents, and the Construction of Identities in Early Modern Avila," in *Culture and Identity in Early Modern Europe: Essays in Honor of Natalie Zemon Davis*, ed. B. Diefendorf and C. Hesse (Ann Arbor, 1993), 83–102. Some problems perceived by contemporary males in confessing women are discussed in chapter 7.

Troublesome Confessors: Brown, *Immodest Acts*, 38; Van de Casteele, "Grauwe Zusters te Nevele," 181–83; AAM, FK, Begijnhof Aarschot/2, visit by Bouckaert, September 7, 1628, and March 29, 1629; AAM, FK, Black Sisters Leuven/32, 1689; AAM, FK, Bethanie Brussels/4, 1590 visitation; C. Harline and E. Put, "A Bishop in the Cloisters: The Visitations of Mathias Hovius, Malines, 1596–1620," *SCJ* 22/4 (Winter 1991): 611–12.

Henri Joos and St. Gertrude's: ARA, KAB, 10752 is a "manuale" of some of his receipts; AAM, FK, St. Gertrude's Leuven/8 contains two other account books by Joos, plus a notarial act of June 8, 1624; AAM, FK, St. Gertrude's Leuven/2, contains other information on the abbey of St. Gertrude's, including its spiritual problems, revealed through visitations of November 1631, among others. Reports of Joos as Pastor, by the Archbishop's visitors, in AAM, Fonds Dekenale Verslagen/L1.

Henri Joos as Confessor of Bethlehem: GZ/5, December 30, 1610; SAL, 7334, fol. 388v and 487; GZ/1, 1616 visitation; Anna Vignarola's short history of 1672, in GZ/8.

Lesken Nijns: Her story is pieced together almost entirely from the journal of Archbishop Hovius, in AAM, FM, 10. In documents written by the sisters of Bethlehem her name is mentioned only once, but this single mention (by Margaret) confirms the events in the journal of Archbishop Hovius and her connection with Bethlehem and Henri Joos. The most important entries in the Manuale are June 22, July 4, 6, 7, 8, 14, 17, 19, August 8, 11, 25, 26, 27, 28, 30, September 2, 7, 11, 16, October 20, 27, 30, November 3, 5, and December 4 and 9, all in 1618; and March 5, 1619.

Margaret and Henri Joos: The entries dealing obviously with Margaret (there are other possibilities as well among the many cryptic entries in the journal) are July 14, August 1, September 20, October 18–20, November 23, and December 12, all in 1618.

The Ties of the Grey Sisters of Leuven with Mechelen, Especially the Black Sisters of Mechelen: "Cession du couvent de Louvain aux Soeurs Grises de Malines," *AHEB* 7 (1870): 217–19; G. Marnef, *Het Calvinistisch Bewind te Mechelen, 1580–1585* (Kortrijk, 1987); AAM, FK, Black Sisters Mechelen/57 (which has much about the Grey Sisters, too); AAM, FM/2, fol. 55, February 7, 1586; AAM, FM/7, fol. 21, October 10, 1606, and AAM, FM/6, fol. 182, same date; ST, folder "Documenten Grauwsusters Leuven, Mechelen."

Henri Joos's Dismissal from Bethlehem, and Margaret's Charges: GZ/5, July 5, 1618. Margaret's later assertions about Joos's advances are from GZ/8, February 23, 1624, a letter by Evangelista to Boonen. The part of the letter that contains Margaret's charge is torn in a crucial place, leaving only the "s" at the end of the name, which I presume is "Henri Joos." The crucial phrases read as follows, with torn segments indicated by [ ] and common abbreviations by { }: "Everyone is of the opinion [that when] she left the convent some years ago, she did this so that she [might be freed] from the possession of the demons; which she denies, but says rather that she did this to avoid [. . . Joo]s, who had spiritual charge of the convent at that time, for he persecuted her very much with his importuning, because of his lust, so that from this [subject verb missing] the diabolical possession which followed." In Latin, "omnium est opinio q[uod] [. . .] [a]nte annos aliquot e monasterio exivit, illud fecerit ut a daemonis posses- [sionem] [. . .]etur; quod it[a] non esse affirmat, sed potius ut per hoc evadere posset [. . . Joo]s, qui eo t{em}p{o}re [mo]nasterii curam habebat, is enim hanc aff{ect} u carnali mu[ltum] [se]quutus [est . . .] importune, ut ex hoc [. . .] sequentem daemonis possession[em]." Obviously there is some guesswork involved here, but especially "affectu carnali" and "who had spiritual charge of the convent at the time" say much. My thanks to Louis Perraud for his comments on this selection.

Possession and Human Agents: Thomas, *Religion and the Decline of Magic;* Midelfort, "The Devil and the German People," 109; Walker and Dickerman, " 'A Woman Under the Influence' "; Walker, *Unclean Spirits,* 8.

Turned Exorcists: AAM, FV, V/11 (Toverye), February 27, 1627, a case involving one Maria Spadens; Vanhemelryck, *Heksenprocessen,* 52; AAM, FV, V/11, October 5, 1616, Frater Guilielmus, the Capuchin; the Spanish example in S. Nalle, *God in La Mancha: Religious Reform and the People of Cuenca, 1500–1650* (Baltimore, 1992), 19–20; and the Brussels scandal in C. Harline and E. Put, *A Bishop's Tale: Mathias Hovius Among His Flock in Seventeenth-Century Flanders* (New Haven, 2000), chapter 7.

Sexuality, Convents, and Possession: Sumption, *Pilgrimage,* 17; Lottin, *Lille,* especially 178; Caron, ed., *Helse en Hemelse Vrouwen* on St. Anthony; Klaits, *Servants of Satan,* 113–14; Reynes, *Couvents de femmes,* 160; Thomas, *Religion and the Decline of Magic,* 478–81; Walker and Dickerman, " 'A Woman Under the Influence,' " 549; M. de Certeau, *La possession de Loudun* (Paris, 1970); J. Bilinkoff, "A Spanish Prophetess and Her Patrons: The Case of María de Santo Domingo," *SCJ* 23/1 (Spring 1992): 21–34.

More on Margaret, Lesken, and Henri Joos: The 1672 account by Anna Vignarola, cited above, does not mention Margaret and Lesken by name, but they are clearly, based on other sources, the nuns Anna had in mind; this account (1) connects the three main players, (2) ties Lesken to the problem of possession and confirms that she too had private sessions with Joos, (3) suggests that Archbishop Hovius removed Joos for causes other than that he disliked him, (4) establishes that soon after the removal of 1618 the sisters came to know or suspect who had made the charges against Joos, and (5) that the sisters were soon telling tales about it themselves, since Anna professed in 1624 and had her knowledge of the events of 1616–18 from other sisters.

The Death of Mater Judoca, the Election of a New Mater in Bethlehem, and the Attempt to Transfer Jurisdiction: Hovius's Manuale, February 1, 2, April 30, and May 21–23, 1619.

Henri Joos After Bethlehem: R. Knaepen, *Mol—Baelen—Desschel, 1559–1795: De oude Keizerlijke Vrijheid en haar Voogdijdistrict* (Mol, 1982), 71–89; and especially BAA, Parochialia, Mol/XI, November 21, 1623; XIII, ca. November 6, 1623, September 16, 1623, October 2, 1623, plus letters of support by various Jesuits for Joos's nomination to Mol. After his appointment, various troubles in XIII, March 20, 1624, June 29, 1624, and July 13, 1624. My thanks to Marie-Juliette Marinus for these last references. See also his account books cited above in this chapter.

CHAPTER 4: DESPAIR

Margaret's Disturbances and Her Plea for Help: GZ/8, January 16, 1624, Petrus Lucius to Boonen; Margaret's plea in GZ/8 is undated, but given the events described, given events from other dated sources, given when the novice's things were scattered (December 1623), given that Evangelista would write his final assessment of these disturbances in February 1624, I think it was written before her attempted suicide on January 17.

Margaret's Attempt at Suicide: GZ/8; Mater Barbara's short note was written on the "27th" but does not name a month. St. Paul's conversion, however, which she mentions as the date of healing, was January 25, and so the 27th was likely in January. Catharina's letter, also in GZ/8, is not dated either, but notes specifically that the attempt was on the night of January 17–18. I think both Barbara's and Catharina's letters were sent on January 27, the same day as the petition from the sisters, in GZ/8. My scenario of the petition's composition is derived from the document itself, knowledge of relationships among the sisters, and the various hands. Likewise my scenario of Barbara and Catharina writing their letters. See on the petition also GZ/5, January 2, 1625, Boonen's response, to the Dean of Leuven. Klaits, *Servants of Satan,* 116, on possessed nuns tearing veils and habits. Other examples of nocturnal disturbances being associated with the devil in C. Thielemans, *Cort Verhael van het Leven der Heylighen van S. Franciscus Oirden met Haer Levende Figuren wt Diversche historie scryvers genomen* (Den Bosch, 1620), and Maes, *Vijf Eeuwen Mechelen,* who cites a victim testifying that disturbances happened especially when she was being exorcised.

Jacob Boonen: P. Claessens, *Histoire des archevêques de Malines,* 1 (Leuven, 1881); J. Lefèvre, "La nomination des archevêques de Malines sous l'ancien régime," *HKKM* 63 (1959): 75–92; L. Ceyssens, "Jacobus Boonen," in *NBW,* 2 (Brussels, 1966): cols. 74–89; L. Jadin, "Procès d'information pour la nomination des évêques et abbés des Pays-Bas, de Liège et de Franche-Comté d'après les Archives de la Congrègation Consistoriale,

1637–1709," *Bulletin de l'Institute historique belge de Rome* (1929): 133–38, 148–55, which is especially helpful for the opinions other ecclesiastical figures held of him; G. de Munck, "Het bisdom Gent van 1609 tot 1621: Carolus Maes (1609–1612), Franciscus van der Burch (1613–1616), Jacobus Boonen (1617–1621)," *Collationes Gandavenses* 14 (1927): 40–45. The comparison to Moses was made by Michel Zachtmoorter, *Thalamus Sponsi, oft t'Bruydegoms Beddeken* (Antwerp, 1623), preface; other praise in KAM, FA, Boonen/73 (Bewind, Varia), a program titled *Tragicomedie, Isaacus Angelus Comnenus, Empereur de Constantinople* (Mechelen, 1628). His active involvement in all institutions of the archdiocese is reflected in such sources as AAM, FK, Aarschot Begijnhof/2, visitation 1631; AAM, FK, Mechelen Leprozije/1, 1632 statutes, which include his hand in the marginal notes; ARA, RSA, 2041/1, March 21, 1625, September 12, 1622, December 31, 1622; AAM, FA, Boonen/186 (his agenda), January 12, 20, April 27, May 10, June 8, October 26, November 10, 1622; January 11, February 4, May 10, 20, July 9, October 5, December 26, 1623; January 5, 1624.

On Model Bishops: P. Broutin, *Le Réforme pastorale en France au XVIIe siècle*, 2 vols. (Paris, 1956), and *L'évêque dans la tradition pastorale du XVIe siècle* (Brugge, 1953; Broutin's French adaptation of H. Jedin, *Das Bischofsideal der Katholischen Reformation*). Last, see the many pleas to Boonen, in AAM, FA, Boonen/157–58, Smeekbrieven, 223.

Boonen and Margaret: Catharina Rijkeboer, GZ/8, March 14, 1624, to Boonen, implies that Margaret had written earlier to Boonen.

Boonen, Nuns, and Exorcising: L. Malherbe, "Le pastorale de Malines: Son histoire," *FM* 28 (1939): 369–88; J. Lacnen, "Heksenprocessen," *FM* 7 (1913): 181–91, 239–47, 407–18, 459–80, 537–60, notes a case of eight nuns, suspected of possession, sent before Boonen; Lottin, *Lille*, 170 ff., and Vanhemelryck, *Heksenprocessen*, 53, discuss scandals and the opinions of churchmen on witchery.

Chapter 5: The Specialist

Capuchins in Leuven: P. Hildebrand, *De Capucijnen*, especially 5:71–78; the learned chronicler who told the story of the reluctant houseseller was Jacobus Baius, nephew of the more famous theologian of the same name.

Johan Evangelista: P. Leonardus, "De Capucijn Joannes Evangelista van 's-Hertogenbosch: Zijn betekenis als geestelijk schrijver," in *FL* 43 (1960): 172–83; P. Gerlachus, "Onze Ascetische Schrijvers: P. Joannes Evangelista van 's-Hertogenbosch, 1588–1635," *FL* 14 (1931): 73–83; Hildebrand, *De Capucijnen*, 5:115–31, 6:558, 7:11, 397, 9:389–93; Fr. Clarentius, "Pater Joannes Evangelista van 's-Hertogenbosch," *OGE* 8 (1934): 369–97; S. Axters, *Geschiedenis van de Vroomheid in de Nederlanden. IV. Na Trente* (Antwerp, 1960), 47–56, 135, 302–4; "Jean-Évangéliste de Bois-le-Duc, capucin, 1588–1635," *DS*, 8 (Paris, 1974): cols. 827–30.

Johan Evangelista and Margaret: GZ/8, February 23, 1624, Evangelista to Boonen.

More on Possession and Suggestion: Klaits, *Servants of Satan*, chapter 5; Thomas, *Religion and the Decline of Magic*; Walker and Dickerman, "'A Woman Under the Influence,'" 535–54; AAM, FK, Begijnhof Aarschot/2, 1629 investigation; also a case in AAM, FK, Bethanie Brussels/4, 1590 visitation.

Diagnosing and Succumbing to Possession: GZ/8, March 28, 1624, Barbara Noosen to Boonen; Bilinkoff, *Avila of St. Teresa*, 119; M. Hovius, *Pastorale ad usum romanum accomodatum* . . . (Antwerp, 1598, 1608), especially 177; Walker, *Unclean Spirits*, especially 8–13; Caron, ed., *Helse en Hemelse Vrouwen;* Maes, *Vijf Eeuwen Mechelen*, 727, on Catherine Janssens; Midelfort, "The Devil and the German People," 109; Vanhemelryck, *Heksenprocessen*, 146; Klaits, *Servants of Satan*, 110.

Various Causes of Possession: Walker, *Unclean Spirits*, 6; Midelfort, "The Devil and the German People," 111; P. Croon, *Onse Lieve Vrauwe van Hanswyck* . . . (Mechelen, 1670), 162–63; Anna Vignarola's 1672 brief history, cited above; Thomas, *Religion and the Decline of Magic*, 480–81; Klaits, *Servants of Satan*, 111; and Walker and Dickerman, "'A Woman Under the Influence.'"

Exorcism Rituals: Those here from Archbishop Hovius's *Pastorale*, 183–86; the most famous from the time, however, was Maximilian van Eynatten, *Manuale exorcismorum* (numerous editions); Walker, *Unclean Spirits*, 46.

The Magus: In Leuven there was a case involving a certain Margareta Smit, whose purported magus was a blacksmith; AAM, Fonds Dekenale Verslagen/D3, 1620.

Johan Evangelista's Works: *Het Ryck Godts Inder Zielen oft Binnen U*

Lieden (Leuven, 1637), and *Het Eeuwigh Leven, Qui manducat meam Carnem, et bibit meum Sanguinem, habet vitam Aeternam . . .* (Leuven, 1644). Though Evangelista's tracts were published after his death, they circulated in manuscript during the 1620s and '30s, and their precepts surely arose while he heard confessions or counseled.

Margaret's Sorrow: GZ/8, March 14, 1624, Catharina Rijkeboer to Boonen.

Archbishop Boonen's Response: March 27, 1624, Margaret to Boonen, GZ/8; March 28, 1624, Barbara Noosen to Boonen, GZ/8.

Chapter 6: Pilgrim

Nuns Going Out: AAM, FK, Thabor Mechelen/3, 1650; AAM, FK, Tienen GZ/6, February 1644; Lucius to Boonen in GZ/8, January 1625; Boonen's letter GZ/5, January 2, 1625; GZ/8, March 14, 1625, from Catharina Rijkeboer; AAM, FM, 10 (Hovius's Manuale), June 29, 1618, plus various entries of 1618 and 1619 on nuns seeking to leave, and Hovius denying them.

Margaret's Leaving and the Potential for Scandal: Walker, *Unclean Spirits;* Walker and Dickerman, " 'A Woman Under the Influence' "; March 27, 1624, GZ/8, Margaret to Boonen; March 28, 1624, GZ/8, Barbara Noosen to Boonen. This letter speaks of the troubles that would befall the convent "once again" if Margaret went to the shrine—suggesting that Margaret may have gone there once before, during her first exile perhaps, or simply referring generally to the problems that came with her going out. GZ/8, December 6, 1624, from Catharina Rijkeboer, notes the "three months" Catharina had been back in the convent.

Scherpenheuvel, Pilgrimage, and Shrines: P. Numan, *Historie vande Miraculen die onlancx In grooten getale ghebeurt zyn, door die intercessie ende voorbidden van die Heylighe Maget* (Leuven, 1604); P. Croon, *Onse Lieve Vrauwe van Hanswyck . . .* (Mechelen, 1670), 162–63; Sumption, *Pilgrimage*, 175; Vanhemelryck, *Heksenprocessen*, 105, 114; Klaits, *Servants of Satan*, 62; Christian, *Local Religion*, chapter on chapels and shrines, 93, 94, 98, 123; Burke, *Historical Anthropology*, "Rituals of Healing"; Thomas, *Religion and the Decline of Magic*; A. Boni, *Scherpenheuvel: Basiliek en gemeente in het kader van de vaderlandse geschiedenis* (Antwerp, 1953); T. Morren, "Bastion op de 'scherpenheuvel,' " in *Spectrum Atlas van Histo-*

rische Plaatsen in de Lage Landen, ed. A. F. Manning and M. de Vroede (Utrecht and Antwerp, 1981), 125 ff; Balduinus Iunius, *'t Huys der Wijsheyt* (Antwerp, 1613).

Joost Bouckaert: Boni, *Scherpenheuvel;* P. Declerck, "De priesteropleiding in het bisdom Ieper, 1626–1717," *Handelingen van het Genootschap voor Geschiedenis te Brugge,* 105 (1968): 56–59; Jadin, "Procès d'information," 30–32; L. Ceyssens, "Joost Boucakert," in *NBW,* 4: cols. 97–99; W. Verleyen, *Dom Benedictus van Haeften, Proost van Affligem, 1588–1648* (Brussels, 1983), 191–92; AAM, Fonds Dekenale Verslagen/Diest; ARA, RSA, 2042/1, and 1947/2; AAM, FK, Diest, Grijze Zusters/1; Hildebrand, "Couvent des Soeurs Grises à Iseghem."

Possible Devotional Works: No one can know what Margaret read. The *Bibliotheca Catholica Neerlandica Impressa, 1500–1727* (The Hague, 1954) lists 5,208 printings of Catholic works between 1605 and 1648, and it is incomplete. I chose here works that were in the vernacular, were specifically or likely directed at religious, belonged to a particular convent of nuns or were written for them, and give some evidence of being popular, such as multiple printings. These included P. van Alcantara, OFM, *Instructie om wel te mediteren, met meer andere Gheestelycke leeringhen ende devote gebeden* (Mechelen, 1618, 11 Dutch printings to 1707, dedicated to the Clares of Mechelen); Bernardin de Balbano, OFM Cap, *Theylich Mysterie Van die Gheesselinghe ons heeren Iesu Christi: Ghestelt in seven Meditatien, voor elcken dach vander weke* (Leuven, 1607; 4 Dutch editions by the early seventeenth century); Fulvius Androtius, SJ, *Een Devoot Memoriael, Van die heylighe Mysterien vander doot ende Passie ons Salichmakers ende verlossers, Jesu Christi* (Leuven, 1607); F. Vervoort, OFM, *De Woestijne des Heeren, leerende hoe een goet kersten mensche, Christum d'licht der warheyt sal navolghen in dese duyster Woestijne des bedroefder wereldts . . .* (Antwerp, 1613; 12 Dutch printings by 1650; belonged to the infirmary of a beguinage); Alphonsus van Madrid, OFM, *Een gulden Boecxken ghenoemt De Conste om Godt Oprechtelyck te Dienen* (Leuven, 1607; 5 Dutch editions in the seventeenth century); G. Spoelberch, OFM, *Sommighe Meditatien ende Devote Oeffeninghen, opde merckelijckste Poincten vande goetheyt Godts . . .* (Leuven, 1615; one other Dutch printing); C. Thielemans, *Cort Verhael van het Leven der Heylighen van S. Franciscus Oirden met Haer Levende Figuren wt Diversche historie scryvers genomen* (Den Bosch, 1620); for other books by Thielemans see B. de Troeyer, OFM, "De Brusselaar P. Cornelius Thiel-

mans: Reanimator van het Franciscanisme Tijdens de Contrareformatie,"
FR 43 (1988): 143; J. Ferraria, OFM, *Vande dry gheloften der Religien, alle Religieuse personen seer oerbaerlyck* (Mechelen, 1618, two other Dutch printings); L. Pinelli (Carthusian), *Den Costelycken Spieghel der Religieuse Volmaecktheydt, Leerende hoe een iegelijc Religieus verbonden is daer toe te arbeyden* (Antwerp, 1605; mostly published in French or Latin); *Contemplationes Idiote*, translated by Jan van Alen OFM, Confessor of the Clares of Antwerp (Antwerp, 1607); Bonaventure's ABCs are appended to *Soliloquium oft Alleenspraecke des H. tSeraphischen Leeraer Bonaventure* (Antwerp, 1624).

Margaret's Vows and Her Penance: AAM, FK, Grijze Zusters Zoutleeuw/1; Psalm 6:2–3, 6, Psalm 38:4, and Psalms 38:19 and 102:8.

The Possibility that Margaret Might Remain in Diest: GZ/8, December 28, 1624, from Bouckaert; GZ/10, visitation of August 20, 1624; GZ/8, undated, from Mater Barbara.

The famous image of furiously raging is from Psalms 2.

CHAPTER 7: FULMINATIONS

Barbara Beli: GZ/8, testimony of June 5, 1624; Catharina Rijkeboer's assessment, November 7, 1624, and December 6, 1624, GZ/8; "Catalogus virginum," July 13, 1624.

Reluctant Confessors: GZ/10, June 25, 1624, from Johan Cranendonck; J. T. Schulenburg, "The Heroics of Virginity: Brides of Christ and Sacrificial Mutilation," in *Women in the Middle Ages and the Renaissance*, ed. M. B. Rose (Syracuse, 1986), 29–72; Moorman, *History of the Franciscan Order*, on the attitudes of the male Franciscans; Hinnebusch, *History of the Dominican Order*, on the Dominicans; Lekai, *Cistercians*, on the Cistercians; Schmitz, *Histoire de l'ordre de Saint-Benoît*, on the Benedictines; Hildebrand, *De Capucijnen*, 9:150 ff., on the Capuchins; Caron, ed., *Helse en Hemelse Vrouwen;* Vanhemlryck, *Heksenprocessen;* J. Delumeau, *Sin and Fear: The Emergence of a Western Guilt Culture* (New York, 1990), 164–65; H. L. De Boer, "De Verlening van de Biechtjurisdiktie in de Germania Inferior van de 17de en 18de eeuw," *FR* 28/1 (1973): 63–125. J. Bilinkoff, "Confessors, Penitents, and the Identities," on the attractions of confessing holy women.

Franciscans of Leuven: S. van Ruysevelt, "De Franciskaanse Kerken: De stichtingen van de dertiende eeuw (vervolg): IX. Leuven," *FR* 27/3 (1972): 107–21; J. Baetens, "Minderbroederskloosters in de Zuidelijke Nederlanden, Kloosterlexicon: 44. Leuven," *FR* 42/2 (1987): 81–105 especially; B. De Troeyer, "Bio-bibliografie van de Minderbroeders in de Nederlanden, 17de eeuw, Voorstudies: 3. Arnold Ab Ischa (Aert van Overijse)," *FR* 32/1–2 (1977): 3–38; Hovius's requests to the friars in his Manuale, July 26 and November 5, 1618, and January 3, 1620; house confessors for Bethlehem in GZ/8, from Barbara Noosen, undated, but early 1624; also from Noosen, GZ/10, June 14, 1622, July 18, 1624, and other letters, plus the visitation of August 20, 1624; Lucius to Boonen, August 21, 1624, GZ/10.

Barbara Noosen's Troubles: News of Margaret's healing in Mater Noosen's undated letter, mentioned above; GZ/8, August 21, 1624, for the sisters' petition; Bouckaert's letter to Boonen GZ/8, September 27, 1624.

Chapter 8: No Balm in Bethlehem

Margaret's Return: G. Hanegreefs, *De steenweg Diest: Leuven, 1777–1797* (Leuven, 1980), treats earlier years as well in the history of the road; GZ/8, December 17, 1624, Catharina Rijkeboer to Boonen on Margaret's "inner sweetness"; GZ/8, November 6, 1624, Bouckaert to Boonen; GZ/1, 1626 statutes, on small rituals.

Reaction to the Return: Summary of the return, and that it happened "in the evening," GZ/8, November 7, 1624, Rijkeboer to Boonen; also her letters of November 6 and December 17, 1624, used as well in other parts of this chapter; bell ringing after Compline in Thielemans, *Heylighen van S. Franciscus Oirden;* Bouckaert's response to Boonen in GZ/8, November 6, 1624; Margaret's letter to Boonen GZ/8, undated, but from the contents it's November 1624, soon after her return; Lucius's in GZ/8, December 18, 1624; Mater Barbara's letters for this chapter from November 13, December 13, 17, and 30, 1624. On recluses, see a third-order example in J. Cruls, *Le S. Sacrement* (Liège, 1881), 186–87; and AAM, FK, Generalia, Statutes for Recluses, in French, undated (before 1620), by Archbishop Hovius.

Joost Bouckaert's Visit to Bethlehem: GZ/8, December 28, 1624, Bouckaert to Boonen; GZ/8, December 26, 1624, Margaret to Bouckaert, and two undated letters to Boonen, probably between December 15 and 31, given events described.

The Controversy over Barbara Beli: GZ/8, undated, but November or December 1624, Barbara van Herssen to Boonen; GZ/5, January 2, 1625, Boonen to Dean Lucius. The petition of the sisters has not survived, but it is alluded to in Boonen's letter of January 8, 1625, in GZ/8, and addressed to Dean Lucius.

Mater Barbara's Demise: C. Vleeschouwers, "Joes van Dormael's Kroniek der Hervorming Binnen de Brabantse Cistercienserinnenabdij Hertogendaal, 1488," *OGE* 47/2 (June 1973): 173–220, especially 192, on the difficulty of Maters resigning; Triest, *Itinerarium*, cites numerous examples; GZ/8, January 16, 1625, Rijkeboer to Boonen; GZ/8, January 22, 1625, Barbara Noosen to Boonen; Bouckaert to Boonen, on Barbara's last hours, GZ/8, January 24, 1625.

CHAPTER 9: THE BURDEN OF BETHLEHEM

Burden as a Message of Doom: Isaiah, such as 13:1.

Margaret's Sources of News: GZ/3, visitation of October 14–15, 1633, two sisters name Joanna Schoensetters, the lay-sister cook, as someone with whom Margaret gossiped in the kitchen. Catharina was mentioned often as the biggest confidante of Margaret.

Elections in Convents: The pattern of shifting power is described in numerous papal conclaves by L. Von Pastor, *History of the Popes,* 40 vols. (London, 1932–50), and L. Von Ranke, *History of the Popes During the Last Four Centuries,* 3 vols. (London, 1913); C. B. De Ridder, "Les élection abbatiales dans les Pays-Bas avant le dix-neuvième siècle," *AHEB,* 5 (1868): 315–28; AAM, FK, Black Sisters Mechelen/4, January 9, 1629, on reasons given by sisters for their choices; AAM, FK, Grijze Zusters Diest/2, 1652 election and the next; AAM, FK, Begijnhof Aarschot/2, September 7, 1628. That Adriana appointed her friends to other offices is in Margaret's letter of February 3, 1628, in GZ/8.

Visitors: GZ/8, May 17, 1626, Van der Wiel's assessment of Margaret, in a letter probably addressed to Boonen; AAM, FA, Boonen/186 (agenda), June 9–10, 1626, shows Boonen in the convent and that he talked with Margaret; GZ/1, for the 1626 statutes.

Reform: See especially the notes under "To the Curious Reader," above; also Vleeschouwers, "Kroniek der Hervorming," 173; Bilinkoff, *Avila of St. Teresa,* 37; Rubinstein, "Lay Patronage," 64; J. Olin, *Catholic Reform* (New

York, 1990); Schmitz, *Histoire de l'ordre de Saint-Benoît,* 238; Trent emphasized the provision of an extraordinary confessor two or three times a year, absolute freedom of profession, enforcement of canonical ages for abbesses, novices, and profession, an interview for profession, the institution of a firm novitiate, a prohibition against cutting hair until profession (to promote freedom to leave), and especially *clausura;* also De Ram, *Synodicon belgicum,* 1:254.

Margaret's State: GZ/11, September 23, 1626, and December 6, 1627, Rijkeboer to Boonen; GZ/9, March 15 or 19, 1628, Adriana Truis to Boonen; Margaret's own letter, February 3, cited above; AAM, FA, Boonen/186, Agenda, November 12, 1627. Evangelista was moved to Tervuren, near Brussels, to begin a friary there, in Hildebrand, *De Capucijnen,* 5: chapter 8. On the virtues of St. Joseph, of whom Margaret sought a relic, see A. De Soto, *Leven van St. Jozef* (Brussels, 1615; 2d edition 1628).

The Relative Anonymity of Visitation: Adriana's suspicions about various sisters are from Margaret's visitation letter of 1633.

Margaret's Literacy and the Composition of Her Letter: After her profession interview, in 1606, cited earlier, Margaret signed a wobbly "X." In Margaret's thirty-two-page letter I find forty-three different groupings, usually indicated by a physical break in the page, but occasionally by an abrupt change of topic.

Chapter 10: Favorites

The Topics of Conventual Life and Visitations: Reynes, *Couvents de femmes,* as background and comparison.

The Visitation Letters of 1628: All in GZ/3, plus notes by the visitors.

Adriana's Example and Office: Triest, *Itinerarium,* May 21, 1624, Black Sisters of Oudenaarde; ARA, KAB, 15307 (an eighteenth-century cartularium), has Adriana signing as Bursaress in 1613, making her no older than twenty-four at the time she held that office; the 1626 statutes review her obligations as Mater. On the reverence owed Mater, see A. de Guevera, *Leeringhe der Religieusen ende Godtvruchtighe Oeffininghen* (Antwerp, 1627); Ferraria, *Vande dry gheloften;* AAM, FK, Thabor Mechelen/4, April 28, 1600, ordinances by Hovius on obedience and reverence.

Favoritism: Bilinkoff, *Avila of St. Teresa,* 131; Lottin, *Lille,* 110; Harline and Put, "A Bishop in the Cloisters," Table 2; AAM, FK, Thabor Mechelen/4, *determinatio* of 1632; AAM, FK, GZ Zoutleeuw/1, statutes of December 1625, chapter 24; 1626 statutes of Bethlehem; AAM, FK, Black Sisters Mechelen/41, visitations of 1615 and 1618; AAM, FK, Bethanie Brussels/4, visitation of March 1590; Brown, *Immodest Acts*, 89, 90.

Duties of the Vicaress: Marchant, *Den Reghel;* GZ/8, January 16, 1625, Rijkeboer to Boonen; 1626 statutes of Bethlehem, chapter 4; AAM, FK, Black Sisters Leuven/32, visitation of 1583, reflects rivalry between Mater and Vicaress.

Lay Sisters: 1626 statutes of Bethlehem, chapter 18.

Property and Annuities: Hereswitha, "Reguliere Kanunnikessen," 424; AAM, FK, Black Sisters Mechelen/39, 1626 ordinance; 1626 statutes of Bethlehem, chapter 2; AAM, FM, 6/234–234v, September 10, 1608, Lesken Nijns' annuity; Susanna Haecht, GZ/6, October 13, 1628, in Catharina Rijkeboer's hand; AAM, FM, 8/fol. 144–45, on St. Monica's Leuven; GZ/5, sheets on grants of 150 florins; RAG, B, M211, Begijnhof Aalst, Account of 1619; Juvyns, "La communauté de Riches-Claires," 207; Brucker, "Monasteries, Friaries, and Nunneries in Quattrocento Florence"; Schmitz, *Histoire de l'ordre de Saint-Benoît;* AAM, FK, Thabor Mechelen/4, 1592 ordinances against private property; GZ/5, January 22, 1597, will of Marie Switten; Ferraria, *Vande dry gheloften der Religien;* Guevera, *Leeringhe;* Alcantara, *Instructie om wel te mediteren;* Lekai, *Cistercians,* 368; GZ/8, Barbara van Craesbeek, undated; Triest, *Itinerarium,* May 21, 1624, Black Sisters Pamele, April 26, 1627, Black Sisters Oudenaarde, and October 18, 1643, Black Sisters Dendermonde.

Common Provisions: 1626 statutes of Bethlehem, chapter 12.

Storytelling: AAM, FK, Bethanie Brussels/4, visitation of March 1590.

Chapter 11: Almsgetting

Debate over Refreshments Before 1628: GZ/1, December 6, 1627, GZ/9, February 3, 1628, and March 15 or 19, 1628, from and to Adriana Truis; GZ/11, July 1, 1625, from Maria Coninxloo; GZ/1, September 23, 1626, from Catharina Rijkeboer; Boonen to Bouckaert, GZ/8, September 19, 1627; the special decree from Boonen in GZ/1, November 17, 1627. Women in Avila who liked contact with nuns, in Bilinkoff, *Avila of St. Teresa.* On grilles provoking even violence, J. E. Sayers, "Violence in the Medieval Cloister," *Journal of Ecclesiastical History* 41 (1990): 533–42;

Schmitz, *Histoire de l'ordre de Saint-Benoît*, 237; Power, *Medieval Women*, 99. Bishop Triest, *Itinerarium,* in Oudenaarde on May 21, 1624, April 26, 1627, May 20, 1640.

More on Dowries: Devos, *L'origine sociale des Visitandines,* 13; Hildebrand, *De Capucijnen,* 5:332; Gruart, "Les Soeurs Grises de Comines," 62, and many others.

Income and Expenses in Convents: Examples in RAG, B, M211/Beguinage Aalst, Account book of 1619; AAM, FK, St. Gertrude's Leuven/9, 1607, for a comparison of a male monastery's income and expenses to a female; also P. Hildebrand, "Le couvent des Soeurs Grises à Iseghem, d'avant 1486 jusqu'en 1796," *NF* 2 (1919): 40; and AAM, FK, St. Niklaasberg/ 1625–26 register on income. Endowments and services in Bethlehem in GZ/7, and GZ/5, undated account book.

Work in Convents: Active orders, AAM, FK, Grey Sisters Zoutleeuw/1, statutes of 1625; Schoonaert, "Onderwijsstructuren Poperinge," 28, and Hildebrand, "Couvent des Soeurs Grises à Iseghem," 25, 44 (sick care and schools); Van de Casteele, "Nevele," 169–70, and Gruart, "Les Soeurs Grises de Comines," 67, 70 (schools, hostels, sewing); Grauwels, "Een lijkbaarkleed der Grauwzusters," 189 (renting of funeral palls). Cloistered orders, see Schmitz, *Histoire de l'ordre de Saint-Benoît,* 254–55, on Benedictines (wine, beer, spirits, hostelry); P. Hildebrand, "De Kapucijnen te Leuven," *NF* 3/3 (1920): 245, on Annunciation sisters who did the laundry, and AAM, FK, Bethanie Brussels/4, visitation of March 1590 (laundry); White Ladies Leuven, ARA, RSA 1947/1, from 1618 (babysitting); AAM, FK, Blijdenberg/8, visitation of 1621 (school); Hereswitha, "Reguliere Kannunikessen," 390 (school); AAM, FK, Black Sisters Mechelen/57 (sewing, boarders, etc.), plus KAM, FA, Hovius/Processen Algemeen, trial of Canon Pussius, 1599, and Van de Castele, "Nevele," 169 (lodgers and boarders).

Balance Sheets: ARA, KAB, 15307, a huge eighteenth-century cartularium containing copies of old documents for Bethlehem, shows the annual average income there from 1645 to 1654 to have been 3,721 florins, with expenses at 3,707—expenses and income were close in other years, too; also GZ/5, February 13, 1631, an example of a typical annuity arrangement; and ARA, KAB, 15306, an approximately six-by-nine-inch book full of official documents; Schmitz, *Histoire de l'ordre de Saint-*

Benoît, 254: "The majority of female monasteries existed in continual discomfort . . . and sometimes in real poverty."

Good Friends: The houses In Den Luypaert and Den Soeten Inval are in Meulemans, *Atlas van Oud-Leuven;* RAA, Kerkarchieven, Mol/236bis, Joos's will includes a bequest to the Luypaert house, hence the assumption that he was a friend there. An example of the steward's charge in AAM, FM, 8/fol. 153, for Groot Bijgaarden in 1619; AAM, FK, Gasthuis St. Peter's Leuven/6, June 20, 1652, reveals fees to a steward; AAM, FK, Jericho Brussels/visitation of September 2, 1628, troubles with the steward.

Children and Nuns: Axters, *Vroomheid,* 128, on Franciscan meditation; Arenal and Schlau, *Untold Sisters,* 119, 190, on children in conventual art.

Devos: In the introduction to *L'origine sociale des Visitandines.*

CHAPTER 12: WORLDLY WAYS

Little Altars: Bange, ed., *Tussen Heks en Heilige,* 86; "Les jardins clos et leurs rapports avec la sculpture Malinoise," *Bulletin du circle archéologique, littéraire, et artistique de Malines* 22 (1912): 51–114.

Less Distinguished Choirs: AAM, FK, Mechelen Thabor/4, February 15, 1610, Hovius ordinances, and 1632 visitation by Boonen; Blijdenberg AAM, FK, Blijdenberg Mechelen/chart. 8, visitation of January 21, 1620; Weemaes, *Visitationes omnium ecclesiarum . . . per Carolum Masium, 1609–1612,* 28–29.

The Superiority of Contemplatives: De Soto, *De Schole van de Eenicheydt;* and Vervoort, *Bruydegoms Mantelken.*

Decorum in Choir: 1626 statutes of Bethlehem, chapter 1; AAM, FK, Black Sisters/32, undated visitation by Van der Wiel; AAM, FK, Grey Sisters Zoutleeuw/1, December 1625; GZ/10, June 20, 1624, on literacy; ARA, RSA/receipt 1594 (signed with an "X" by the Bursaress); Tomizza, *Heavenly Supper,* 73, on "religious sounds"; on number of masses in a male monastery, M. Ultee, *The Abbey of St. Germain des Prés in the Seventeenth Century* (New Haven, 1981); Corstjens, "De Franciscanessen van OLV-Ter-Rivieren," 116; *Monasticon Belge,* 4(1):262; Arenal and Schlau, *Untold Sisters,* 95.

Other Forms of Worship: M. Cloet, *Karel Filips van Rodoan* (Brussels, 1970), 190; Pinelli, *Costelycken Spieghel der Religieuse Volmaecktheydt;* P.

Camporesi and T. Croft-Murray, *The Incorruptible Flesh: Bodily Mutation and Mortification in Religion and Folklore* (Cambridge, 1988); chapter 9 of the house statutes of Bethlehem; Marchant, *Den Reghel;* Alcantara, *Instructie om wel te mediteren;* Thielemans, *Heylighen van S. Franciscus Oirden;* Guevera, *Leeringhe;* Vervoort, *Woestijne;* GZ/10, Anna Vignarola to Nuncio, February 28, 1673; Am. van Dijk, ed., *Verspreide Sermoenen van Johannes Brugman* (Amsterdam, 1948); Van de Putte, *Claren Spiegel der Waerachtiger Christelijcker Maechden;* Evangelista, *Rijk Godts.*

Play and Ritual: N. Davis, *Society and Culture;* Darnton, *Great Cat Massacre;* E. Van Autenboer, *Volksfeesten en Rederijkers te Mechelen, 1400–1600* (Gent, 1962), 72; E. Weaver, "Spiritual Fun"; Guevera, *Leeringhe,* chapter 28; AAM, FK, Grey Sisters Diest/1, undated letter from Mater.

Cloister: Van de Castele, "Nevele," 184; Ferraria, *Vande dry geloften;* Brucker, "Monasteries, Friaries, and Nunneries in Quattrocento Florence"; Bange, ed., *Tussen Heks en Heilige,* 84; Schmitz, *Histoire de l'ordre de Saint-Benoît;* A. de Vogüé, "Caesarius of Arles and the Origin of the Enclosure of Nuns," in *Women in Monasticism,* ed. J. Leclerq et al. (Petersham, Mass., 1989), 16–29; J. T. Schulenburg, "Strict Active Enclosure and Its Effects on the Female Monastic Experience, ca. 500–1100," in *Medieval Religious Women. I. Distant Echoes,* ed. J. A. Nichols and L. T. Shank (Cistercian Publications, 1984), 51, 58, 63; Moorman, *History of the Franciscan Order,* 36; 1626 statutes of Bethlehem.

Scandals and Laxity Regarding Cloister: De Brouwer, *Land van Aalst,* 255, 260; Hinnebusch, *The History of the Dominican Order,* chapter 13; AAM, FK, Groot Bijgaarden, various bundles regarding the confessor Kerremans; Harline and Put, "A Bishop in the Cloisters," 239, on the nuns of Zichem; AAM, FK, Bethanie Brussels/4, February 28, 1592, and October 8, 1608, visitations by Dean Vinck.

Enforcement of Cloister and Netherlandish Nuns: Triest, *Itinerarium,* 52, Cruybeke, May 1626; R. De Ganck, "Marginalia to Visitation Cards for Cistercian Nuns in Belgium," *Citeaux* 40 (1989): 236–37.

Prestige of Cloister: AAM, FM, 8/130, visitation of 1618 to Blijdenberg, and AAM, FK, Blijdenberg Mechelen/72; Brown, *Immodest Acts,* 114–15; Rubinstein, "Lay Patronage and Observant Reform in Fifteenth-Century Florence"; AAM, FK, Grey Sisters Diest/9, November 28, 1628, Pastor to Boonen.

More on the Grille: Sayers, "Violence in the Medieval Cloister";

Schmitz, *Histoire de l'ordre de Saint-Benoît,* 237; Ferraria, *Vande dry ghelof-ten;* Bilinkoff, *Avila of St. Teresa;* chapter 16 of the 1626 house statutes of Bethlehem; Marchant, *Den Reghel;* Hereswitha, "Reguliere Kannuni-kessen," 402; J.-B. Thiers, *Traité de la clôture des religieuses* (Paris, 1681); AAM, FK, Grey Sisters Zoutleeuw/1, December 1625, point 11 on the Portress.

Church Grilles in Convents: P. Octave D'Angers, "Le chant liturgique dans l'ordre de Saint François aux origines," *Études Franciscaines* 75/3 (1975): 300; AAM, FK, Forst/3, on Sister Barbara; Triest, *Itinerarium,* May 16, 1624, Oudenaarde.

CHAPTER 13: THE VISITORS

Peter van der Wiel: GZ/10, undated, summary of past visitations to Bethlehem; see his hand and signature in many files in AAM, FK, as well as numerous other collections of the archive; AAM, FK, Black Sisters Meche-len/42, December 17, 1637; Jadin, "Procès d'information"; numerous vis-itations such as in AAM, FK, Poor Clares Mechelen/1; AAM, FK, Tienen Cabbeeck/1633 visitation; AAM, FK, Beguinage Tienen/1, undated *deter-minatio,* plus interview summary in bundle 5, October 9, 1630; AAM, FK, Mechelen Leprosy House/3, visitation of November 7, 1624, and 1631; AAM, FK, Brussels Leprosy House/2, visitation of 1632 probably by Van der Wiel; AAM, FK, Mechelen Hospital/3, visitation of October 4, 1635, and March 16, 1620; AAM, FK, Bethanie Brussels/4, visitations of March 19, 1613, June 27, 1614, January 29, 1624; AAM, FK, Forst/3, visitation undated, but after 1626. Sensitive questions put to the Vicariaat in AAM, Fonds Amatus Coriache, 3:62, 215, 217, 221, 223, 226, 227, 229, 296. Serious troubles in AAM, FK, Groot Bijgaarden/3, visitation of April 1630; AAM, FK, Beguinage Vilvoorde/2, visitations of April and May, 1629. His interview book in AAM, FM, 9. The example of the German convent from Eckenstein, *Women Under Monasticism,* 417.

Difficult Visitations: AAM, FK, Bethanie Brussels/4, 1590 visitation; Power, *Medieval Women,* 99; Hovius's Manuale on Groot Bijgaarden; AAM, FK, Diest Cellesusters/Statutes 1625, fol. 42; Harline and Put, "A Bishop in the Cloisters"; Power, *Medieval People,* 76.

Peter Lucius: AAM, Fonds Dekenale Verslagen/L3, 1619–29; AAM, FK, Florival (unsigned, but the text in his hand).

The Protocol of Visitation, and What the Visitors Knew of Bethlehem: The rings for each nun are mentioned in a letter by Adriana Truis in GZ/9, March 15 or 19, 1628. Also GZ/1, December 6, 1627, and February 3, 1628; GZ/3, visitation of May 24, 1669, on protocol of an earlier visit; Lucius's notes and all the visitation documents for 1628 in GZ/3.

Resignations of Maters: AAM, Black Sisters Mechelen/4; election of January 9, 1629.

Letters of the Other Sisters: All in GZ/3.

Factions: Aleidis Doelmans, Jacomyn de la Haye, Maria de Smet, Anna van den Broek, and a couple of others were willing to criticize both factions.

Anna's Motto: "Spijs der wormen," or Worms for Lunch, was not exclusive to Anna, for it was taken as well by Catharina van Habroeck, a beguine of the late seventeenth or early eighteenth century, who owned Alcantara's *Instructie* (copy in possession of the ST).

Compiling the *Determinatio:* Van der Wiel, Memoriale, GZ/3, 1628, and his summaries; the hand in the margin of Van der Wiel's various documents for this visitation is very sloppy but appears to be Boonen's.

Failure to Conclude the Visitation Promptly: AAM, FA, Boonen, Agenda, 1628 bis, August 14; GZ/11, November 1628, Bouckaert to Boonen; GZ/3, February 5, 1629; AAM, FK, St. Niklaasberg Aarschot/9, fol. 63; Margaret to Boonen, GZ/8, February 3, 1629; Catharina to Boonen, GZ/8, February 5, 1629; Maria Coninxloo to Boonen, GZ/8, April 21, 1629; Lucius to Boonen, September 1629, GZ/11; Boonen Agenda, an unlabeled entry between June 6–23, 1628 bis, in which he notes the need to visit Bethlehem; October 8, 1629, March 4, 1630; the preacher à la mode in AAM, FA, Boonen/223. A 1637 letter from Adriana Truis alleged that a written *determinatio* was never issued to the convent for the 1628 visitation, in GZ/3, March 19, 1637, thus confirming why there was no final document.

Concern for Mater's Authority: This was evident not only in how *determinatios* were put together but in such decrees as AAM, CK, Grey Sisters Zoutleeuw/1, statutes, point 4, where Mater confessed her sins to no one but God or her confessor, "lest her authority be damaged."

Election of a Bursaress: GZ/8, August 6, 1629, from Catharina Rijkeboer; also Dean Lucius's summary of the votes, GZ/4, August 20, 1629.

The Inquest into Margaret's Condition: GZ/8, September 12, 1630.

An Easy Visitation: Triest, *Itinerarium,* May 21, 1624, Black Sisters

Pamele: *Omnia hic utcunque bene ordinata fiunt et tranquille et exemplariter vivunt.*

CHAPTER 14: JUSTIFICATION

The Siege of Leuven and the Flight of Certain Orders: Claessens, *Histoire des archevêques,* 277; P. Guilday, *The English Catholic Refugees on the Continent, 1558–1795* (London, 1914), 383.

The 1633 Visitation to Bethlehem: All documents in GZ/1 and GZ/3. Some of Van der Wiel's random, undated notes in these files could be from any year but seem most pertinent for 1633. That some could be from 1633 or 1637 suggests how common the same themes were.

The Lost *Determinatio* of 1633: GZ/3, March 19, 1637, from Adriana Truis.

The Plague in Leuven: Guilday, *English Catholic Refugees,* 383.

Margaret's Return: GZ/8, various undated documents, but especially Van der Wiel's letter of April 16, 1636, and Hubert's and Bergaigne's of May 23, 1636; the documents of return are all in the same hand, namely Bouckaert's. They include: "Heymelijcke Instructie" (July 10, 1636), "Secreta Instructio Matris," and "Jacob byder gratie Godts."

Catharina's Death: No Necrology for the house remains, and there's no direct evidence of when she died; but in GZ/3, March 13, 1637, Van der Wiel laments that Catharina was no longer with them. The best clue of the time of her death was the election of the new Vicaress in 1635.

Election of Anna Vignarola as Vicaress: GZ/2, interviewer's notes, February 14, 1635, and Paridanus's letter of the next day.

On Semipermanent Official Visitors to Convents: Verleyen, *Benedictus van Haeften,* 181; AAM, FM, 140/fol. 199v, 1616, and 8/163, 1619, for the convent of Jericho; AAM, FM, 8/fol. 147, Black Sisters of Leuven, 1618.

The Banning of Henri Joos in 1637: Boonen's agenda, March 9, 1637. The scenario of Joos's receiving the news is my construction, based on broader events of the moment, and subsequent communications of Joos with Bethlehem, especially Adriana's letter of March 19, 1637, to Van der Wiel, in GZ/3. It is my inference that Adriana and Joos corresponded about the visitation of Joost Bouckaert, because they had certainly corresponded over the upcoming novice-clothing of March 22. Dean Mannarts also asked Van der Wiel, after the visitation of 1637, for documents relating to the removal of Joos back in 1618; March 13, 1637, in GZ/3, from Van der Wiel. The confessor in Bree in Corstjens, "De Franciscanessen van OLV-Ter-Rivieren," 91.

Peter van der Wiel's Reaction to the Visitation and His Knowledge of Old Events: His letter from March 13, 1637, and an undated letter from around the same time, provide the best clues of his feelings and knowledge.

The Reaction of Joost Bouckaert: That other nuns wrote letter after letter to Peter van der Wiel to complain about the visitation of 1637, and perhaps undo it, was stated by Bouckaert himself, whose reaction may be found in several letters of March 21, April 6, and April 14, 1637. His *determinatio* in GZ/1, dated May 20, 1637, plus an earlier draft.

On the Possibility of Regular Elections: In Thabor in 1634 a new subprioress and Bursaress were elected, and in 1637 Van der Wiel returned to see whether the sisters wanted these women to continue in their offices; AAM, FK, Thabor Mechelen/3. At the Grey Sisters' house in Diest, an election was held in 1652 because the current Mater's three-year term was up, the only justification given; AAM, FK, Grey Sisters Diest/2. In the Brigitinne convent of Gent an abbess and her prioress were not only removed but sent to the convent of the Grey Sisters in that city; Triest, *Itinerarium,* 240. Verleyen, *Van Haeften,* 188, on the Black Sisters of Aalst, 1623, notes another way to solve difficult messes in leadership: bring in an outsider, supposedly neutral in her feelings. See also AAM, CK, Grey Sisters Zoutleeuw/1, Statutes, December 1625, chapter 3, "On Electing a New Mater": it was to be done every three years, as per the rule of Leo X, unless the current Mater was deemed satisfactory. In Our Lady Ter-Rivieren in Bree, one woman was elected nine different (non-consecutive) times as Mater in the early seventeenth century, reflecting the back-and-forth swing typical of in-fighting. Rarely did anyone there serve more than one three-year term in this period; Corstjens, "De Franciscanessen van OLV-Ter-Rivieren," 96–100. Gruart, "Les Soeurs Grises de Comines," 84–85, shows that the length of tenure for Maters in this house between 1481 and 1787 (with several missing bits of information along the way), was about eight years, among the twenty-seven Maters known. Several of them quit to lead a new convent; five of them were Mater at two different times (indicating that elections were held besides at time of death). One of them was superior for twenty-eight years, between 1582 and 1610. In the Poor Clares convent of Mechelen there were twenty-three abbesses between 1500 and

1783, an average tenure of about twelve years; see De Backer, *Het Arme Klaren Klooster*, 111. Lengths of tenure varied from house to house, but where a Mater was powerful or respected or both, a de facto tenure for life was probably not unusual.

On Boonen's Approval of Bouckaert: Among many other signs of trust, in December 1637 Boonen noted happily that Bouckaert was being considered for the vacant see of Den Bosch; Agenda, December 10.

CHAPTER 15: CAPITULATION

The Challenges of Enforcement: The Bishop of Antwerp's comment in C. B. De Ridder, "Rapport adressé au Souverain Pontife, Paul V, par Malderus . . . en 1615," *AHEB* 1 (1864): 113. The fictional priest in G. Bernanos, *Diary of a Country Priest* (New York, 1986; translated from the French original), 83. The number of parishes and convents in the archdiocese fluctuated, usually upward, in the reports by Boonen to Rome; see J. Paquay, *Les rapports diocésains de la province ecclésiastique de Malines et du diocèse de Liège* (Tongeren, 1930), 2–4, 9–10, 14, 23.

Boonen's Limitations: Comment on the Grey Sisters of Diest from AAM, CK, 1625 statutes. Failure in Tienen is from AAM, CK, Beguinage Tienen/1. The Bishop of Grenoble in P. Broutin, "Les visites pastorales d'un évêque au XVIIe siècle," *Nouvelle revue theologique* 71 (1949): 942.

Van Haeften's Opinions on Women: Verleyen, *Van Haeften*, 194–95.

Van der Wiel's Visit of 1638: Recounted in his letter in GZ/1, May 27, 1638. His tensions with Bouckaert could certainly not have been helped by the fact that it was Van der Wiel to whom Bouckaert sent reports of his Deanery and it was Van der Wiel who would write small notes of instructions to Bouckaert in the margins. Yet because of his position at the shrine of Scherpenheuvel, and his connection to Margaret, Bouckaert enjoyed as well a privileged position with Archbishop Boonen.

Adriana's Letter on the Lost *Determinatio* of 1637: GZ/10, August 6, 1639. Bouckaert's response to Adriana's excuse on August 19, 1639, in GZ/10. Regarding the altering of documents, two of the twenty questions put to the Black Sisters of Leuven in a 1689 visit had to do with accusations certain sisters had made about the Dean's falsifying of recent visitation decrees; AAM, CK, Black Sisters Leuven. Such things were therefore hardly unheard of.

Jurisdiction over Bethlehem: Boonen's letter is dated April 8, 1639, in GZ/10. Probably at Boonen's request, Van der Wiel also drew up in 1638 or 1639 a document that showed the frequency of episcopal visitation to Bethlehem over the years. Based on his memory and written records, Van der Wiel noted visitations for 1611, 1616, 1624, 1626, then 1628, 1633, 1637, and 1638. See the document in GZ/10, undated, but certainly after 1638.

Official Letters from Rome and Elsewhere Regarding Jurisdiction: GZ/10, dated 1638 and 1639; the documents by the cathedral chapter are in Bundle 73 of KAM, FA, Boonen, full of pieces on jurisdiction, one dated March 30, 1639, another June 8, 1640, and several others that are undated.

CHAPTER 16: FINIS

Care for the Dying: GZ/1, rule, and 1626 statutes, chapter 14; C. Leutbrewer, OFM, *Gulde biecht-konste om op den tijdt vanmin als twee uren sich te bereyden tot een generale biechte van heel syn leven, sonder peryckel van eenighe doodt-sonden achter te laten* (Brussels, 1646), with 13 editions afterward; J. van Gorcum, *Troost der Siecken* (Antwerp, 1644), with numerous earlier editions; Marchant, *Af-beeldinghe.*

Announcement of Margaret's Death: GZ/3, December 18, 1648, Gerard van Reijden, perhaps Dean of Leuven at the time (no one knows for sure who was Dean then, but he seems a possibility), to an officer of the archdiocese. No Obituarium of the convent has survived.

EPILOGUE

Other Margarets? AAM, FK, Black Sisters Leuven/32, undated visitation by Van der Wiel; AAM, FK, Bethanie Brussels/4, 1590 visitation; Triest, *Itinerarium*, 65, 121, 158, 492; GZ/10, undated letter from around 1666, from Anna Vignarola.

The Fate of Henri Joos: AAM, FK, St. Gertrude's Leuven/3–4; AAM, Dekenale Verslagen/L3, 1628, by Lucius; RAA, Kerkarchieven, Mol/3–4, 82, 796, 236bis, and BAA, Parochialia Mol, 11–13; T. I. Welvaerts, "Geschiedkundige Bijdragen over de Voogdij van Molle," *Het Kempisch Museum* (1890), on his tomb and expiration in Diest; RAA, Voogdij Mol-Balen-Dessel, 208/1. Note that his age is mentioned in none of the available documents. If he began at St. Gertrude's, and Bethlehem, in 1604, he was likely between twenty-five and thirty, which put him at thirty-five to forty at the time of Margaret's first scandal around 1615, about forty-five to fifty when he left for Mol in 1624, and about sixty to sixty-five when he died in Diest in 1638.

The Fate of Peter van der Wiel: Boonen agenda, July 22, 1641; KAM, Personalia/438; J. Baetens, *Verzameling van Naamrollen betrekkelijk de kerkgeschiedenis van Mechelen,* 3 vols. (Mechelen, 1881); J. Schoeffer, "Archidiaconorum Ecclesiae Metropolitanae Mechliniensis Notitia Chronologica" (Ms. 1845, AAM).

The Fate of Joost Bouckaert: Jadin, "Procès d'information"; P. de Clerck, "De Priesteropleiding in het bisdom Ieper, 1565–1626," *Annales de la Société d'émulation de Bruges* 100 (1963): 7–67; J. Philippen, "Joost Bouckaert, Pastoor van Scherpenheuvel, Overste van de Oratorianen Aldaar, Landeken van Diest, Bisschop van Ieper," *Oost-Brabant* 28 (1991): 56–61; AAM, FA, Boonen/192; ARA, KAB, 23349 (an inscription from what appears to have been his tombstone).

The Fate of Jacob Boonen: ARA, RSA, 945, AAM, FA, Boonen, 223, and KAM, FA, 223, for expenses; KAM, FA, Boonen/73, August 13, 1644, on worship; Ceyssens, "Boonen," *NBW,* and "Les dernières années de Boonen, archevêque de Malines," *Augustiniana* 11 (1961): 87–120, 320–35, 564–82; KAM, FA, Boonen/74 (will); KAM, FA, Boonen (library inventory).

The Fate of Bethlehem: P. Carolo van Coundenhove, OFM, *Provinciae Germaniae Inferioris Compendiosa Descripto* (n.p., 1680), 8; GZ/10, October 17, 1646, from Steenbergh; GZ/3, GZ/1, 1663, 1664, 1669, and 1671 visitations; Anna in numerous files in GZ between 1635 and 1660 as "Vicaress," plus in ARA, KAB, 15307, while Adriana was clearly always Mater; GZ/8 and GZ/5 and GZ/11 on temporal troubles; GZ/10 on dragging on of jurisdiction; SAL, 3331, 3332, 4272, for other documents on lawsuits in Leuven; after their deaths, also ARA, KAB, 15309, November 7, 1693; GZ/3, October 3, 1693, more pleas for aid; GZ/11, November 7, 1695; GZ/3, visitation of 1695; SAL 4279, for wealthy entrants of 1717 and 1793; Van de Castele, "Nevele," on closing of convents during the French Revolution; Mater Maria Theresa of Bethlehem refused to hand over documents, in ARA, Dijledepartement, 2035, Sequestration of Goods of Closed Convents, Trente Vendémiaire, neuf heures du matin, Ans 5.

Acknowledgments

Thanks to the National Endowment for the Humanities, the University of Idaho Research Council, the History Department, College of Family, Home, and Social Sciences, and Women's Research Institute of Brigham Young University for supporting my research. It was while working on another project, under a research grant from the American Philosophical Society, that I found the crucial documents for this book.

A historian can never praise enough the usual host of archivists and librarians behind a book, and so I take occasion again to do so, starting with the still extraordinary Professor Dr. Constant van de Wiel, who has worked so tirelessly to bring the rich collection of the Archive of the Archdiocese of Mechelen-Brussels into order, as well as his successor at the archive, Mr. Aloysius Jans. I thank further Brother Joseph Baetens, then of the Franciscan provincial archives in St. Truiden, his assistant Mr. Alfred Perry, and the staffs of the Algemeen Rijksarchief in Brussels, the Rijksarchief in Gent, the Rijksarchief in Antwerp, the Stadsarchief of Leuven, the Stadsmuseum of Leuven, and the Royal Library in Brussels.

My debt to colleagues and friends in Belgium remains as great as ever, especially to Michel Cloet of the Katholieke Universiteit van Leuven, who welcomed and encouraged me from the time of my first visit there, Jan Roegiers of the same institution, and Eddy Put of the Algemeen Rijksarchief in Brussels. Many thanks as well to Marie-Juliette Marinus, Guido Marnef, Walter Prevenier, Hans Storme, Marc Therry, Georgi Verbeeck, Herman and Monique Van der Wee, Johan Verberckmoes, and still others, for their suggestions about archives, interpretation, and the finer points of modern and archaic Dutch.

Closer by, Rudy Bell, Jodi Bilinkoff, Tom Brady, Karen Carter, Kent Hackmann, Martha Howell, Karin MacHardy, Sherrin Marshall, Theodore Rabb, Herbert Rowen, Carlos Schwantes, Walter Simons, Bob Scribner, and James Tracy all contributed to the making of this book. I owe special debts to Erika Rummel, who first suggested I prepare a shorter paperback version suitable for classes, and to Louis Perraud, whose expertise in the subtleties of ecclesiastical Latin was the least of his many kindnesses to me. I am grateful as well to John Ware for taking on the manuscript not once but twice, to Tom Cahill, Rob Radick, and Trace Murphy at Doubleday, and especially to Charles Grench and Philip King at Yale University Press, who gave the book new life.

Last I thank Paula, Andrew, Jonathan, and Kate, for traveling willingly, enthusiastically, and at times inconveniently to foreign places, for making my life richer, and for helping me keep my work in perspective with regular questions about why I study nuns and other such things at all.

Index

Pilgrimage. *See* Shrines

Pinelli (spiritual author), 154

Pius V, Pope, 211

Plague, 12, 17, 194, 196

Portress, office of, 89, 104, 166

Possession, demonic, 24–28, 35–37, 42–44, 52, 55–65, 67, 78, 80, 85, 90, 94, 108, 196, 215. *See also* Witchcraft

Postulants, 7, 43–44, 78–79, 124; training, 15–16. *See also* Novitiate and novices

Poverty, vow of, 11, 18, 75–76. *See also* Community, monastic ideal of; Material life; Vows, monastic

Prayer, 131, 151–55, 216. *See also* Divine Office; Worship

Preaching, 28, 51, 81, 154–55, 163, 197–98, 201–3

Prime, 151. *See also* Divine Office

Private property. *See* Material life; Poverty, vow of

Profession of nuns, 7, 17–19, 106, 167

Protestantism, 9, 33

Public relations, attention to by convents, 21, 68, 96–99, 124–25, 127–45, 150, 156, 168. *See also* Laity

Punishment, 106, 157

Recluses, 91, 92

Recreation: excesses of, 134, 141–42, 155–58, 179, 184; types of, 140–41, 155–58, 165

Recruitment and entry of nuns, 7–10, 15–19, 137–38

Refectory, 19, 124, 148, 149, 157, 180

Reform and Reformation, 85, 99, 105–9, 170–71, 174, 176, 184, 187–88, 193, 197, 220; enforcement, 205–7, 211–12, 218–19, 223. *See also* Counter Reformation

Relics, in convents, 2–3, 13, 15, 22. *See also* Shrines

Remmens, Magdalena (lay sister of Bethlehem), 21

St. Renildis (martyr of Brabant and a favorite in Bethlehem), 13, 153

Reverence. *See* Divine Office

Rijkeboer, Catharina, 2, 44, 46–47, 57, 64–65, 66, 68–69, 72, 77, 84, 85, 90–93, 95, 99, 100, 103, 108, 128, 129, 137, 170–71, 176, 178–83, 184–87, 192, 196; as Vicaress, 104, 115–16, 120, 121, 122, 137, 177, 193

Roermond, diocese of, 55

Routine, monastic schedule and, 151, 153

Rule, of a monastic order, 10–11, 75, 106–7

Sacristan, of nuns' choir, 104, 123, 140, 145, 164

Saints, in convent life, 13, 18, 22, 56, 60, *146,* 147–50, 153, 214, 215

Satan. *See* Devil

Scandals, dealing with, 31, 33–34, 38–39, 159–60, 174–75